**Please check all items for damages
before leaving the Library.
Thereafter you will be held
responsible for all injuries
to items beyond reasonable wear.**

l   12/13
l   11/14
l   3/16

AT LIBERTY TO DIE

At Liberty to Die

The Battle for Death with
Dignity in America

Howard Ball

 NEW YORK UNIVERSITY PRESS New York and London

NEW YORK UNIVERSITY PRESS
New York and London
www.nyupress.org

References to Internet websites (URLs) were accurate at the time of writing.
Neither the author nor New York University Press is responsible for URLs
that may have expired or changed since the manuscript was prepared.

Library of Congress Cataloging-in-Publication Data
Ball, Howard, 1937-
At liberty to die : the battle for death with dignity in America / Howard Ball.
p. cm.
Includes bibliographical references and index.
ISBN 978-0-8147-9104-2 (cl : alk. paper)
ISBN 978-0-8147-6975-1 (ebook)
ISBN 978-0-8147-4527-4 (ebook)
1. Right to die — Law and legislation — United States.
2. Assisted suicide — Law and legislation — United States.
3. Euthanasia — Law and legislation — United States. I. Title.
KF3827.E87B36   2012
344.7304'197 — dc23   2011052258

New York University Press books are printed on acid-free paper,
and their binding materials are chosen for strength and durability.
We strive to use environmentally responsible suppliers and materials
to the greatest extent possible in publishing our books.

Manufactured in the United States of America

10 9 8 7 6 5 4 3 2 1

DEDICATED TO THE MEMORY
OF A GOOD FRIEND,

DON BEXTERMUELLER.

He loved his Linda and his mules. He died in Hospice.

◆ CONTENTS

Acknowledgments   ix

Introduction   1

1   The Changing Nature of Death in America   13

2   The Plight of the Incompetent Patient   27
       in a "Permanent Vegetative State" (PVS)

3   Terri Schiavo's Tragic Odyssey, 1990–2005   51

4   What Freedom Do We Have to Die with Dignity?   67
       The U.S. Supreme Court Decides, 1997

5   The Second Path to PAD: Passing Legislation   105
       Allowing Death with Dignity

6   The Pioneering PAD States: Oregon and Washington   131

7   America's Transplants   163

Notes   173

Cases Cited   205

Bibliography   207

Index   217

About the Author   229

◆ ACKNOWLEDGMENTS

During research and writing of this book, I have had the great pleasure of meeting with a variety of medical practitioners across the nation. They include pathologists at the University of Vermont's Medical School and the Dartmouth-Hitchcock Medical School. Their discussions with me and my students regarding how humans die in this new century was of great help to me in gaining insight into this key issue. In addition, I have had the insights of many doctors and nurses, both pro and con on the issue of death with dignity, in Vermont, Arizona, Utah, North Carolina, Montana, and Oregon about physician-assisted death (PAD). I gratefully thank the Center for Disease Control and Prevention for basic data on American mortality.

While teaching at the University of Utah in the 1980s, I had the pleasure of discussing the general issue with a preeminent scholar, Margaret Battin, a professor in the Philosophy Department. She has been thinking and writing about a person's liberty to die with dignity for decades and has been in the forefront of thinkers whose ongoing task is to teach about the liberty one has of dying with dignity.

During the late fall 2008, en route to Arizona, I had a heart attack and triple bypass surgery in North Carolina. I had excellent care by the cardiac care team at Forsyth Medical Center in Winston-Salem, led by my "plumber," Dr. David Duncan. While recovering, I had insightful discussions about the medicalization of death with a variety of personnel, including the members of the hospital's palliative care center. They are in the forefront of compassionately caring for the terminally ill.

Thanks also to my friend and companion for nearly fifty years, my wife, Carol. Nor can I forget the rest of my family, Susan, Sheryl, Jay, Lila, Nate, Melissa, Tim, Sophie, Stormin' Norman, Candyman, Harry, Charlie, and Cooper. I love all of you.

Finally I gratefully acknowledge my editor, Deborah Gershenowitz, for her work on my behalf from the very beginning of this project. She is a gem, and it was my good fortune to work with her for the past four years.

None of these men and women is responsible for any errors in the book. I take responsibility for all of them.

Dudley Clendinen is a sixty-six-year-old author and columnist dying of amyotrophic lateral sclerosis (ALS, known as Lou Gehrig's disease). In a recent essay, he discussed his existential situation.[1] There is no meaningful treatment for ALS nor is there a cure. "Lingering would be a colossal waste of love and money. I'd rather die," he wrote. Although leaving his daughter "is the one thing I hate. But all I can do is to give her a daddy who was vital to the end, and knew when to leave. . . . When I can't tie my bow tie, tell a funny story, walk my dog, kiss someone special—I'll know that life is over. It's time to be gone."[2]

The central thesis of the book is that the liberty found in the U.S. Constitution's Fifth and Fourteenth "Due Process" Amendments extends to Dudley Clendinen and other terminally ill competent persons' right to choose to die with dignity—with the passive assistance of a physician—rather than live in great pain or live a quality-less life. While federal judges and most state legislatures have not yet moved to accept this view, the book will show that there has already been some modest movement in that direction, one that presently allows terminally ill patients to die with the assistance of a physician in two states, Oregon and Washington. Recently, Montana's Supreme Court ruled that the state constitution does not prohibit physician-assisted death (PAD) but, to date, there has been little legislative action to establish the necessary guidelines for medical practitioners to follow when ministering to their terminally ill patients who wish to die on their own terms.

However, there is an unusual consequence if there is no further movement toward either judicial expansion of the meaning of liberty or the passing of laws enabling terminally ill patients to die with the assistance of a doctor: terminally ill people crossing state lines to enter those states that allow such medical assistance. It is these persons—strong-willed, competent and dying adults who want to die with dignity when faced with a terminal illness—who are the eight-hundred-pound gorillas in this book.

This transient activity is not a hypothetical situation. It is presently occurring throughout the world and goes by a number of names: the "Switzerland syndrome," "Death tourists," "Suicide Tourists":[3] these are men and women who transplant themselves to obtain medical assistance in taking their lives because of terminal disease that either leaves them in great pain or robs them of a decent quality of life.

In America, there is the specter of some terminally ill people—"Oregon Transplants" one Arizona lawyer labeled them[4]—in America traveling to Oregon, Washington, and now Montana in order to obtain passive physician assistance in dying.[5] Hospice and palliative care developments have lessened this kind of transient movement to die a good death in a state where that is possible. In addition, for decades physicians have used the "double effect" practice to assist their dying patients. (This protocol allows a doctor to give painkilling medications to a terminally ill patient to relieve pain, with the possibility that the treatment will indirectly hasten the patient's death.)

A small number of Americans will still travel in order to seek out a place to die with some dignity. This possibility parallels earlier actions Americans once took in order to obtain an abortion (which was illegal in their home state)[6] or to marry because of their state's prohibitions against marriage of persons of different races or of the same gender.[7]

For more than a century, the U.S. Supreme Court's decisions have acknowledged that a person has the constitutionally protected liberty to travel from state to state. The first case decided by the Court was *Crandell v Nevada*, 1868,[8] where the Justices unanimously struck down a Nevada law that levied a $1 tax on persons leaving the state by public transportation. The right to travel from state to state was a right of national "citizenship" found in the "privileges and immunities" clause of the Fourteenth Amendment. And in 1941 another unanimous Court decision invalidated a California statute that sought to keep nonresidential indigent "Oakies" out of the state.[9]

Furthermore, because of legal and medical events that have taken place in America since the 1970s, described in this book, there has developed—in society and in the medical community—a growing awareness of the needs, choices, and rights of dying patients. There is also a greater understanding of the dying process and a corresponding ease when talking about death and dying that did not exist until the last decades of the twentieth century.

Americans live much longer now than a century ago. The average life expectancy for a person born in 1900 was forty-seven years; for a person born in 2010, it is more than seventy-eight years. Seniors are not only living longer but most are dying ever so slowly. For many, their families see them in great pain. A friend of mine told me that her dying father "dropped from around 250 pounds . . . down to about 80 in the time it took him to die. All I recognized the MONTH before he died . . . were his eyes. It was a terribly gruesome and undignified death."

A majority of Americans now believe that a terminally ill person has the right to determine how her life will end. Public opinion polls over the years indicate that a growing number of Americans support a person's right to choose to die with the assistance of a physician. A typical poll result: a 2005 Pew Research Center Survey noted that 84 percent of those polled approved of patients being able to decide whether to be kept alive through medical treatment or choosing to die with dignity—with only 10 percent opposed. However, religious, medical, political, and ideological communities have, to date, successfully countered the public's positive view of this personal liberty. They have defeated most efforts to transfer this idea into legislation.

There is, also, a significant change in the way the medical community views and treats pain. There is a growing acceptance of the importance of minimizing pain by all means necessary—even if this effort leads to the death of the individual. In 1974, there was just one palliative care hospice facility in America providing a handful of terminally ill cancer patients relief from excruciating pain. In 2010, nearly five thousand hospice-palliative care programs in all fifty states and American territories are caring for more than one million terminally ill patients. In less than forty years, America has moved from a minimum number of patients treated and dying in hospices to, in 2009, nearly 42 percent of all deaths (1.2 million) occurring in a hospice program. Between 2000 and 2008, the number of hospital-palliative care programs grew exponentially.[10] While there has been significant change, more than half of American terminally ill patients still die in hospitals, some in great pain, without palliative care.

For all those who have experienced the way most Americans die in the twenty-first century, the solution to the horror of a delayed degenerative disease such as cancer is death with dignity: palliative care, hospice, and, for a few, physician-assisted death.[11] It is, Margaret Battin argued, *not suicide* but the "least worst" death.[12] An eighty-six-year old man in Oregon, diagnosed with terminal COPD,[13] reflected Battin's thoughts when he said to a reporter: "I'm not suicidal. I'm sane. When the time comes, I'm going to swallow that bottle of Lethe[14] and say goodbye."[15] As changes in American attitudes toward death occur, it is increasingly important to consider how the meaning of liberty in the U.S. Constitution relates to one's personal choice regarding death.

For nearly a half century, there has been an insistent constitutional argument made by individuals whose personal choice to die, by receiving a prescription for lethal medications, state law prohibited. There is a fundamental liberty interest, they claimed, found in the U.S. Constitution's "Due Process" Clause.[16] It enables a person to make personal, intimate, and ultimate choices without interference by government.

For some dying persons, liberty is their right to choose death over life. They claim that the right to die with dignity is a constitutionally protected choice a person has under both the common law and the Constitution. This concept of liberty as personal privacy and autonomy saw its constitutional life begin in 1965 in a marital privacy case that came to the U.S. Supreme Court from Connecticut. In 1965, in *Griswold v Connecticut*,[17] a seven-person U.S. Supreme Court majority ruled that the liberty concept in the U.S. Constitution extended to a married couple's *right to marital privacy* in the bedroom.

There is, the lawyers argued, a "fundamental personal right of privacy" possessed by married couples. The challenged Connecticut law, an 1879 statute that made it a crime for any person to use any drug, article, or instrument to prevent conception, was declared unconstitutional. Justice William O. Douglas for the Court majority, argued that the Connecticut law interfered with the right of privacy found in the "penumbras"[18] of the Constitution's Bill of Rights, specifically the First, Third, Fourth, Fifth, and Ninth Amendments.

Justice Arthur Goldberg's concurring opinion in *Griswold*, joined by Justice William J. Brennan and Chief Justice Earl Warren, featured a much more expansive definition of a person's liberty interests found in the nation's constitutional history: "Liberty protects those personal rights that are fundamental, and is not confined to the specific terms of the Bill of Rights."

For Justice Goldberg, judges and justices adjudicating a controversy between an individual's use of a "fundamental right" and a state law prohibiting such an action had to determine whether that claimed right was "so rooted in the traditions and conscience of our people so as to be ranked as fundamental [in our constitutional law]."[19]

Justice John M. Harlan II, joined by Justice Byron White, refused to accept either constitutional justification offered by his colleagues. Instead, he argued in his concurring opinion, the Due Process Clause and specifically its liberty component "stands on its own bottom." For Harlan, the Connecticut statute violated basic historical, cultural, and legal principles "implicit in the concept of ordered liberty."[20]

This "right" of marital privacy—the right to choose to use or not to use a contraceptive—until *Griswold* was not specifically found in the language of the Constitution. The majority, however, based on a trio of differing legal arguments written by Douglas ("*penumbras*"), Goldberg ("fundamental rights *rooted* in America's traditions"), and Harlan ("due process"), concluded that the state statute was unconstitutional.

The two dissenters, Justice Hugo L. Black and Justice Potter Stewart, argued that the statute was a nineteenth-century anachronism; it was essentially "a silly law." However, they concluded that it did *not* infringe upon a fundamental and enumerated constitutional right. Unless there was a specific, constitutionally authorized liberty or right infringed by a state law, even an admittedly "silly" law is constitutional. Their basic fear: "Use of any such broad, unbounded judicial authority [seen in the three majority and concurring opinions] would make of this Court's members a day-to-day constitutional convention."[21] Interestingly, their understanding of judicial constraint in constitutional interpretation became, in the 1980s, the majority's position. It remains the dominant view of the Court majority today.

The *Griswold* decision, despite its different interpretations and understandings of the U.S. Constitution's liberty clause, was a watershed opinion regarding a person's right to choose to act in certain ways so long as the action did not injure others. All competent persons have a self-determined liberty to make choices they believe will benefit them.

A few years later *Griswold* was followed by another important decision that expanded upon the marital privacy principle. In 1972 *Eisenstadt v Baird* was decided by a seven-person U.S. Supreme Court.[22] (Justices Black and Harlan retired in September 1971 and their replacements, Justices William Rehnquist and Lewis Powell, had not yet taken their seats on the Court.)

By a 6:1 vote,[23] in an opinion written by Justice William J. Brennan, the Court majority ruled that a Massachusetts law banning the distribution of contraceptives to *unmarried* persons was unconstitutional. In an expansion of *Griswold*, Justice Brennan concluded that "If the right of privacy means anything, it is the right of an *individual*, married or single, to be free from unwarranted governmental interference into matters so fundamentally affecting a person as the decision whether to bear or beget a child."[24]

The following year, the U.S. Supreme Court heard *Roe v Wade*,[25] the case that determined whether and under what conditions a woman could choose to have an abortion. By a 7:2 vote, with Associate Justices William Rehnquist and Byron White in dissent, Justice Harry A. Blackmun, for the majority, concluded that the challenged state statutes from Texas and from Georgia, which prohibited abortion, were unconstitutional on the ground that they violated a woman's right of privacy.

A woman has a liberty interest in determining the fate of the fetus she was carrying, Blackmun wrote. Although the right to an abortion was a right not specifically found in the Constitution, nevertheless the majority believed that a woman's liberty extended to her right of privacy to choose or not to choose to have an abortion.

Between 1965 and 1973, then, U.S. Supreme Court majorities laid down some very fundamental but, in the minds of its conservative critics, extra-constitutional principles regarding a person's right to choose in very personal, very private, very intimate circumstances: marital relations, sexual relations, and the right to have an abortion. For all those who believed that liberty extended to the right of a competent terminally ill adult to die with the assistance of a physician, these opinions were very encouraging ones. When these terminally ill men and women became plaintiffs and went into court to argue that they had a constitutional right to end their lives, these earlier cases were used as precedent for their position.

These pre-1973 decisions are the constitutional arguments that plaintiffs have made from the very first case brought into a court that challenged a state law which interfered with the decision to receive physician assistance in choosing to hasten death rather than continue life in a vegetative state, or life in constant pain, or life without dignity. They were the stepping-stones to litigation regarding the most profound personal decision a person can make—dying.

Those who defend the right to die with dignity insist that, like the privacy right, the right to die with dignity should fall under the protective mantle of the liberty found in the Constitution. They argue that a terminally ill person has a fundamental liberty to choose to die with the assistance of a physician. There is no difference between the liberty a woman has to have an abortion and the liberty a competent terminally ill patient has to die under the person's own terms.

This book, in part, focuses on the legal and constitutional arguments and debates, in state and federal courts, and in the U.S. Supreme Court, regarding the argument that a dying person has a right to choose to die with a physician's assistance. Those seeking to expand the meaning of liberty contend that a state law barring physicians from providing that patient with a prescription for the necessary lethal drugs violates the person's liberty protected by the Due Process Clause.

By the mid-1970s, the first of the end-of-life cases came into state courts involving non-competent patients. In 1990, another set of political, ethical, and legal questions arose in state and federal courts. Can a competent terminally ill patient, suffering from a crippling, and at-times-painful illness, request a prescription for lethal drugs from a medical practitioner that would allow that patient to die with dignity? As the book shows, there were efforts in many states to draft legislation that would allow physician-assisted death of terminally ill patients. These battles were political, ideological, and religious ones, which for the most part led to political defeat for pro-PAD advocates.

There has always been in America the freedom to travel unimpeded to seek a better life. The prospect—in the twenty-first century—of dying persons traveling to a state that offers them the liberty to choose a good death necessitates telling the story of the constitutional history and the controversial debates—beginning in the 1970s—regarding a person's constitutional liberty to choose to die with dignity.

At the heart of this American story is a competent person's right of freedom of choice, a freedom over one's body that allows a person to die with the help of a doctor. It is a story that involves legal disputes regarding termination of life support for incompetent patients, medical arguments that start with the notion that a doctor must do no harm to the patient, and political battles over the meaning of liberty in the Constitution. One general consequence of these clashes of ideas over the past four decades is that there has been significant change in Americans' attitudes and beliefs about death and dying. Public perceptions of this controversial subject are far ahead of the views of federal and most state judges, and much more open to legislative change to reflect these attitudes than are the political leaders in the legislature and in executive mansions.

The story begins in chapter 1 with an examination of the "Medicalization" of death phenomenon that emerged during the twentieth century. This reality has led some people to seek out a merciful way to end their lives with the assistance of a physician. Over the past century, the nature of how we die has changed considerably. Science has discovered many ways to prolong a person's life. In so doing, it has created new problems associated with living too long. Many terminally ill patients are in great pain and are unable to live the life they had before the illness.

The end-of-life debates began in America with legal cases that addressed the fate of incompetent patients in a permanent vegetative state. Chapters 2 and 3, examine these contentious debates. Competent persons have the freedom to choose to refuse or to discontinue life-sustaining medical treatment. What about the incompetent patient? Three watershed cases—*Quinlan, Cruzan,* and *Schiavo*—raise and answer important constitutional, medical, religious, and political questions associated with the right of personal privacy and the constitutional liberty found in the Fifth and Fourteenth Amendments. More importantly, these cases have forced Americans to confront the reality of end-of-life problems that all must face.

The cases (1975–1990) that opened the controversial right-to-die legal, medical, and ethical debates raised the question of whether withholding or withdrawing of life support mechanisms from *incompetent* and *incapacitated* persons in a Permanent Vegetative State (PVS)[26] can take place without civil or criminal liability facing those who act to remove the life support systems from such patients.

In the *In Re Quinlan* (1976); the *Cruzan* (1990), and the *Schiavo* (1997–2005) litigation, state and federal courts for the very first time reviewed the facts and the law and the medical ethics issues in order to determine whether and under what conditions life support could be withheld or withdrawn from an incompetent patient. In *Quinlan,* the New Jersey Supreme Court based its ruling on the 1965–1973 right to personal privacy arguments presented by U.S. Supreme Court majorities. Drawing upon the decisions of that Court, especially *Roe v Wade,* the state court concluded that the life of a PVS patient could be ended by withdrawing life support.

By *Cruzan,* in 1990, the U.S. Supreme Court accepted the Missouri state standard for withdrawing life support systems: There must be shown "clear and convincing evidence" that the PVS patient, *when competent,* indicated—

verbally or by an advanced directive—that he or she did not want to be kept alive by machines if there was no quality of life possible. Moreover, the Court said that both the common law and the U.S. Constitution allow a *competent* patient to instruct medical professionals to remove life support systems so that the patient could die.

Terri Schiavo's case began when she was diagnosed as PVS by her doctors in 1990. Eight years later her husband, claiming that he was following her verbal instructions before her cardiac arrest, asked for a court order to have the hydration and nutrition tubes removed. However, Terri's parents disagreed with him and petitioned the courts to continue to keep their daughter on life support.

These battles, in the Florida courts, and in the state's executive and legislative branches, went on for seven years. By the time the international spectacle ended in March 2005, state courts,[27] federal courts, the U.S. Congress, and President George W. Bush[28] were enmeshed in the exploited tragedy of an incompetent patient who had been in PVS since 1990. In the end, Terri Schiavo's life support tube was removed, and she died on March 30, 2005—nine days after President Bush signed Terri's law, which momentarily prevented removal of her life-sustaining tube.

Chapter 4 takes the story to its next plateau, moving from a general awareness of the end-of-life choices for caregivers of incompetent patients to focus on the public debates that addressed the question of whether a terminally ill competent patient who wants a "good death" has the constitutionally guaranteed liberty to achieve his or her goal. This issue became very visible due, in part, to the actions of Dr. Jack Kevorkian. His medical actions—beginning in 1990—brought into sharp focus the dilemma of persons suffering from illness and who wanted to die. Although the medical community and others condemned Kevorkian's aggressive actions to help patients die—many of them not suffering from a terminal illness—they opened the door to the next set of questions regarding the fate of competent patients. One major problem that faced these terminally ill competent patients was that the medical community, as a matter of principle and policy, was opposed to passive assistance by doctors to enable these dying patients to take their own lives.

Throughout the 1990s, grassroot efforts to pass death with dignity legislation came into existence, and there were pitched battles and highly emotional debates surrounding the rightness of such legislation. Very critical to these discussions was the constitutional question regarding the scope of the liberty clause in the Constitution. Was the liberty, found in the Fifth and Fourteenth Amendments of the Constitution, as interpreted by the federal courts, a fundamental right that extended to a person's choice to end life with the help of a physician?

The U.S. Supreme Court in 1997 entered the discussions because of legal actions taken by PAD proponents—a few doctors joined with their terminally ill patients—in the federal courts. The Court concluded that the liberty sought by the plaintiffs was not a fundamental one. The liberty concept does not extend to a person's right to seek medical assistance in taking one's life. Its conclusions did not satisfy those who argued for the constitutional right to die. However, these decisions continued the discussion of the basic question: does liberty mean that a terminally ill competent person has the constitutional right to choose to die with dignity—with the assistance of a physician—rather than live in great pain or live a quality-less life?

Chapter 5 examines the alternative strategy of the PAD advocates: passing legislation that allows PAD. The chapter examines and analyzes the battles in the states over whether physician assistance in dying would become law. Nearly two dozen states, beginning in 1990, experienced intense political battles regarding PAD legislation. Over the course of two decades, most political battles led to the defeat of PAD legislation.

There were, however, two successes in the battles to pass legislation. Chapter 6 examines these political and legal battles. Oregon became the first state to pass a death-with-dignity law in 1994, although it was litigated in state courts until 1997. Additionally, at the federal level President George W. Bush's U.S. Justice Department attempted to invalidate the bill in 2001. The effort failed when, in 2005, the U.S. Supreme Court, invalidated the administration's strategy.[29] Oregon's success was replicated by its neighbor, Washington State, in 2008. In addition, in 2009 the Montana Supreme Court interpreted the state constitution in a way that allows medical practitioners to provide terminally ill patients with prescriptions so that they may end their lives on their own terms. This chapter discusses these breakthroughs and whether they will impact the future of the death-with-dignity movement.

Are we at the end of the death-with-dignity story? This is the essential question raised in chapter 7. Americans at this moment have the freedom of movement, accompanied by their right to decide for themselves how they want to live or die, and the liberty to choose to die in Oregon, in Washington, or in Montana. They will move if they feel that is the only way for them to go as they face their life's end.

Unless, of course, future interpretations of the Constitution by federal judges allow the terminally ill patient to use the liberty provided to all in the U.S. Constitution to seek out physician assistance in dying without becoming "Oregon transplants." This end-of-life drama will continue because in the federal court system significant changes in the makeup of U.S. Supreme Court personnel regularly occur. With new Justices deciding cases, there is the probability of new ways of interpreting the liberty clause in the Constitution. The PAD issue will continue to percolate in the state and federal courts because more and more people are succumbing to those chronic end-of-life illnesses (chiefly cancer and heart failure).

Unless there is continued expansion of the hospice and palliative care program in America, the death-with-dignity movement will continue to champion legislative changes in state law. (In 2010 nearly 60 percent of patients who died in America—2,450,000—did not have the vital assistance of palliative care professionals to make their final days less stressful and less painful.)

The right-to-die issue will continue to roil in controversy because it, like the right to an abortion, confronts the very essential beliefs of "sanctity of life" proponents. Religious groups, especially the Roman Catholic Church, continue to seek ways to ban abortion ever since *Roe v Wade* came down in 1973. They and other groups representing disabled persons and other Americans have fought to block PAD legislation since the 1970s and will continue to do so in the future.

Will more states pass death-with-dignity legislation similar to the existing legislative and legal decisions in Oregon, Washington, and Montana? Will federal judges, especially the Justices on the U.S. Supreme Court, enlarge the scope of liberty in the U.S. Constitution? Will palliative care and hospice programs continue to grow in the effort to deal mercifully with the dying patient's final days? These answers will probably be forthcoming in this decade. The book's final chapter examines these options and speculates about their success.

1

THE CHANGING NATURE
OF DEATH IN AMERICA

In the long run, we are all dead.

—John Maynard Keynes[1]

Old age is no place for sissies.

—Bette Davis[2]

Except for those who die suddenly, death is a gradual process[3] common "to all living organisms in the earth's biosphere."[4] The clinical definition of death, however, has evolved over the centuries because medical science developed new techniques and instruments that doctors used to treat their patients. As these new protocols and technology became available, new insights emerged regarding how humans die and when they are pronounced clinically dead.

I. How We Die

The cell is the basic unit of all living organisms. When cells die (cell necrosis) in humans,[5] because of physical trauma or biological invasion (hypothermia, oxygen deprivation, immunological attack, or toxin exposure), the death of organs can follow if the patient goes untreated. "Successive organic failures (such as the liver and the kidneys) eventually reach a point at which brain death occurs and this is the point of no return. . . . [When the entire brain dies], "a person becomes truly dead."[6]

The definition of death has changed substantially over the past century. Until the invention of the stethoscope in 1816, death was declared when a person stopped breathing. The invention of the stethoscope allowed physicians to add the absence of heart sounds as another criterion of death.

Scientific and technological advances, for example, the mid-twentieth-century development of the process of cardiopulmonary-cerebral resuscitation (CPR), the establishment of the Intensive Care Unit (ICU), and other medical technological advances, have forced definitional changes in the characterization of clinical death. With these developments in the emergency department, treatment of patients, cardiac arrest, and respiratory arrest could be overcome. However, "while medical science had figured out how to start a heart that had stopped, it had made no similar progress with the brain."[7]

In a growing number of cases, a person was revived but was unresponsive. While breathing and heartbeat were restored through the use of CPR and intubation of the patient, there was unconsciousness, a deep, irreversible coma—the permanent vegetative state (PVS).

This was the new reality: a patient breathing and with a heartbeat but, because of near–brain death, without "meaningful contact with the environment,"[8] led to monumental ethical, legal, and medical dilemmas.

By 1968 the international medical community determined that there was a second definition of death: "The death of an individual could be equated with the death of his or her brain and that 'cerebral death' could be diagnosed with reasonable certainty. . . . [This] was a most momentous development in the history of medicine and mankind."[9]

In the twenty-first century, clinical death is when there is *either* (1) total brain death,[10] or (2) when there is no heartbeat and no respiration. Either reality means that recovery to a conscious state is impossible. Total brain death is irreversible. It occurs when destruction of nerve cells—due to lack of oxygen (*anoxia*) or increased pressure inside the skull due to severe head trauma (1) in the brainstem (the center for reflex responses such as swallowing and respiration) *as well as* (2) in the cerebral cortex has taken place.[11]

In 2011, there are four universally accepted criteria of total brain death: (1) unresponsive coma, (2) inability to breathe spontaneously, (3) absence of brain stem reflexes, and (4) absence of electrical activity of the brain.[12]

Just as the definition of death has evolved over the centuries, so too have the *causes* of death changed over the same time. The changing definitions of death occurred simultaneously with medical, scientific, and technological creations and breakthroughs. The changes in how humans die reflect the political and cultural dynamics that occur in society over time: from eating habits to the development of the public health institution to the length of the average life expectancy of the person.

II. The Etiology of Death in 1900

In 1900 the doctor had but a few basic tasks: deal with lethal diseases and disabilities, deliver live births, manage pain, and participate in the deathwatch along with family and friends. "[The doctor] performed these with meager success."[13]

The doctor's goal was fairly simple: do the best one could to care for the sick individual until death came to the patient. "Back then," wrote one doctor about her predecessors, "although the weapons at their disposal were meager, they took more time to talk with the dying patient."[14]

Treatment of the sick changed dramatically a few hundred years ago. During the nineteenth century, two schools of medical practice emerged that were to fundamentally change the way medicine was practiced.

In Paris, France, early in the century, the pathological anatomy movement, practiced in the hospital, began. To understand the dynamics of disease, doctors had to start cutting dead bodies open so that "obscurity will disappear."[15] In Germany, at about the same time

> medical training focused primarily on *laboratory* medicine based on microscopy, vivisection, chemical investigations, and everything else measurable, weighable, and testable. The hospital was fine for observing but the laboratory was tailor made for experimenting.[16]

These two new medical schools of thought, combined, led to the transformation of the practice of medicine in the twentieth century. Through the nineteenth century, "disease called the shots. Persons were stricken by dangerous infections which in [those] pre-bacteriological days could not even be diagnosed with exactitude, let alone cured." Individuals were plagued by infections, lethal to young and old alike. All the family doctor could do was to make comfortable the ill or dying patient until the patient expired. From the Greek and Roman era through the nineteenth century, a doctor had but a few options for treating the patient: "blood letting, sweating, purging, vomiting, and other methods of purging the body of bad humours."[17]

Until the twentieth century, humans did not live very long. Our hunter-gatherer ancestors' life expectancy was about twenty-five years. In 1700 in Great Britain, the second richest country in the world (after Denmark), life expectancy at birth was thirty-seven years of age. By 1820, however, life expectancy at birth in England was up to forty-one years of age. That figure remained stable for another eighty years.[18]

For centuries medicine was an atomized art, a hodgepodge of patient-doctor dealings. There were no clinical studies; there were no medical instruments that could assist the doctor in determining the nature of the illness; there were no regional or national medical institutions to share new medical information with colleagues. Remember, the stethoscope was not invented until the nineteenth century nor were there laboratories the doctor could send blood samples to for analysis. And high-quality precision microscopes were developed only in the last decades of the nineteenth century.

In 1900, the chance of a marriage lasting forty years was just one in three because of early mortality. And, quite different than today, death and post-mortem events accompanying death took place in the home following a protracted deathbed watch. According to the National Center for Infectious Diseases, Centers for Disease Control and Prevention, the top ten causes of death in America were:

TABLE 1.1. Top 10 Causes of Death, 1900

Tuberculosis	11.3%
Pneumonia	10.2
Diarrhea	8.1
Heart Disease	8.0
Liver Disease	5.2
Injuries	5.1
Stroke	4.5
Cancer	3.7
Bronchitis	2.6
Diphtheria	2.3

Tuberculosis, called the "White Plague," killed almost 150,000 Americans in 1900, "three times as many deaths as those from all types of cancers combined." Since there were no antibiotics to treat the illness, "doctors could offer little treatment other than fresh air, sunshine, nutrition and bed rest."[19] Through the middle of the twentieth century, most deaths were due to infectious diseases. "And such deaths were relatively quick—a matter of days between the onset of a terminal illness and death. . . . Those deaths also came much earlier, often in what we call the prime of life."

> People who became debilitated or bedridden also did not last long. They developed a pneumonia and, since pneumonias couldn't be effectively treated, they died. The threat of being bedridden for years and years did not loom large. Pneumonia—"the old man's friend"—would reliably deliver a person from that peril.[20]

Improving mortality numbers from 1900 to 2000 was initially due to improved nutrition and the elimination of the most pernicious of the industrial revolution's characteristics (child labor, twelve-hour workdays, poor working conditions, extreme poverty of the workers), and the development of vaccines.[21] Tuberculosis deaths fell by 80 percent "*before* there was any effective [medical] treatment for the disease. The same is true for other infectious diseases as well."[22]

The emergence—in the early twentieth century when the evils of industrialization and urbanization were at their brutal apex—of the state-developed public health service organizations at the local, state, and national levels was a key factor in addressing the many illnesses faced by the community.

Public health is a new field of medicine. Its practitioners—doctors, nurses, dentists, health educators, lab technicians, and others—focus on preventing disease, prolonging life, and the promotion of good community health practices by government agencies. The modern public health organization emerged in the nineteenth century in all nations going through the industrial revolution. The health problems that infected Americans, Germans, French, and English were very similar—smallpox, cholera, yellow fever, and typhus—and called for communitywide efforts in each nation to prevent and eradicate those contagious diseases that bred in the industrial slums. "The dramatic reduction of water- and food-borne diseases after that time—typhoid, cholera, dysentery, and non-respiratory tuberculosis—highlights the role of public health. From a mortality rate of 214 per 100,000 in 1900, these diseases were virtually eliminated in the U.S. by 1970."[23]

By the middle of the twentieth century, due to scientific and clinical developments, "many of these infectious and once deadly diseases were controlled or their morbidity and mortality substantially reduced. Advances in medical technology, including diagnostic imaging technologies, procedures (the respirator), and new prescription drugs (sulfur, penicillin and other antibiotics) have extended and improved the quality of countless lives."[24]

III. Death's Path in 2000

Medical advances mean that these days we are living longer, but paradoxically, longevity means more time for chronic illnesses to emerge, to debilitate, and to kill us. "The epidemiology of how we die is changing," wrote Margaret Battin, "and an individual's chances of dying in certain highly predictable ways are increasing. [In 2010,] seventy to eighty percent of deaths are the result of degenerative diseases marked by a long, downhill decline."[25]

In the twenty-first century, the three most common ways people over sixty-five die are cancer, organ failure, heart and lung disease, and extended frailty accompanied by dementia, principally Alzheimer's disease.[26] Researchers have uncovered some basic generalizations about these three paths to death. Cancer deaths, according to Dr. Joanne Lynn, generally appear in patients in their sixties and come after many years of good health and "peak functioning."[27]

Organ failure (heart and lung diseases) generally peaks about the age of seventy-five and exhibits a "far bumpier course." The patient experiences bouts of severe illness that alternate with periods of relative stability. However, at some point, medical intervention fails and there is the sudden death of the patient.[28] Extended frailty and dementia, generally occurs in people in their eighties. At present, more than 40 percent of the "old-old" live long enough to die of dementia. This figure will only increase with improvements in the prevention and treatment of cancer, heart disease, and pulmonary disease. These three chronic illness trajectories across time are the consequences of the medical scientific breakthroughs of the late twentieth century.

The times have changed quite dramatically. In the first decade of the twenty first century, the average person "knows *three* years in advance what she will die of." The average male experiences increased medical problems for five years before he dies while the elderly female experiences serious medical problems for eight years. "We now live facing death for a very long time."[29]

According to the CDC's National Center for Infectious Diseases, the top ten causes of death in America in the first decade of the twenty-first century are very different from the top ten causes of death in 1900.

TABLE 1.2. Top 10 Causes of Death, 2010

Heart Disease	29.6%
Malignant Neoplasms (Cancer)	23.0
Stroke	7.0
Chronic Lower Respiratory Disease	5.1
Accidents[30]	4.1
Diabetes Mellitus	2.9
Pneumonia and Influenza	2.7
Alzheimer's Disease	2.1
Kidney Disease	1.5
Septicemia (toxins in blood)	1.3[31]

According to the CDC, the leading cause of death in America differs by age group. In infants, the leading cause of death was congenital malformations; for children, adolescents, and young adults (1–44 years of age), unintentional injuries; cancer for middle aged adults (45–64 years); and heart disease, dementia, and cancer (65 years or older).[32] By the end of the twentieth century, the three major chronic diseases—heart disease, cancer, and stroke—accounted for 67 percent of the deaths for persons age sixty-five or over.

Socioeconomic status and the race of a person also account for differences in mortality statistics. "Better educated, and thus richer, people smoke less than less educated people, perhaps because they know more about the true risks of disease. . . . Richer people may demand better health."[33]

Social policy, evidenced in legislation and government regulations, in a society is another factor that influences mortality in a population. In America, Medicare and Medicaid are two clear examples, along with the critically important Social Security policy.

A final significant difference between dying in 1900 and dying in 2000 is that "we no longer die at home. Starting in the 1930s, the locus of our dying moved from the home to the hospital or some other health care facility. "[This] simple move had hidden, undreamed of consequences."[34]

This change in the death venue of most Americans (more than 80 percent of Americans die in hospitals in the twenty-first century[35]) came about toward the middle of the twentieth century. The nineteenth-century hospital was essentially a poorhouse; it was a place where the destitute, the homeless, the sick, went to die. It was a place where nuns gave solace to them. It was not a place to go to get better.

By the 1930s this poorhouse perception of the hospital had changed radically; the hospital became the "first port of call for the sick." Sick people went to the hospital to get better, not to die. This new role of the hospital took place because the help sick people needed to recover was there: doctors, nurses, laboratories, new diagnostic and therapeutic technologies."[36]

To sum up, the history of increased life expectancy in humans, over the past three centuries, encompasses three phases. The first phase lasted about one hundred years, from 1750 to 1850. This era was highlighted by improved nutrition, economic growth, and, in reaction to the evils of the industrial revolution, the beginning of the public health system. The second phase, 1850–mid-1930, focused on new developments in the medical laboratories and the growing impact of public health institutions in cities, states, and nation. The third phase, from the mid-1930s to the present day, is "the era of big medicine, starting with vaccination and antibiotics, and moving on to the expensive and intensive personal interventions that characterize the medical system today."[37] Death has become medicalized; the extension of life is now largely due to new medical technologies such as organ transplants, and the use of laser technology in once-impossible medical procedures.[38]

IV. The Third Phase: The "Medicalization" of Death

The Oxford English Dictionary defines "medicalization" as follows: "To give a medical character to [death]; to involve medicine or medical workers in [the death process]; to view or interpret [death] in medical terms."[39] It was coined to reflect the radical changes that were being introduced in the treatment of the dying. Death no longer was managed by the dying person, his or her family, the cleric, and the local community. Instead, death primarily involved the dying patient and medical personnel in hospitals employing the latest medical technologies to forestall death.

The nature of the physician changed in the twentieth century because science-based medicine had finally emerged. The doctor became a professional medical practitioner because of the transition of medicine into medical science. By the end of World War I, medical science "became a profession based on newly acquired diagnostic skills that stressed rigorous diagnosis with the emphasis on laboratory, microscopic, and bacteriological routines—thermometers, fever charts, blood pressure machines, stethoscopes, microscopes, [and] staining techniques."[40] Moreover, with better living standards, better nutrition, an improved environment, behavioral changes, and the rapid growth of medical science and medical interventions, there was a dramatic change in the understanding of disease.

The emergence of the clinical medical study and the emergent research-orientation of medical schools attached to premier universities, led to new innovations in the treatment of historically chronic killers. Clinical lab work and monitored medical research studies produced new knowledge about the treatment of disease. These breakthroughs captured the interest of the general population who believed that scientific progress would cure them of the disease they harbored in their bodies—or at the very least give them more years of quality of life before the disease won out—unless, of course, medical science discovered a cure for the disease.

Medical innovation and discovery have, in the twentieth century, increased the life spans of Americans. However, and in this "however" lies the other consequence of these new medical capabilities; we are living longer, but now two-thirds of the population die of the three major chronic diseases, with most facing incapacity at the end.[41]

New medical techniques have led to the saving of untold number of lives, the restoration and preservation of health, and living longer with chronic illnesses. One unfortunate and unavoidable by-product of these medical breakthroughs, rarely seen severe brain damage, emerged. These new syndromes include brain death, the minimally conscious state, "and, probably the most widely known example, the permanent vegetative state (PVS)."[42]

Originally described and labeled by famed neurologist D. Fred Plum in 1972, PVS is a neurological consequence of a person's loss of oxygen for more than four to six minutes, followed by resuscitation by Emergency Medical Technicians (EMTs) using cardiopulmonary resuscitation(CPR), rapid transportation to a hospital's emergency department and then, if the patient has survived, to the ICU. (As chap. 2 points out, the very first right-to-die cases involved once-competent young adults who were without oxygen for more than twelve minutes and then resuscitated, only to enter into a PVS.)

The PVS is a consequence of extensive damage to the higher brain centers, especially the cerebral cortex that contains a person's cognitive functions. If there is a loss of oxygen to the brain for *only* four to six minutes, the cerebral cortex dies and the patient enters the twilight zone of the vegetative state.

A patient is in a permanent vegetative state when, after repeated X-ray computed tomography (CT scans), electroencephalograms (EEGs),[43] and other medical tests determine, with a very "high degree of certainty, that the brain damage is extensive and irreversible."[44] Over this time, the cerebral cortex has atrophied, lost almost half its original weight. In all cases, this part of the brain dramatically loses weight. (After clinical death, autopsies indicate that the weight of the brain of the PVS patient is more than 50 percent less than its estimated original weight prior to extensive loss of oxygen.)

"How to come to death" in the twenty-first century is one of the major dilemmas raised by the consequences of contemporary medical technologies. Indeed, this quandary lies at the core of this book. These medical efforts—which include chemotherapy, pacemakers, defibrillators, and transplanting organs—may very well lengthen a patient's life. And most *patients,* especially the dying ones, want these medical interventions because they "extend dying."[45]

V. The Questions Raised by Medicalization of Death

Given the existence of these new medical technological developments that have led to the prolongation of life, occasionally accompanied by the paradox of PVS, there emerged in the late decades of the twentieth century some very fundamental questions regarding the consequences of medically extending life.[46]

Should a patient whose breathing and heartbeat have been restored—by CPR or other methods but who is in a —be kept alive by artificial nutrition and hydration and a mechanical ventilator? A medical ethicist phrased the quandary in the following way:

Either the person in a PVS is dead, in which case it is permissible to withdraw therapy; or such a person is alive, and the issue then is whether the withdrawal of therapy is permissible, even though such an individual is not dead [but will die when the therapy is withdrawn].[47]

Or is a person in a PVS—essentially incompetent and without the possibility of a minimal quality of life ever returning—even alive? Some "have maintained that permanently unconscious patients should be declared dead, on the grounds that they are no longer persons."[48]

For the parents of Karen Ann Quinlan and Nancy Cruzan, and for the husband of Terri Schiavo, their loved one in a PVS is a lost personhood. They *died* when the higher brain functions ceased to exist—even though Karen and Nancy and Terri lived for ten, seven, and fifteen years, respectively, each felled by a terrible accident.

This dreadful situation illuminates the weighty medical, moral, and political reality: the medicalization of death distinguishes *social* from *biological* death. It has led to some fundamental questions, discussed in succeeding chapters, regarding continuance of medical treatment for incompetent patients and whether a terminally ill competent person can end her life with the assistance of a physician.

Social death occurs when family members believe that their parent, or sibling, or spouse has "died" because of a stroke, PVS, or another serious condition "that destroys or masks the personality of the individual."[49] Karen Ann Quinlan's[50] mother poignantly addressed this reality when she wrote:

We could prolong [her] life, but we could not make that life better. No, we could not heal or cure [Karen, who was] surviving only by machines. We could only prolong [our daughter's] dying.[51]

This *social* death occurs days, weeks, months, or years before medically determined *biological death*, when the patient is declared clinically dead. The discrepancy between them is one of the most difficult features of contemporary medical decision making. And it has become an equally difficult ethical, political, and legal problem as well.

Americans and all people living in highly industrialized societies have barely begun to address these unanticipated questions generated by the actuality of medicalization of death. This new reality has raised serious, painfully difficult questions that were not on the minds of patients, families, doctors, nurses, lawyers, judges, priests, rabbis, ministers, politicians, economists, and a myriad of others persons and organizations as recently as forty years ago.

Can a competent patient who is in severe pain, and who will not recover from the illness wracking his or her body, instruct the physician to withdraw life support or refuse to have the medical/technological procedure attached to him or her in the hospital? Does such a patient have the legal, constitutional right to choose to die? Further, can a physician assist the dying patient who makes this choice?

What about a person who *was* competent prior to a traumatic event, given CPR by EMTs at the scene of the accident, and then becomes incompetent in an irreversible coma. The patient is kept alive by an artificial respiratory machine and/or a nutrition and hydration tube. Can life support be withdrawn under these circumstances? And if the person is an incompetent adult because of the trauma, who is it that can request the termination of life support?

What about the relationship between these medical conundrums and the law? In succeeding chapters, we will see judges struggling to avoid applying traditional criminal law principles to these radically evolving medical standards and practices. These essential questions have led to controversial and conflicting responses since the 1970s in courtrooms, medical schools, and hospitals, in the media, in religion, and in legislatures across the nation.

Ironically, the very first set of constitutional cases that became controversial media stories came about because *young adults*—not elderly patients with chronic, debilitating illnesses—had their hearts and breathing restored by emergency medical personnel. However, because CPR began *after* ten to twelve minutes of heart stoppage and nonrespiration in the young adult, the patient suffered severe brain damage because of the lack of blood circulation and was in an irreversible coma—in a PVS. These early landmark cases, beginning in the mid-1970s, grappled with what kind of medical treatment is permitted, when can such treatment be terminated, and under what circumstances.

Could parents and husbands and wives, facing the medical calamity of near–brain death in their loved one have the hospital remove the breathing and/or feeding/hydration tube that is keeping the patient alive? Or would they—and the medical staff—be violating state laws that prohibit such actions?

These are some of the troubling questions—legal, ethical, and political—that have emerged in this era characterized by the medicalization of death. Do the participants in these end-of-life dramas have the liberty, protected by the words of the U.S. Constitution, to make such fateful choices? Can the state, in the name of preserving life, refuse to accept this broad definition of liberty?

To understand the questions and explain the answers is the focus of this book. In order to accomplish these tasks, it is important to view the legal, constitutional, and political history of this drama as it has unfolded since the 1970s. In the end, this analysis will lead to an answer to fundamental human issue: Does a patient who is facing death have the liberty to choose to die with the assistance of a physician rather than live with pain or live without any quality of life?

2 THE PLIGHT OF THE INCOMPETENT PATIENT IN A "PERMANENT VEGETATIVE STATE" (PVS)

> *Quinlan* was the *Brown v Board of Education* of the right-to-die movement.
>
> —Ian Dowbiggin[1]

This chapter explores the initial set of questions that arose when one consequence of the medicalization of death—PVS—first appeared in state and federal courts. Because of the intensive media coverage of the cases, public discussions of the questions ensued. The answers are legal and constitutional stepping-stones to the question that is the central focus of the book: Does a competent, dying person have the liberty to choose to die with a physician's assistance?

The cases that initiated the right-to-die debates raised the following questions: Who decides when life support is withheld, or discontinued and withdrawn, from a competent patient? Who decides the fate of the once-competent but, because of catastrophic injury, now-incompetent patient who is in a PVS?

The chapter focuses primarily on the leading early cases: *In Re Quinlan*, 1976, and *Cruzan v Director, Missouri Dept of Heath*, 1990. Chapter 3 examines the highly controversial *In Re Schiavo* case that began its fifteen-year odyssey in 1990.

These two chapters address two central legal and constitutional principles intimately bound to the questions raised by the litigation. First, the centuries-old common law doctrine of *self-determination* or *personal autonomy*,[2] which is a person's right to make decisions involving one's life, including the decision to end it. Second, the *constitutional defenses* for a decision to withhold or withdraw medical assistance found in the U.S. Supreme Court's individual privacy decisions, essentially *Griswold*, 1965, and *Roe*, 1973, as well as in opinions that interpreted the meaning and scope of a person's liberty found in the Constitution's Due Process clauses.

In the right-to-die litigation, as in all other areas of constitutional law, there is a balance struck by the judges between the interests of the state in preserving life and the individual's freedom to refuse medical treatment and hasten death.[3] Even a fundamental right is not absolute. The state or federal government can interfere and prevent a person from using such a right if the restrictive statute is (1) narrowly tailored and (2) compelling reasons are presented that explain the necessity for the state's infringement of a fundamental right.

The U.S. Constitution contains the important concept of federalism: the division of governmental power between a central government and local governments. The document's preamble spells out the important functions of the central government: "to insure domestic Tranquility, provide for the common defense, promote the general Welfare, and secure the Blessings of Liberty."

Article I enumerates the powers the federal government uses to achieve these goals, especially Article I, section 8, which lists these powers, ending with the broad power to "make all Laws which shall be *necessary and proper* for carrying into Execution the foregoing Powers, and all other Powers vested in this Constitution in the Government of the United States, or in any Department or Officer thereof."[4]

The Tenth Amendment is the key to understanding the powers of the states in our constitutional system. Ratified in 1791, with the other nine amendments that make up the Bill of Rights, the Tenth Amendment states: "The powers *not delegated* to the United States by the Constitution [Article I, section 8], *nor prohibited* by it to the States [Article I, section 10], are reserved to the States respectively, or to the people [my emphasis]."[5]

Our history illustrates the broad powers state governments have to pass legislation, which protects the sovereign people from all types of harm. Since the ratification of our system of republican government in 1789, the states are allowed "great latitude under their police powers to legislate as to the protection of the lives, limbs, health, comfort, and quiet of all persons."[6]

One state responsibility is the regulation of the medical profession under its *police powers*. Another, very basic, state "police power" is the passage of legislation for the preservation of the lives of all persons who live within its jurisdiction. Using these powers, most state legislatures prohibited a physician licensed to practice in the state from writing prescriptions for lethal medications for use by their dying patients to hasten their deaths.

As against the individual competent and informed patient's rights of self-determination and liberty, then, there are a number of primary state concerns, codified in the criminal laws passed and in the regulations promulgated, that judges take into consideration in the balancing process when asked to resolve the conflict between the individual rights and the state's police power.

"First, and the most significant, [there is] the preservation of the lives of the patient and others; second, the prevention of suicide; third, the protection of innocent third parties [the impact of the patient's death on the family, especially minor children]; and fourth, the protection of the ethics of the medical profession."[7]

This balancing of interests is done by judges, men and women, politically elected or appointed, who have to examine, in the right-to-die cases, the blizzard of medical "facts"—often containing contradictory assessments—before them in a case in light of precedent and practice. Equally true is the very subjective nature of this decision making. As this chapter will indicate, in a federal system there are a number of standards—often contradictory—for making these judgments. They exist in the common law, in statutes, in the U.S. and state Constitutions, and in state and federal court decisions.

Concepts and values such as "informed consent," "substituted judgment," "the right to be left alone," "personal autonomy," "right to privacy," "best interest," "clear and convincing evidence," and the "sanctity of life" abound in legal, political, and medical discussions about withdrawing or withholding medical devices that keep people alive. However, when there are conflicts between government officials (including medical administrators) and patients, and their guardians and families, regarding the appropriateness of withdrawal requests, the judge is the final authority. While each case involves one or more of the above values, each case's *fact* situation is different from all those that preceded it. And each case, therefore, calls for a new balancing of interests by the adjudicator.

Although judges and courts have been making such choices since the medicalization of death began in mid-twentieth century, they are often reluctant, painful judgments. A New Jersey Supreme Court Justice said, ruefully, in 1987, about the then still relatively new problem: "Science has forced medical choices upon us that we have yet fully to resolve in the context of our values."[8]

I. The Competent Person's Decision to
Refuse Life-Sustaining Medical Treatment

A patient, so long as she is competent and has been fully informed of the consequences of her decision, has a near absolute right to refuse life-sustaining medical treatment even if that means that the person will die. A knowledgeable patient, said the Michigan Supreme Court in 1990, "may refuse life-sustaining medical treatment because the treatment itself is a violation of bodily integrity."[9] The concept of bodily integrity "has ancient roots in Anglo-American law, in the common law right to be free of unconsented invasion, in penal codes' prohibitions on battery, and in state constitutional provisions."[10]

Even if the competent patient is a young adult, *not* terminally ill *nor* in severe, unremitting pain, he can refuse medical assistance or request the withdrawal of medical aid if that is his informed desire. In *Bouvia*, involving a young female quadriplegic suffering from cerebral palsy, the California Supreme Court allowed the woman to refuse continued forced feeding even though she was not a terminally ill patient. The decision to refuse continuing treatment was hers alone to make:

> It is incongruous, if not monstrous, for medical practitioners to assert their right to preserve a life that someone else must live, or more accurately, endure for "15 to 20 years." We cannot conceive it to be the policy of this state to inflict such an ordeal upon anyone.[11]

Whether the patient's argument to the court is based on the common law right of personal autonomy, or on the constitutional rights to privacy, or the liberty interest "to live and die according to his own values,"[12] his choice is paramount. This choice, said one court, "protects the patient's status as a human being."[13]

As early as 1891, the U.S. Supreme Court concluded that "no right is held more sacred, or is more carefully guarded, by the common law, than the right of every individual to the possession and control of his own person, free from all restraint or interference of others, unless by clear and unquestionable authority of law."[14] This right is at the very core of the legal questions raised in recent decades regarding a person's right to terminate treatment.

The 1990 *Cruzan* majority decision, acknowledged this legal axiom when, in *dicta*,[15] it stated that a competent person's constitutionally protected liberty interest means at least that the person has the right to be free of bodily invasion. Chief Justice Rehnquist, writing for the Court, wrote that "the principle that a competent person has a constitutionally protected liberty interest in refusing unwanted medical treatment may be inferred from our prior decisions. . . . [We] assume that the Constitution would grant a competent person a constitutionally protected right to refuse lifesaving hydration and nutrition."[16]

Justice O'Connor's concurrence in *Cruzan* was even more emphatic:

> Because our notions of liberty are inextricably entwined with our idea of physical freedom and self-determination, the Court has often deemed state incursions into the body repugnant to the Due Process Clause.[17]

Clearly, although formally noted as *dicta*, all five *Cruzan* opinions, in part, "stand for the proposition that there is a protective liberty interest in rejecting invasive treatment, even when the predicted consequence is death."[18]

II. When a Competent Person Becomes Incompetent and in a PVS

The natural follow-up question is what happens when a competent adult suffers a catastrophic trauma? When a competent person, for whatever medical reason, becomes incompetent and is in a PVS,[19] the medical and the legal context shifts focus. In this new scenario, the prime decision-maker is not the patient but the person appointed guardian[20] for the now-incompetent patient. And the prime legal question the court has to wrestle with, when the guardian asks for a court order to withdraw or withhold medical assistance, is whether there is sufficient evidence presented by the guardian (respecting the patient's intentions regarding life support *when she was competent*) to warrant issuance of an order to discontinue the treatment.

In 1976 the New Jersey Supreme Court, in *In Re Quinlan*, was the first court in the nation to grapple with this emergent medical, legal and moral dilemma.

a. In Re Quinlan, 1976

Twice during the evening of April 15, 1975, the twenty-one-year-old New Jersey resident Karen Ann Quinlan stopped breathing. According to her friends, Karen had been dieting and, on that day, had had nothing to eat. That evening they celebrated a friend's birthday by having a few drinks at a local pub. Karen, evidently, had a few gin and tonics "and then started to nod off."

Her friends drove her to her apartment (shared with two other young women), brought her to her bedroom, and then left. Later, one of the friends checked on Karen and found her not breathing. She attempted to resuscitate her with CPR. The EMTs arrived, resuscitated Karen, and rushed her to the hospital. She had sustained two lengthy respiratory arrests, each lasting about fifteen minutes, prior to coming to the hospital.[21]

While Quinlan received extraordinary medical treatment in the hospital, she did not regain consciousness. Urine and blood samples revealed only a "'normal and therapeutic' level of aspirin and the tranquilizer Valium in her system. . . . Tests were taken for [the presence of] harder drugs (cocaine, barbiturates, inhalants, etc.) All the tests came back negative—which meant that Karen had no drugs in her system."[22] Clearly, Karen's lack of oxygen (*anoxia*) for all those minutes produced severe brain damage, left her in a PVS, with a respirator breathing for her, and with a hydration and nutrition tube sustaining her.

Karen's heartbroken parents initially instructed the neurologist to do everything possible to keep their daughter alive. They visited their comatose daughter every day. However, after three months of no improvement in Karen's condition and with the somber prognosis that she would never "regain any level of cognitive function,"[23] her parents, after consulting with their local parish priest (who supported their decision), sought to have the respirator removed by the medical staff.

As her mother wrote, "by late May, 1975, I faced the reality that there was no medical help for Karen."[24] The parents signed a statement instructing the doctors to "to discontinue all extraordinary measures, including the use of a respirator for our daughter, Karen Quinlan.[25]

Dr. Morse, Karen's physician, however, refused to withdraw the respirator, "asserting that to do so would deviate from standard medical practice and would require making a 'quality of life' determination, which he would not do."[26] In response, Karen's father, Joseph, on September 12, 1975, "appealing to the power of equity,[27] and relying on claimed constitutional rights of free exercise of religion, of privacy, and of protection against cruel and unusual punishment,

> sought judicial authority to (1)withdraw the life-sustaining mechanisms temporarily preserving his daughter's life, and (2) his appointment as guardian of her person to that end.[28]

Judge Robert Muir heard the case, and the trial was set for October 20, 1975. The next day, headlines blasted the story on front pages: "Father Asks the Court to Allow Him to Kill His Daughter." As Julia Quinlan would write, "from that moment on our lives would never be the same. We were literally thrust into the public eye. . . . Overnight, Karen, as well as Joe and I, became what the press called *celebrities*, but not by choice."[29]

On November 10, 1975, Judge Muir announced his decision. For Muir, judicial conflict resolution in equity cases rested with his "*judicial conscience* and [that would] govern the court in the determination of disputes between litigants" (my emphasis).

Equating his "judicial conscience and morality" with that of the medical profession, which Muir saw as the guardian of morality in situations like Karen Quinlan's, and "charged by society to do all within its human power to *favor life against death*," he ruled in favor of Dr. Morse and the hospital in *Quinlan*.[30]

Specifically, he concluded that Dr. Morse's behavior in refusing to act on the Quinlans' request, was "exemplary." The doctor was a "man who demonstrated strong empathy and compassion, and a man who has directed care that impressed all the experts."[31]

Muir rejected the Quinlans' argument that, before her tragedy, Karen said she had no desire to live on a machine. Her statements, when she was just twenty years old, were not sufficiently probative enough (not enough proof or evidence presented) to persuade Muir to rule in her parent's favor. The judge could not provide the equitable relief sought by the Quinlans.

Further, while the Quinlans could agree with medical treatment decisions, they could not order the medical staff to act contrary to Dr. Morse's decisions. Additionally, Muir barred them from playing *any* role in medical decision making.[32] And he appointed a lawyer, Daniel Coburn, as guardian *ad litem* to protect Karen's interests. In the end, Muir

> concluded that the constitutional right to privacy claimed by Karen's parents on her behalf was weaker than, and trumped by, both the medical profession's duty to provide life-giving care and the judicial obligation (as *parens patriae*)[33] to act in Karen's best interest by choosing her life over her death.[34]

A week later, the Quinlans filed an appeal with the appellate division of the New Jersey Supreme Court. Bypassing the intermediate state appeals court, the Supreme Court granted the petition, due, they said, to the important issues presented by "the tragic plight of Karen and the Quinlan family."[35]

The justices heard arguments on January 26, 1976, and, very quickly, announced their unanimous opinion on March 31, 1976. The case was seen by the Court, not as a case in equity but as "a matter of transcendent importance," involving questions of constitutional law and statutory meaning.[36]

Quinlan, said the court,

> involves questions related to the definition and existence of death, the prolongation of life through artificial means developed by medical technology undreamed of in past generations of the practice of the healing arts;[37] the impact of such durationally indeterminate and artificial life prolongation on the rights of the incompetent, her family, and society in general; the bearing of constitutional right and the scope of judicial responsibility, as to the appropriate response of an equity court of justice to the extraordinary prayer for relief of the plaintiff, Joseph Quinlan, to guardianship of the person of his daughter.[38]

Joseph Quinlan's lawyer urged the New Jersey Supreme Court to rule in his favor by presenting three constitutional and legal arguments: the First Amendment's free exercise of religion clause, the Eighth Amendment's prohibition against cruel and unusual punishment, and the constitutional right of privacy.

The Court speedily rejected the first two contentions, finding neither right applicable in the case.[39] The opinion then turned to the argument that privacy rights, including "what have been called rights of 'personality,'" were paramount as against the state's right to preverve life. Joseph Quinlan's argument was that the constitutional right of privacy, a right that "has given us most concern,"[40] extended to the grave, tragic situation the Quinlan family faced.

The justices, after talking about the U.S. Supreme Court's recent opinions that created a constitutional right of personal privacy, said: "Presumably this [personal privacy] right is broad enough to encompass a patient's decision to decline medical treatment under certain circumstances, in much the same way as it is broad enough to encompass a woman's decision to terminate pregnancy under certain conditions."[41]

The Court *balanced* the state's responsibility for the "preservation and sanctity of human life and defense of the right of the physician to administer medical treatment according to his best judgment," against the right of personal privacy interests of Karen Quinlan, "as seen by her surrogate," to terminate life support, which only maintained her vegetative existence.

> We think that the State's interest weakens and the individual's right to privacy grows as the degree of bodily invasion increases and the prognosis dims. Ultimately there comes a point at which the individual's rights overcome the State interest.[42]

Although Karen "is grossly incompetent, . . . we have concluded that Karen's right of privacy may be asserted on her behalf by her guardian under the peculiar circumstances here present. . . . The only way to prevent destruction of the right is to permit the guardian and family of Karen to render their best judgment, subject to the qualifications hereinafter stated, as to whether she would exercise it in these circumstances."[43]

The opinion was unanimous and had an immediate impact. The public, which had followed the case closely since 1975, learned about the emergent problem and the importance of living wills and advanced care directives. Ethics committees began to appear in hospitals, nursing homes, and hospices after *Quinlan*.

The constitutional right to privacy is not destroyed if a person becomes incompetent; it can be transferred to those who know the patient best—the family of the victim. However, the hospital did not act to create a consultative group and, after a meeting with its lawyers, the hospital refused to comply with and carry out the Court decision.

Furthermore, the doctors initially refused to bring their views to the hospital administrators. However, after almost two months, Dr. Morse and his associate spoke to the Quinlans to tell them "that they would like to attempt to wean Karen off the respirator."

The effort began on May 17, 1976. "By May 22 the weaning process was successfully completed. Karen appeared tired but peaceful. . . . We had no idea how long she would survive"[44]

By that time, the hospital wanted Karen Quinlan out. The family was turned down by twenty-two New Jersey hospitals. Finally, the Morris View Nursing Home in Morris County, New Jersey, accepted Karen. The hospital administrators established an Ethics Committee in order to comply with the Supreme Court declaratory order, and Karen was moved in early June 1976.

The expectation held by most medical professionals, and by the New Jersey Supreme Court, was that Karen, once off the respirator (but still on the nutrition and hydration tube), would not live very long. Everyone was mistaken.

Karen existed in a PVS for another decade. It was not until June 11, 1985, that Karen died.[45] The statement given to the press the evening of her death was a short one: "Miss Quinlan developed pneumonia five days ago. She died of respiratory failure following acute pneumonia. We ask the press to respect the family's wishes, which is to be left alone to mourn the loss of their daughter in private."[46]

The New Jersey Supreme Court, in *Quinlan*, "recognized that the federal constitutional right to privacy was broad enough to encompass an individual's decision to decline medical treatment, even if that decision would lead to the individual's death."[47] Even more important than that extension of the right to privacy was the Court's judgment that such decisions not rest with the medical doctors. In a case involving an incompetent patient, the guardian could make the decision.

The *Quinlan* decision, however forward looking it was, was the rule of law only in New Jersey. There was no rush on the part of state legislators to pass statutes incorporating *Quinlan*'s guidelines into laws regarding the rights of non-competent PVS patients. The sanctity of life remained the dominant value held by most physicians, nurses, politicians and judges.

When the U.S. Supreme Court, in 1990, heard the case of *Cruzan v Director, Missouri Department of Health*,[48] a case very similar to *Quinlan*, the Justices took a very different path to reach their decision than did the New Jersey justices.

b. Cruzan v Director, Missouri Department of Health, 1990

Nancy Beth Cruzan[49] was a young, twenty-seven-year-old adult when, in January 1983, she lost control of her automobile and was thrown into a ditch, where she lay in respiratory and cardiac arrest between twelve and fourteen minutes. Like the Quinlan event, EMT personnel, using CPR, were able to restore breathing and heartbeat at the crash site and then transport her to the hospital.

Nancy needed a gastrostomy tube to provide nutrition and hydration.[50] Neurologists who examined her in the emergency room were concerned about the *anoxia* she experienced immediately after she was thrown from the car.

A week after the January 11, 1983, accident, a medical report noted: "Patient is out of coma, but has no verbal response and does not follow commands."[51] The family and the doctors had to wait and see if there was any improvement, if Nancy could respond to commands. A month after the accident, everyone noticed that Nancy's arms and legs "had started to stiffen and atrophy, drawing in slowly toward her trunk. The doctors and nurses called this stiffening 'contractures.'"[52]

During time immediately after the accident, Nancy "progressed to an unconscious state in which she was able to orally digest some nutrition."[53] The CT scans (pictures of Nancy's brain) in the ER were very bad, indicating severe brain damage.

An EEG taken the night of the accident indicated significant abnormality in her brain. It showed a "nearly flat background."[54] Another EEG taken two months later was even worse than the initial one; it showed *further* deterioration. By February 1984, three months after her accident, the latest EEG report brought no change: "Flat background activity, coupled with patient's history, is suggestive of a vegetative comatose state."

In August 1986, given the extremely poor prognosis, the Cruzans signed a "No CPR Form" in the event Nancy's heart or lungs ceased functioning. This form, also known as a "do not resuscitate" (DNR) order, was witnessed by a notary and copies given to the hospital administrators, nurses, and doctors. The parents were prepared to let her go.

In May 1987, after four and one-half years of Nancy existing in a PVS, the parents took the next, inexorable step. They requested that hospital personnel "discontinue the life support system that provides nutrition and hydration to our daughter." The hospital refused and, like the Quinlans, the Cruzans sought a court order authorizing the withdrawal of the feeding tube.

In 1985, Missouri passed a "living will" statute, so that citizens of the state could prepare advance living wills. The person specified which medical treatments she would not want, as well as parameters for DNR orders, if she became terminally ill or incompetent. The law, however, specifically stated "that feeding tubes were not considered medical treatment in Missouri, and that a person could *not* list a feeding tube as a treatment to forgo in a Missouri living will." Given this statutory prohibition, the state response to the Cruzan request was a categorical negative. The official letter from the Missouri Department of Health said: "*We will not consider such a procedure without a specific Order of the Courts of Missouri* in a case in which we are a party and a final decision is issued."[55] (The emphasis is in the original letter.)

The Cruzans had to go into court to discontinue use of Nancy's feeding and hydration tube. Because they were of very modest financial means, they needed a lawyer who would take their case *pro bono*.[56] And in May 1987, they were put in touch with William Colby, a young, thirty-something lawyer who worked for a law firm in Kansas City, Missouri. For the next three years, from 1987 to 1990, Colby spent a substantial amount of time preparing briefs and oral arguments for appearances in two Missouri courts and in the U.S. Supreme Court.

As soon as Colby took the case, he began reading the literature on the withdrawal of medical machines that maintained life for incompetent patients, including the *Quinlan* case. A view of his initial jottings of legal questions surrounding the Cruzan tragedy is an important insight into the mind of a lawyer embarking on this difficult and controversial road.

The right to privacy was everywhere [in the literature], but should that controversial right be the foundation of our case?[57] Some cases suggested treating a patient against her wishes might legally be considered *battery*, defined as the touching of another person without consent or legal justification. Would a simple claim of *battery* under Missouri law solve the Cruzans' case?. . . I was trying to start a lawsuit—did I need both common law and constitutional rights? Which of these theories made the most sense in Missouri? . . . Where should we file, state or federal court? Should we try to find a way to have a jury trial? . . . Did we need to sue anyone, such as the state hospital or the Missouri Department of Health?[58]

After meeting with Judge Teel, the probate judge already involved in the case, Colby filed a petition in Teel's court seeking a declaratory judgment that would proclaim that the Cruzans, as guardians of Nancy, had the authority to act in their daughter's "best interests."

Colby's strategy in the brief and then in court was threefold:

(1) Present the medical evidence and medical witnesses who would testify about Nancy's status as an unconscious patient in a PVS.

(2) Present evidence indicating Nancy's views, before the accident while she was conscious and competent, about being kept alive by medical machines.

(3) Present evidence from medical doctors and medical ethicists who supported the parents request for discontinuation of the medical feeding and nutrition.

In addition, Colby had to deal with the 1985 Missouri living will statute. In particular, there was the specific rejection by the Missouri legislators of "any procedure to provide nutrition or hydration" as a *medical* procedure. This prohibition was "the exact medical procedure our lawsuit would seek to withdraw."[59]

The arguments took place in March 1988. Judge Teel spent months agonizing over the decision he had to make. By mid-July 1988, he had reached judgment and his decision was delivered on July 27:

> There is a fundamental right expressed in our Constitution as the right to liberty which permits an individual to refuse or direct the withholding or withdrawal of artificial death prolonging procedures when the person has no more cognitive brain function than our Ward [Nancy] and all the physicians agree there is no hope of further recovery while the deterioration of the brain continues with further overall worsening physical contractions. The Respondents, employees of the state of Missouri, are directed to cause the request of the Co-guardians (Nancy's parents) to withdraw nutrition or hydration to be carried out. Such a request having Court approval, shall be taken the same as a request for discontinuance of any other form of artificial life support systems.[60]

The respondents, the hospital administrators, and the Missouri Department of Health, immediately appealed to the Missouri Supreme Court, bypassing the intermediate state appellate court. The Missouri Supreme Court accepted the petition and docketed the appeal for a hearing in September 1988.[61]

Oral argument in the Missouri Supreme Court took place on September 28, 1988. A few weeks before Christmas, on December 14, 1988, the opinion came down. The Court ruled 4:3 to reverse Teel's opinion, concluding that Missouri law did not allow Nancy's parents to choose to have the patient die.

> In the face of this State's strongly stated policy in favor of life, we choose to err on the side of life, respecting the rights of incompetent persons who may wish to live despite a severely diminished quality of life.[62]

The three dissenters deferred to the family's judgment: "I am not persuaded that the State is a better decision-maker than Nancy's parents," said one dissenting judge. Another wrote that Judge Teel's opinion "was a courageous voyage in an area not previously charted by Missouri courts."

Totally rejecting New Jersey's *Quinlan* precedent, the majority opinion concluded that there was *no* broad right of privacy to refuse life-sustaining medical treatment in either the Missouri or the U.S. Constitutions.[63] The Missouri justices stated that the state's policy in such medical cases was to respect "the sanctity of life."[64]

Only when guardians produce documentary evidence reliable enough to meet Missouri's "clear and convincing evidence" standard ("the most rigid of formalities") for withdrawal of life-sustaining medical care from an incompetent individual could the state's protection of Nancy Cruzan end.[65] In the absence of such evidence, the "substituted judgment" of Nancy's parents acting in her best interest, a key factor in the *Quinlan* decision, would not be the basis of termination of medical care for incompetent patients in Missouri.

In the *Cruzan* decision, the Missouri Supreme Court concluded that there was only insufficiently reliable evidence that Nancy would have wanted an end to all extraordinary medical care. Therefore the feeding tube would not be removed.

On March 13, 1989, the Cruzans appealed the Missouri Supreme Court decision to the U.S. Supreme Court and the Justices granted *certiorari* to hear the arguments.[66] The Cruzans petition for *certiorari*[67] asked the justices to consider:

Whether a State may, *consistently with the Due Process Clause*, require clear and convincing evidence that an incompetent person would want life-sustaining medical procedures withdrawn before it approves the termination of such procedures.[68] (my emphasis)

Given the conservative makeup of the Court sitting in 1989, the last thing Colby wanted was to raise the privacy specter to the conservative Justices: "Trying to win our case using the right to privacy just didn't make sense with this Court. We stayed as far away from *Roe v Wade* as we could."[69] Instead, the focus of the appeal was on the scope of liberty found in the U.S. Constitution's Due Process Clause.

Colby hoped that the U.S. solicitor general's office would file an *amicus* in support of Nancy Cruzan. However, in early September, the Justice Department, reflecting the conservative pro-life views of the Republican Party and of President George W. H. Bush, filed a friend of the court brief *supporting* the Missouri position on the question.

This was a very critical event in the *Cruzan* litigation. Historically, when the U.S. government files a petition for *certiorari*, it is successful *between 70 and 80 percent of the time.* Furthermore, when the solicitor general files an *amicus* petition in a case which is of "interest to the United States," a majority of the time the federal government supports the eventual "winner" in the litigation before the Court.[70]

When Colby and others read the *amicus* brief filed by the solicitor general Kenneth Starr, they were not surprised at the quality of the brief; it was about two dozen pages long and very well written. Nor was anyone surprised by its contents. As Colby knew, Starr's brief categorically rejected any use of the "privacy" principle constructed by the liberal Warren Court in *Griswold*. It urged the Justices to "decline petitioner's invitation to extend the 'right of privacy' to cover all types of decisions about medical treatments and procedures. Such an approach invites judicial intervention based on little more than the 'predilections of those who happen at the time to be Members of the Court.'"[71]

Instead, the Starr brief maintained that the liberty in Due Process "approach is more in keeping with the Court's teachings. . . . Historical sources—including the Framers' understanding of our Nation's long-standing traditions[72]—provide a more objective basis for identifying liberty interests entitled to heightened judicial protection."

By limiting the scope of substantive due process to those interests that have received the sanctions of history, tradition, and law, the Due Process clause serves "to prevent future generations from lightly casting aside important traditional values" without at the same time becoming a judicial license "to invent new ones."[73]

Although conceding that, "at a minimum, the Framers understood 'liberty' to mean [a competent person's] freedom from state-imposed physical restraints, [and that has] always been recognized as the core of the liberty protected by the Due Process Clause," this constitutional principle did not extend to an incompetent person in a PVS. The same argument was made by Starr regarding the common law protection of bodily integrity. Both the constitutional and the common law protections are not unqualified. Under certain conditions the state can intervene to prevent a competent person from refusing medical treatment.

But what about incompetent patients such as Nancy Cruzan? The solicitor general's brief argued that *even if* the Court assumed that a competent patient had an absolute right to refuse treatment, "it does not follow that any such right would extend to an adult who is currently incompetent." The state, historically, has had a "profound interest in preserving human life. *The State's interest is not in quality of life*. The State's interest is an unqualified interest in life (my emphasis).[74]

Given the "compelling governmental interests in protecting incompetent persons and in assuring accurate determinations of an incompetent patient's wishes, decisions by the States and the federal government about appropriate evidentiary standards and procedures for giving effect to decisions by previously competent adults should not be subject to any heightened standard of judicial review." If Missouri has designed a standard for deciding whether a feeding tube can be disconnected—if it is "reasonably designed"—it will pass constitutional and common law muster. Missouri's evidentiary rule, the "clear and convincing evidence" standard of proof, was a "reasonably designed" standard that the U.S. Supreme Court should validate in the *Cruzan* case.[75]

In focusing extensively on the solicitor general's *amicus* brief, the U.S. Supreme Court followed the government's suggestions. Indeed, reading the majority opinion is almost like reading the Starr *amicus* brief.

The U.S. Supreme Court opinion came down on the last day of the 1989 Term. The majority opinion concluded that Missouri could require clear and convincing evidence of an incompetent's wishes regarding withdrawal of life-sustaining treatment.[76]

All nine Justices concluded that a competent person has a liberty interest under the Due Process Clause in refusing unwanted medical treatment. However, it is not an absolute right; stating that a person has a liberty interest "does not end the inquiry; whether Cruzan's constitutional rights have been violated must be determined by balancing his liberty interests against the relevant state interests."[77]

Missouri's establishment of a "reasonably designed" procedural safeguard—the clear and convincing evidence rule—to assure that the surrogate's action conforms as best as possible to the wishes expressed by the patient while competent is a "permissible" exercise of the state's police powers to protect its citizens.

Furthermore, the Missouri Supreme Court did not commit constitutional error in concluding that the evidence presented in Judge Teel's court did not rise to the level of the clear and convincing evidence standard.

The Due Process Clause, said the majority, did not require Missouri to accept the "substituted judgment" of Nancy's parents in the absence of substantial proof that their judgment reflected the patient's views.[78]

Two Justices in the majority, Sandra Day O'Connor and Antonin Scalia, also wrote short concurring opinions. O'Connor's concurring opinion said: "Today we decide only that one State's practice does not violate the Constitution; the more challenging task of crafting appropriate procedures for safeguarding incompetents' liberty interests is entrusted to the 'laboratory' of the States, in the first instance."[79]

Justice Scalia "would have preferred that we announce, clearly and promptly, that the federal courts have no business in this field."

The various opinions in this case portray quite clearly the difficult, indeed agonizing, questions that are presented by the constantly increasing power of science to keep the human body alive for longer than any reasonable person would want to inhabit it. . . . [The answers to these heartbreaking questions] are neither set forth in the Constitution nor known to the nine Justices of this Court any better than they are known to nine people picked at random from the Kansas City telephone directory.[80]

His final words were spoken like a true constitutional originalist: "The Constitution has nothing to say about the subject. To raise up a constitutional right here we would have to create out of nothing (for it exists neither in text nor tradition) some constitutional principle."[81]

The four dissenters disagreed with the majority on every issue. The right to be free from unwanted medical attention, wrote Justice William J. Brennan (joined in his dissent by Justices Harry Blackmun and Thurgood Marshall), was "deeply rooted in this Nation's traditions."[82] Because the dissenters believed that the right to refuse life-sustaining treatment was a "fundamental" right protected by the Constitution, a state had to show a "compelling" state reason to prevent the discontinuation of the medical assistance. Missouri had not shown such a compelling need to intervene in the *Cruzan* case.[83]

Brennan categorically rejected the Missouri "clear and convincing evidence" standard; the state court's application of the standard in *Cruzan* demonstrated "disdain" for the patient's views about death made before she became incompetent.[84]

Missouri and this Court have displaced Nancy's own assessment of the processes associated with dying. They have discarded evidence of her will, ignored her values, and deprived her of the right to a decision as closely approximating her own choice as humanly possible. They have done so disingenuously in her name and openly in Missouri's own.[85]

Justice Stevens's dissent was the most heart-rending of the five opinions written in *Cruzan*. He raised the normative question about the meaning of life and death: Was mere existence in a PVS truly "life"?

Nancy Cruzan is obviously "alive" in a physiological sense. But for patients like Nancy Cruzan, who have no consciousness and no chance of recovery, there is a serious question as to whether the mere persistence of their bodies is "life" as the word is commonly understood, or as it is used in both the Constitution and the Declaration of Independence.[86]

For Justice Stevens, as it was for Justice Brennan, the

critical question, however, is not how to prove the controlling facts but rather what proven facts should be controlling. In my view, the constitutional question is clear: the best interests of the individual, especially when buttressed by the interests of all related third parties, must prevail over any general state policy that simply ignores those interests.[87]

All four dissenting Justices believed that Nancy Cruzan "has a fundamental *right* to be free of unwanted artificial nutrition and hydration, which right is not outweighed by any interests of the State." In addition, all four maintained that the state's standard of "clear and convincing evidence" was an "improperly biased procedural obstacle [that] impermissibly burdens that right."[88] However, in the U.S. Supreme Court, five votes beat four votes.

In *Cruzan*, the U.S. Supreme Court majority upheld the right of a state to set high and rigid standards regarding evidence that showed an incompetent patient's wishes regarding withdrawal of life-sustaining processes. Furthermore, all nine Justices accepted the fact that artificial nutrition and hydration was a form of medical assistance that must "not be forced on a patient, even though the obvious outcome will be starvation."[89]

After the June 25, 1990, opinion, the case returned to Missouri. Colby prepared for a new hearing before the chancery court judge and, with the assistance of Nancy's parents and friends, began the search for new witnesses who could testify regarding Nancy's views about "living" with the assistance of medical devices. Judge Teel needed to see and hear additional witnesses and had to receive the latest, detailed update on Nancy's medical condition.

There was the required one-day trial on November 1, 1990. Judge Teel announced his decision on December 13, 1990. His order was a short one:

The court, by clear and convincing evidence, finds:

(1) That the intent of our ward [Nancy], if mentally able, would be to terminate her nutrition and hydration.
(2) That there is no evidence of substance to cause belief that our ward would continue her present existence, hopeless as it is, and slowly progressively worsening.

(3) That the allegations in the petition are true and it is sustained.

(4) That the co-guardians. Lester L. [Joe] and Joyce Cruzan, are authorized to cause the removal of nutrition and hydration from our ward, Nancy Beth Cruzan.[90]

The following day, December 14, 1990, Colby, the Cruzan family, and Nancy Cruzan's doctor met with hospital officials and read them the Teel opinion. After a few minutes of hesitation, the hospital administrators reluctantly agreed to comply with the judge's order. The patient's doctor immediately went into Nancy's room, withdrew the gastrostomy tube, and bandaged the wound at 3:30 in the afternoon. Nancy was moved to the hospice unit of the hospital that night.

As soon as the Teel order took effect, pro-life groups in Missouri protested the action. The Missouri Citizens for Life immediately asked the governor to order the Missouri attorney general to go to court to ask for a writ of prohibition, which, if granted, would have stopped the judge's order from being carried out and would have forced the doctors to reinsert Nancy's feeding and hydration tube.

The Missouri governor John Ashcroft,[91] himself a conservative evangelical Republican, called the hospital and requested that the doctors reinsert Nancy's tube. Nancy's doctor refused: "The tube's already out and there's no medical reason to put it back in." When the hospital administrator repeated the governor's request, the doctor pulled out the Teel order. "I have a court order," and he walked away.[92] The state attorney general did not appeal the Teel order.

Unfortunately, the state's announcement was not the final chapter in the *Cruzan* drama. Over the weekend, pro-life leaders in Missouri began to plan a last-ditch effort to marshal public opinion in order to have the feeding and hydration tube reinstalled. The pro-life group, however, failed to stop the withdrawal of the tubes.

Finally, in the early morning of December 26, 1990, Nancy Cruzan was pronounced dead. Two days later, the Cruzan family buried Nancy Cruzan. The grave marker had three dates carved on it: "Born: July 20, 1957; Departed: January 11, 1983; At Peace: December 26, 1990."

The tumult that erupted after Judge Teel's second ruling in favor of the Cruzan co-guardians was a harbinger of the future. The *Cruzan* opinion, much more than *Quinlan*, opened a festering wound in the body politic. First of all, it was an opinion rendered by the nation's highest court; its ruling therefore extended to the legislatures and courts in all fifty states. Also, the Court's conservative majority's *imprimatur* on a very tough, very rigid state standard reflected the views of a large, vocal, politically active community in America that vigorously defended the sanctity of life principle.

In sum, the five-person Court majority said that the right of persons to choose to die was not a fundamental common law right of self-determination nor was it a fundamental liberty protected by the Due Process Clause in the U.S. Constitution. A state, in order to preserve the lives of its residents, could pass legislation such as Missouri's "clear and convincing evidence" rule, even though such state action would keep a PVS patient in an "endless twilight state between life and death."[93]

The five-person Court majority instructed state and federal judges and legislators that there was no fundamental right of self-determination, nor right to privacy, nor liberty interest found in the Constitution that extended to a person's right to choose to die. No state was required, by either the words in the Constitution or in the common law, to protect such a right, unless the values, culture, and politics of the state led lawmakers and judges in that direction.

The *Cruzan* case clearly reflected the diametrically opposed views of the nine members of the U.S. Supreme Court. The minority maintained that there was a fundamental right of self-determination—including the decision to end life. The majority, however, concluded that there was no such fundamental liberty found in the Constitution and that the state could reasonably act to prevent action that would end life.

III. State Responses to *Cruzan*

What were the legal consequences in the states after the U.S. Supreme Court majority, in 1990, dismissed the argument that the right to die was a *fundamental* liberty interest of any person, competent or not, in America?

After *Cruzan*, state legislators and judges viewed the choices they had if legislation was passed that addressed the issue of due process for an incompetent PVS patient and legal challenges came into their courts. There were at least three choices: the Missouri standard of "clear and convincing evidence," there was the "substituted judgment" rule, and the "best interest of the PVS patient" standard.

In a 1995 Pennsylvania case, *In Re Daniel Joseph Fiori, an Adjudged Incompetent*, these options were discussed by the state court. The appellate court decided that the patient's mother, with the consent of two physicians but without court involvement, could remove life-sustaining treatment from her adult son who was in a PVS (because of two separate head traumas) and who did not leave any advanced directives or a living will. The court noted that the "facts here are tragic. This state [PVS] has been described as a *twilight zone* of suspended animation where death commences while life, in some form, continues."[94]

The Missouri standard was not employed by the court because applying it "requires nothing less than unequivocal proof of the patient's express wishes as to the decision to terminate life support."[95] Instead, the appellate court agreed with a lower court "that the 'substituted judgment' standard, in Pennsylvania, is the proper approach."

> We believe that where a PVS patient has not left instructions as to the maintenance of life sustaining treatment, the only practical way to prevent the destruction of the PVS patient's right to refuse medical treatment is to allow a substitute decision maker (such as a close family member) to determine what measures the PVS patient would have desired in light of the patient's prognosis.[96]

Florida's judicial response to the *Cruzan* opinion, in a 1990 case, was similar to the views held by the New Jersey Supreme Court's *Quinlan* opinion. The case that established precedent in Florida in this area of law was *In Re Guardianship of Browning*.[97] The question answered was "Whether the guardian of a patient who is incompetent but not in a PVS and who suffers from an incurable, but not terminal condition, may exercise the patient's right of self-determination to forego sustenance provided artificially by a nasogenic tube."[98]

The court answered in the affirmative: Under the Florida Constitution, the patient's "fundamental right of self-determination, expressed as the right of privacy, controls this case."[99] In this case, the Court extended this fundamental right to an incompetent patient's guardians even though the patient was not in a PVS and was not terminally ill.

Another example of the inconsistent impact of *Cruzan* is the Wisconsin Supreme Court case of *In Re Guardianship of L. W.*, decided in 1992. The Wisconsin Supreme Court held "that a guardian may only direct the withdrawal of life-sustaining medical treatment, including nutrition and hydration, [without court approval,] if the incompetent ward is in a PVS and the decision to withdraw is in the *best interests* of the ward."[100]

The court rejected the use of what the judges labeled a "subjective" *substituted judgment* test, which called for the guardian to consider "the ward's past values, wishes, and beliefs." It also rejected the *clear and convincing evidence* standard because it was "too strict." The court settled on the *best interests* standard because it was an "objective" rule: "the only thing that matters in the decision-making process is what would be in the ward's best interests."[101]

There was, however, no distinct difference described by the court between the "subjective" *substituted judgment* standard they rejected and the "objective" *best interests rule* that became the law in the State.

Also, if one compares the Wisconsin Supreme Court opinion with the Missouri Supreme Court opinion, one sees that what was unclearly differentiated by the Wisconsin jurists (substituted judgment and best interests) were terms that were used *interchangeably* by the Missouri judges.

In a case heard by the Wisconsin Supreme Court five years later, involving a seventy-one-year-old woman suffering from Alzheimer's disease but *not* in a PVS, the Wisconsin court refused to extend the *L. W.* precedent.[102]

While the states, as Justice O'Connor pointed out in her *Cruzan* concurring opinion, can serve as "laboratories" for the development of responses to problems their residents faced, there can be unwelcome consequences. When the U.S. Supreme Court eschewed labeling the right to die as a *fundamental* liberty interest that all persons in America possessed, it left open the consequent reality that states would generate legislation that, in some cases, significantly stifled the right to die for incompetent patients in a PVS in that state.

At the very least, if the right to withdraw life-saving medical devices from patients in a PVS was a *fundamental* personal right by the U.S. Supreme Court in *Cruzan*, then a state had to show *compelling* reasons for interfering with a person's right—even an incompetent patient's right. Furthermore, if a state made the effort to interfere with the fundamental right, and it was challenged in court, judges and justices had to apply the toughest, highest, level of judicial review—*strict scrutiny*.[103]

The New Jersey, Pennsylvania, Florida, Wisconsin, and Missouri cases reflect this unwelcome reality when a right is determined to be non-fundamental. Because the U.S. Supreme Court did not underscore the fundamental nature of a person's right to self-determination, or liberty, or privacy, treatment of incompetent patients in a PVS will vary dramatically based on the state the person resided in when tragedy struck.

The next chapter takes this story to the linkage made between the right of a woman to choose to have an abortion and the right to end the life of a patient in a PVS. Both issues reflect the raging conflict in American politics regarding the sanctity of life principle. In the Terry Schiavo tragedy, which began in 1990, the world's communities were onlookers to these fierce battles.

3

> In *Schiavo*, extraordinary legislative and political
> intervention with the judicial system . . . leave
> everyone wondering where the lines between morality,
> lawmaking, and judicial interpretation truly lie.
> —Marisa Martin[1]

Nancy Cruzan finally died on December 26, 1990. Months earlier, on February 25, 1990, Theresa Marie (Terri) Schiavo, a happily married twenty-seven-year-old woman suffered a major cardiac arrest as a result of a potassium imbalance. Like others who were felled by a cardiac arrest or other acute trauma, EMTs, using CPR, restored her heart beat—after more than twelve minutes without oxygen to her brain. The rescuers transported her to a local Florida hospital. She never regained consciousness. She was in a PVS.

The Schiavo story, while very similar to *Quinlan* and *Cruzan* regarding the horrible impact of PVS on the decision to terminate life support, was unlike the other cases already discussed. Her case turned into a multiyear legal, political, and cultural epic because of the conflation of medical treatment and ethics, fundamental family disagreements, political demagoguery in the state and in Congress, as well as sustained protest and activism by sanctity of life groups.

Schiavo did not add to the case law on the subject of withdrawing medical aid from someone in a PVS. It does underscore, as the *Cruzan* case did, the many controversies surrounding the ideas of privacy, due process, and the right to die.

The Terri Schiavo tragedy was a fifteen-year-long "bitter battle"[2] between her husband, Michael Schiavo, and her parents over whether Terri's feeding and hydration tube should be removed in order to end her life. After eight years in a PVS, her husband, appointed as Terri's guardian (at the time with Terri's parents consent), petitioned a Florida court to have her feeding tube removed. Her parents strongly resisted such a drastic action, and this opposition led to extraordinary judicial and political efforts to leave the tube untouched. In February 2000, the Florida court granted the petition. Both the Florida Supreme Court[3] and the U.S. Supreme Court[4] declined to hear the appeals.

Undeterred, pro-life advocates urged action in the political process to reverse the decision to end Schiavo's life. At various times in that long battle, Florida politicians, including Republican Governor Jeb Bush and Republican state legislators, became participants in the drama. At the national level, conservative politicians, including Governor Bush's brother, Republican President George W. Bush, and leading Republicans in the Congress, passed and signed legislation in attempts to overturn judicial rulings of Florida courts and to restore the medical devices into Terri's body no less than three different times.

Thanks to CNN, MSNBC, and Fox News, by 2005 Terri's fate had also become a global spectacle with billions of people reading about the legal and political battles and watching, again and again, televised videos of Terri Schiavo sitting up in her hospital bed with what seemed to be tears dripping from her eyes.

The Schiavo tragedy did not have *any* impact on state and federal precedents in this area of the law.[5] Indeed, *all* the Florida judges who became involved in the case supported the husband's request to withdraw the medical assistance that was keeping his incompetent PVS wife alive. The Florida Supreme Court *declined* to review these lower court judgments. And the U.S. Supreme Court declined to review the Florida Supreme Court's judgments every time it received another *certiorari* petition. However, *Schiavo* became one more example of the efforts of ideologically driven groups and politicians to influence state and federal judges and Justices of the U.S. Supreme Court.

Schiavo also clearly shows the deep religious and ideological cleavages that continue to exist in twenty-first century America regarding the scope of a person's liberty and personal autonomy ostensibly protected by state and federal constitutions and by the common law. (Unlike the Cruzan family, the Schindler's were conservative, devout, deeply religious parents who believed in the absolute "sanctity of life," even the "sanctity of life" of a person in a PVS.)

The same forces that battled in this case have continued to wage war over the question of whether a person's liberty and autonomy extend to her right to seek the assistance, passive or active, of her physician, in ending life. The *Schiavo* case was another springboard that led to intense, emotional debates surrounding the right of a person to end his life with physician assistance.

I. The Beginning: Terri Schiavo's Cardiac Arrest and PVS, 1990

Given the twelve or so minutes Terri was in cardiac arrest, "nearly twice as long as is generally necessary to cause profound, irreversible brain damage,"[6] she experienced *anoxia* and unconsciousness. A hydration and nutrition tube was placed in Terri in the hospital. That intervention became the focal point of almost seven years of litigation when, in 1998, her husband sought to remove it.

After many months of nonresponsiveness immediately after the accident, and after many clinical physical examinations of Terri by her doctors, all the doctors concluded that she was in a persistent vegetative state, one that, over time would turn into a permanent vegetative state (PVS). Her 2005 autopsy led to findings consistent with clinical descriptions of PVS. "Her brain weight was approximately half of the expected weight. Of particular importance was the hypoxic damage and neuronal loss in her occipital lobes, which indicates cortical blindness."[7]

II. Attempts to End Terri's Existence in State Courts, 1998–2005

From 1990 to 1998 Michael Schiavo did all he could to improve his wife's condition—which was hopeless given the clinical reality that she was in a PVS. On May 11, 1998, Michael petitioned the court to authorize the removal of his wife's feeding and hydration tube. His in-laws, however, adamantly opposed his decision. Unlike the Quinlan and Cruzan misfortunes, in this case there was a categorical objection by the Schindlers to Michael's request to withdraw the feeding and hydration tube. They believed that Terri's death, when it came, would be a natural one, with the grace of God.

They argued that Terri had the same deeply religious beliefs that they held and that she would not want the feeding tube withdrawn.[8] Additionally, unlike their son-in-law, in 1998 and throughout the seven-year ordeal that followed, they still held out hope that Terri would improve.

They insisted that Terri could see objects and persons, and could follow these movements. (As already noted, the 2005 autopsy report clearly rejected their view.)

In response, the court appointed a *guardian ad litem* (GAL) to prepare a report for the court regarding what action would be, in the GAL's view, in the "best interest" of Terri Schiavo. In December 1998, the GAL reported that Terri was in a PVS with no chance of improvement and that her husband's request was motivated "by the potential to inherit the remainder of Ms. Schiavo's estate."[9]

After the GAL report, the Pasco-Pinellas county circuit court judge, George Greer, scheduled a trial to determine Terri Schiavo's fate. The week-long trial without jury began on January 24, 2000.

Over the next five years, Judge Greer would issue almost thirty separate rulings and orders in the case, nearly all of them favorable to Michael Schiavo. In addition, there would be numerous appeals to the district court of appeals (DCA) and close to one dozen appeals to the Florida Supreme Court. There would also be more than one dozen appeals to the federal courts: the U.S. District Court, Middle District, Florida; the Eleventh Circuit U.S. Court of Appeals; and to the U.S. Supreme Court in Washington, D.C.

In all, more than thirty judges at the county, district, state, and federal judicial levels heard appeals, most coming from the Schindlers and conservative support groups, including Randall Terry's Operation Rescue organization as well as Roman Catholic bishops and cardinals in the United States. Even Pope John II, speaking from the Vatican, entered the discussion of Schiavo's fate. Three times Judge Greer ordered the withdrawal of Terri's feeding and hydration tube,[10] and twice the DCA ordered reinsertion of the tube.

On February 11, 2000, less than a month after Judge Greer had heard testimony in his court, he announced his opinion. He concluded, because of the evidence presented at trial, that Terri Schiavo would have chosen to have the feeding tube withdrawn. Testimony before the judge revealed that Terri made comments or statements about end-of-life care to five persons, including her husband and her mother.

Was there, as Florida law commands, "clear and convincing evidence of [Terri's] intent?" Judge Greer indicated that the "court had the testimony of the brother [Scott Schiavo] and sister-in-law [Joan Schiavo,] has reviewed their testimony and finds nothing contained therein to be unreliable." Greer concluded his opinion:

> The court specifically finds that these statements are Terri Schiavo's oral declarations [to Michael's brother and sister-in-law] concerning her intention as to what she would want done under the present circumstances and the testimony regarding such oral declarations is reliable, is credible, and rises to the level of clear and convincing evidence to this court.[11]

The order granting Michael Schiavo's petition was granted;[12] he was "authorized to proceed with the discontinuance of said artificial life support for Theresa Marie Schiavo." However, Greer issued a stay until thirty days after the Schindlers had exhausted all their appeals.

The parents appealed the order to the DCA and on January 24, 2001, that court upheld Greer's order. They concluded "that the trial court's decision is supported by competent, substantial evidence and that it correctly applies the law. Accordingly, we affirm the decision."[13]

After the Schindlers effort to get that court to grant a rehearing was denied, on April 12, 2001, they appealed to the Florida Supreme Court to stay the removal of their daughter's feeding tube. In the jurisdictional brief filed in the state's Supreme Court, they argued that Judge Greer's judgment, based on Terri's oral statements, and upheld on appeal, was erroneous and insubstantial. Less than one week later, the Florida Supreme Court chose not to review the decision of the Second District Court of Appeals.[14]

The Schindlers next received a temporary stay from a federal district court judge, in order to file an emergency petition for *certiorari* with the U.S. Supreme Court. On April 23, 2001, Justice Anthony Kennedy, for the Court, refused to issue the stay and denied *certiorari*.

One day later, on April 24, 2001, another order of Judge Greer ordered the removal of the feeding tube. According to medical testimony, Terri would die, painlessly, in seven to fourteen days.

The Schindlers, however, were not finished. Two days later, on April 26, 2001, they filed a new civil suit against Michael Schiavo, claiming that he had perjured himself when he testified that Terri told him she did not want to remain on life support. The new judge, Frank Quesada, immediately ordered Terri's feeding tube reinserted.

Four days later, Michael filed an emergency motion in the DCA to allow the removal of the feeding tube. On May 9, 2001, the DCA announced a date for the hearing of oral arguments regarding Michael Schiavo's motion.

On July 11, 2001, the DCA remanded the case back to Judge Greer's courtroom, instructing the trial judge to weigh the new evidence in making another determination of what Terri would have wanted to do. The DCA denied Michael's request to withdraw the tube.

On August 7, 2001, Judge Greer once again ordered the tube to be withdrawn on August 28, 2001. In addition, he denied the Schindlers motion to have their own doctors examine Terri, to remove Michael Schiavo as Terri's guardian, and to disqualify himself from the proceedings. That meant another delay in tube removal to give the Schindlers time to appeal his ruling.

At this point, both Schiavo and the Schindlers were exhausted, mentally and physically, from the legal battles and agreed to sit down with a mediator to discuss what additional tests medical doctors could run on Terri to ascertain her current medical condition. In January 2002, the Florida Supreme Court stayed all legal proceedings and the withdrawal of the feeding tube to give the mediation process a chance to succeed. A month later, both parties walked away from the failed mediation effort.

With a second wind, the Schindlers pressed forward with another attack on Michael Schiavo in mid November 2002. This time they alleged that the husband constantly abused Terri and that abuse led to her cardiac arrest. One of their claims, repeated in nearly every petition and appeal, pointed to their unrealistic understanding of the utter hopelessness of their daughter's PVS and concerned her husband.

They argued in their briefs that Michael knowingly did all he could "to increase [Terri's] incapacity through the denial of basic health and rehabilitative services such as range of motion therapy, other physical therapy, orthopedic evaluations and treatment, *speech therapy*, standard diagnostic tests and procedures, gynecological care, dental care, rehabilitation evaluations and *cognitive therapy*. He has intentionally withheld information concerning Terri's true condition: *that she is conscious, aware, and can swallow*"[15] (my emphasis).

They asked Judge Greer to stay the withdrawal of the feeding tube; they needed more time to collect their evidence against Michael to have the judge remove Michael Schiavo as the legal guardian.

On November 22, 2002, Judge Greer once again authorized Michael Schiavo to remove the feeding tube on June 6, 2003. Once more, for the fourth time, the DCA reviewed and affirmed the Greer order. In August 2003, the Florida Supreme Court once again declined to review the DCA decision. And, on September 17, 2003, Judge Greer once again ordered the removal of the feeding tube on October 15, 2003.[16]

III. Florida's Legislators and Governor Enter the Conflict, 2003–2005

The tragedy then moved into the state political arena. On October 7, 2003, Florida's governor Jeb Bush—a devout Roman Catholic—filed an *amicus curiae* brief in support of the Schindlers Motion for a Preliminary Injunction in the U.S. District Court, Middle District of Florida, Tampa Division.[17] This intrusion by Florida's chief executive marked the first of many such intrusions into the legal process by conservative politicians and right-to-life organizations—in Florida and in Washington, D.C. The brief argued that the governor had a right to intervene in support of the Schindlers' motion for a preliminary injunction.[18]

However, a few days later the federal District Court judge, Richard Lazzara, ruled that there was a lack of federal jurisdiction to hear the case and the *Schiavo* litigation returned to the Florida courts.

On October 15, 2003, Terri's feeding tube was, for a second time, withdrawn. Governor Bush, for a second time, petitioned the court in order to intervene in the case. The DCA rejected his argument.

Florida legislators, at this point, were angry about the looming death of Terri Schiavo and entered the fray. On October 20, 2003, the Florida House of Representatives passed a bill, "Terri's Law." The bill passed in the Senate the following day. Terri's Law authorized the governor to issue a one-time stay "to prevent the withholding of nutrition and hydration from a patient if, as of October 15, 2003:"

(a) the patient has no written advance directive;
(b) the court has found that patient to be in a PVS;
(c) that patient has had nutrition and hydration withheld; and
(d) a member of that patient's family has challenged the withholding of nutrition and hydration.[19]

As soon as the bill passed, Governor Bush issued an Executive Order, 03-201: "Effective immediately, continued withholding of nutrition and hydration from Theresa Schiavo is hereby stayed."[20]

Immediately after the issuance of Bush's EO, Michael Schiavo filed a suit in the DCA. He argued that "Terri's Law" was unconstitutional and sought an injunction to stop the reinsertion of the feeding tube. The DCA, however, ordered the tube reinserted and briefs filed by both parties on the constitutional arguments for the challenged state law.

For the first time in this extended tragedy, the American Civil Liberties Union (ACLU), joined with Michael in the filing. For them the question was straightforward: Can legislators and the governor nullify decisions of Florida courts by issuing a stay blocking the removal of the tube?[21]

The Schindlers' brief was filed with the DCA the same day. Quoting from the Florida Constitution, they argued that "The Ward has a Florida constitutional right not to be 'deprived of any right because of race, religion, national origin, or physical disability' and a further constitutional right to 'enjoy and defend life.'"[22]

In early May 2004, Michael Schiavo's suit against "Terri's Law" reached judgment. The law is unconstitutional, said the circuit court Judge Douglas Baird: "The court finds that [the law] constitutes an unconstitutional delegation of legislative power."[23]

Governor Bush appealed the ruling to the DCA. However, that appellate court, because of the importance of the issue, instructed Michael Schiavo to ask the DCA to send the case directly to the Florida Supreme Court. On June 16, 2004, the Florida Supreme Court, noting the "great public importance of the issue," accepted jurisdiction and scheduled oral argument for August 31, 2004.

On July 27, 2004, an *amicus* brief in support of Michael Schiavo was filed by "55 Bioethicists and Autonomy, Inc.," with the Florida Supreme Court.[24] For these *amici*, personal autonomy was the central value, and they filed to lend support to Schiavo's brief. They argued that when a patient was "incapable of making decisions about health care, an appropriate surrogate [Michael Schiavo] . . . should make decisions on the patient's behalf. [He has considered] the patient's best interest in deciding that proposed treatments are to be withheld or that treatments currently in effect are to be withdrawn. . . . The judicial process is better suited than the political arena for implementing proxy exercise for the right of personal autonomy."[25]

After the Florida Supreme Court heard oral arguments on August 31, 2004,[26] less than one month later the judges unanimously declared "Terri's Law" unconstitutional.

> This court . . . concludes that the law violates the fundamental constitutional tenet of separation of powers and is therefore unconstitutional both on its face and as applied to Theresa Schiavo. Accordingly, we affirm the trial court's order declaring the law unconstitutional.[27]

Once again, that court transferred jurisdiction back to Judge Greer. However, because Governor Bush planned to file a *cert* petition with the U.S. Supreme Court, the Florida Supreme Court held its mandate to Judge Greer pending the outcome of the Bush petition.

On December 1, 2004, Governor Bush filed his petition with the U.S. Supreme Court. On January 24, 2005, the high court again denied *certiorari*. With the denial, the case returned to Judge Greer's court once more.

The Schindlers once again petitioned Judge Greer to rescind his order to have the feeding tube removed from Terri Schiavo's body. Once again, he denied their request. Once more, they appealed to the DCA. And, once again, on February 21, 2005, the DCA denied their motion. Judge Greer, on February 22, 2005, extended the stay on the withdrawal of the feeding tube until 1 p.m., Friday, March 18, 2005.

Undeterred, the Florida legislature tried again to enact legislation that would prevent Terri's feeding tube from being withdrawn. In mid-March 2005, the legislature passed H 701. It provided that medically supplied hydration and nutrition could not be stopped from a patient in a PVS if (1) the tube withdrawal would end the life of that patient; (2) a conflict existed between members of the family; and (3) the patient had not prepared an advanced directive.

IV. The Congress and the President
Insert Themselves in the Battle, 2005

The Schiavo case now began to see political involvement by members of Congress. On March 3, 2005, David Weldon, a U.S. House of Representative congressman from Florida introduced in the House HR 1151, titled the "Incapacitated Persons' Legal Protection Act of 2005."[28] It provided for the removal of a state case involving an incapacitated person "to the U.S. district court for the district in which the claim or cause of action arose, or was heard."

The House of Representatives, by voice vote, passed a different version of Weldon's bill, HR 1332 on March 16, 2005. On the House floor the following morning, Representative Joe Pitts applauded his colleagues action. We "did a good thing." The bill "will allow her to challenge the ruling that she is to starve to death.[29]

Not to be left out of the story, on March 17, 2005, the U.S. Senate entered the picture by passing a "private bill,"[30] "S 653 ES, For the Relief of the Parents of Theresa Marie Schiavo," that specifically applied to the Schiavo case but differed from the just-passed HR 1332. The bill gave jurisdiction to the U.S. District Court for the Middle District of Florida to take the case from state court and "shall issue such declaratory and injunctive relief as may be necessary to protect [her rights]."[31]

While the national lawmakers were passing differing legislation, and stalemating, the Schindlers—who were in Washington to lobby lawmakers—turned once again to the U.S. Supreme Court. This time—March 17, *the day before Terri's feeding tube was to be withdrawn*—they asked the Justices for an Emergency Application for Stay of Enforcement of the Judgment Below. The U.S. Supreme Court, *on the same day*, denied the application for the stay.

On March 18, 2005, the U.S. House Committee on Government Reform, in an unprecedented action, sought to intervene in the case before Judge Greer. It requested the judge to stay his removal order. Greer, although nonplussed by the congressional committee behavior, denied the motion.

That same day, the House committee requested the U.S. Supreme Court to review the Florida Supreme Court's denial of its motion. Justice Kennedy, *once again*, denied this request for federal intervention in the Schiavo case.

As scheduled, Terri Schiavo's feeding and hydration tube was removed—*for the third time*—on March 18, 2005. The Congress, in an effort to do something to prevent Terri from dying, delayed its scheduled Easter recess and, on March 20, 2005, passed S 686, which was a carbon copy of the Senate's "Private Bill."

In addition, the U.S. House Committee on Government Reform issued a most unusual subpoena: it *commanded* that Terri Schiavo, along with her attached feeding tube, come to Washington, D.C., and appear before the committee! (Such an action, if the subpoena were obeyed, would necessitate the reinsertion of Terri Schiavo's feeding tube.)

President George W. Bush flew into the capital the following day to sign the bill. Bush spoke briefly at the signing:

> In cases like this one, where there are serious questions and substantial doubts, our society, our laws, and our courts should have a presumption in favor of life. This presumption is especially critical for those like Terri Schiavo who live at the mercy of others.[32]

On the same day, the Schindler's lawyers, joined by the federal government, presented arguments to federal district court judge James D. Whittemore for a temporary restraining order or preliminary injunction "requiring that Theresa Schiavo be provided hydration and nutrition necessary to keep her alive in order to maintain the status quo during the pendency of the suit."[33]

The next day, March 22, 2005, Judge Whittemore declined to order the reinsertion of the feeding tube. He reasoned that the federal court did not have the constitutional authority to consider temporary injunctive relief. "A preliminary injunction is 'an extraordinary and drastic remedy' and is 'not to be granted unless the movant clearly established the burden of persuasion.'"[34]

The Schindlers immediately appealed that decision to the U.S. Court of Appeals for the Eleventh Circuit. On March 23, 2005, the CA11 denied the appeal by a 2:1 vote. On March 23, 2005, now five days after the feeding tube was withdrawn, sitting *en banc*, the CA11, refused to rehear the Schindler appeal.

They then desperately sought to have the U.S. Supreme Court grant their emergency petition for *certiorari*, joined by five members of the U.S. House of Representatives who filed an *amicus curiae* brief with the Court.

On March 24, the U.S. Supreme Court, for a final time, denied the *certiorari* request. In Florida on the same day, Judge Greer denied another petition from the Florida Department of Children and Families (DCF) to intervene on behalf of the Schindlers. (The DCF had produced an affidavit from a medical doctor, William Polk Cheshire Jr. He was a neurologist and maintained that she was not in a PVS. "She demonstrates a number of behaviors that I believe cast a reasonable doubt on the prior diagnosis of PVS." He listed seven behaviors "in a variety of *cognitive domains*"[35] that, for him, showed that her medical condition "differs fundamentally from end-of-life scenarios where it is appropriate to withdraw life-sustaining medical interventions that no longer benefit or are burdensome to patients in a terminal stages of illness."[36])

V. The Clinical Death of Terri Schiavo, 2005

At 9:05 a.m., March 31, 2005—thirteen days after the feeding and hydration tube left her body, Terri Schiavo died. An autopsy immediately took place. It laid to rest the views of so many who argued on her behalf, believing that she would recover cognition and awareness. Her medical condition was consistent with a person in a PVS. "This damage was irreversible," wrote the medical examiner. "No amount of therapy or treatment would have regenerated the massive loss of neurons" in Terri's brain.

Editorials in newspapers the day following her death were legion. Most asked readers to leave the Schiavo and the Schindler families alone, and to let them grieve privately. The *New York Times* editorial, however, reflected on the *consequences* of the extremely high level of grief in the case, anguish that "seldom brings out the noblest emotions. In the case of Terri Schiavo, the whole world witnessed what happens when that natural emotional frailty is held captive by politics. It was awful and according to the polls, the American public shrank from the sight of it."[37]

On April 15, 2005, the Harris Poll published its Schiavo findings. Almost 70 percent of Americans *closely* watched the Schiavo case. "Most people approve of how both Michael Schiavo, Terri's husband, *and* the Schindlers, Terri's parents, behaved. A 55 to 39 per cent majority of the public approved of Michael Schiavo's behavior but a similar 53 to 41 percent majority also approved of the behavior of Robert and Mary Schindler." Additionally, 58 percent disapproved of the role of the U.S. Congress in the tragedy; 57 percent disapproved of the actions of the Florida legislators; 54 percent disapproved of President Bush's actions, and 51 percent disapproved of Governor Jeb Bush's behavior in the appalling affair.[38]

Governor Jeb Bush, however, was not yet through with the Schiavo affair. On June 17, 2005, he asked the State Attorney's Office to investigate the circumstances of Terri Schiavo's February 1990 cardiac arrest. Somehow the governor believed that an undue amount of time elapsed between the time of her collapse and her husband's 911 telephone call.[39]

Politically, the Schiavo matter continued to bubble along after Terri's death. In August 2005, John Roberts, President Bush's nominee to replace the retired U.S. Supreme Court Justice Sandra Day O'Connor,[40] was quizzed by

Democratic senator Ron Wyden (D-Ore.). Should the Congress have intervened in the Terri Schiavo case? The nominee's answer criticized the Congress:

> I am concerned with judicial independence. Congress can prescribe standards, but when Congress starts to act like a court and prescribe particular remedies in particular cases, Congress has overstepped its bounds.[41]

Earlier in 2005, the legal counsel to U.S. Senator Mel Martinez (R-Fla), admitted to his boss that he authored a memo "citing the *political advantage* to Republicans for intervening in the case of Terri Schiavo."[42] The memo said, in part: "This [the *Schiavo* case] is an important moral issue and the pro-life base will be *excited* that the Senate is debating this important issue"[43] (my emphasis).

And, during the early days of the lengthy 2007–2008 Democratic primaries campaign, Senator Barack Obama (D-Ill.), said that "he regretted not fighting Republican-led efforts in March 2005 to reconnect Mrs. Schiavo's feeding tube. A lot of us, including me, left the Senate with a bill that allowed Congress to intrude where it shouldn't have."[44]

VI. Politicizing the Right-to-Die Issue

Schiavo is the story of the unvarnished politicalization of the right to die in America. Between 1998 and 2005, legislators and executives—at the state and federal levels—aware of the relationship of the case to the right-to-life beliefs of religious and conservative groups, sought to turn the case into a fundamental ideological and political issue. As subsequent chapters will show, Schiavo was the catalyst for many emotional diatribes in the political arena as public debate and votes on PAD occurred.

Also present throughout the litigation battles, and an extremely important factor in the next generation of right-to-die issues and litigation, was the intense ideological fervor surrounding and invading the *Schiavo* petitions and briefs. "Some on the right [saw Schiavo] as validation of their conviction that the judiciary was out of control," wrote Joan Didion.[45]

Cal Thomas, a well-known conservative media commentator, provided an example of the unbridled passion exhibited during the Schiavo debates:

Theresa Schiavo will quickly become a saint to the pro-life movement as well as a metaphor for what is wrong with our federal and many state courts. . . . This will be the beginning, or the continuation on the line of death that began in the womb in 1973 with *Roe v Wade* and will now quickly advance toward the "retirement" villages. The angel of death that moved through ancient Egypt at the first Passover was called the "destroyer." Our courts are his modern incarnation.[46]

U.S. Senator Orrin Hatch (R-Utah) hit the issue on its head when he remarked: "The torrent of accusations reflects the bitterness over the life-and-death issues in the *Schiavo* case. [These accusations] were a proxy on both sides for what provokes every ugly political conversation—that's abortion."[47]

Interestingly—and paradoxically—Joseph Cruzan, Nancy's father, could never understand the logic behind Senator Hatch's comments as well as those of the conservative pro-life movement leaders. Their co-joining of the abortion issue with the right to die of patients in a PVS made absolutely no sense to him. This was because abortion was the ending of a life *before* the fetus had time to *become* somebody, before the fetus had the opportunity to live life. For incompetent patients like his daughter, such a future was *not possible* because of the massive brain injuries that ended cognition and any possibility of a normal life.[48]

Legally, as the tortuous *Schiavo* litigation illustrated, by the beginning of the twenty-first century end-of-life decisions by surrogates—and judges—for incapacitated and incompetent patients in a PVS followed state protocols that grew out of decades-earlier end-of-life cases such as *Quinlan* and *Cruzan*. *Schiavo* was, however, the most publicized of end-of-life cases where family members disagreed about discontinuing treatment.

In the eyes of the medical bioethics community, the extensive media coverage greatly skewed the case and story. as seen by their coverage of the *Schiavo* litigation. Political and ethical aspects of the litigation made the headlines more than accurate scientific and medical information. "Only 1 percent of the articles examined gave a definition of the 'persistent vegetative state,' an essential concept to understand the issues at stake," wrote a team of researchers from Stanford University, the University of British Columbia, and the Institut de Recherches Cliniques de Montreal.[49] And one-fifth of all the articles indicated to readers that Terri's condition *would* improve. The report concluded:

Our observations show that the press capitalized on the controversy to a large extent, and selling copies mattered more than delivering scientific information. *Media coverage sustained myths and false hopes.*[50] (my emphasis)

The *Schiavo* case reveals the depth of the feelings held by many Americans when they hear or participate in discussions regarding questions about the right to die. These new public policy issues emerged because of the impact of medicalization of death.

Furthermore, because so few Americans, even in the light of the Quinlan, Cruzan, Schiavo, and other publicized personal tragedies, have prepared advanced directives or living wills, there is still the reality of medical and moral quagmires when the next PVS patient's family tries to end the life of their loved one.

Schiavo is a sad story; it is also an ugly story accounting for seven years of "mass hysteria and political manipulations that turned one woman's death into a horrifying public spectacle."[51] If *Schiavo* revealed the clash of core values and triggered such unconstrained and emotive responses, imagine the emotions and rage triggered by the actions of "Dr. Death," the late Dr. Jack Kevorkian, and by the issue of physician-assisted death, reflected in his and other doctors' actions that first seared itself in the public's consciousness in 1990.

Clearly, 1990 was a watershed year for the right-to-die issue. "The movement for compassion and choice in dying dates not from the 1960s or 1970s but rather from 1990."[52] The nation saw the final act of the Cruzan family tragedy and the opening act of the Schiavo misfortune. In 1990, Congress passed the Patient Self-Determination Act, which required hospitals to inform all patients of their right to prepare and sign an Advanced Directive demanding or refusing treatment at the end of life. Derek Humphry, who founded the Hemlock Society, published a how-to-commit-suicide book, *Final Exit*, which found a home at the very top of the *New York Times* best-seller list. Dr. Timothy Quill's article about counseling his dying leukemia patient—and then giving her a prescription for a lethal dose of medicine—was also published in the *New England Journal of Medicine* (hereafter *NEJM*) in 1990.

That year also saw, in the state of Washington, the first voter referendum, the Washington Initiative, on whether a death with dignity process would be adopted by Washingtonians. If passed, it would have legalized physician-assisted death (PAD).[53]

Furthermore, the very conservative American Medical Association (AMA), at its 1990 annual meeting, formally adopted the position that if a terminal patient gave informed consent, a medical doctor could withhold or withdraw life-supporting medical assistance and that a physician could discontinue life support of a patient in a PVS.

What follows next is the question of physician-assisted death in America. If the nonrational noise and hysteria were shrill surrounding the *Cruzan* and *Schiavo* litigation, the maddening cacophony dramatically increased when the issue shifted to the question of whether PAD legislation would pass in America.

The following chapter discusses the political, legal, medical, and moral controversies surrounding a competent person's right to choose to die—with the assistance of a physician—under his own terms. These arguments are as contentious as the abortion controversy has been since 1973.

The essential question addressed in chapter 4 is the central theme of the book: Can a competent person, who is terminally ill, not clinically depressed, and in pain or not, hasten death with the assistance of a physician?

4

WHAT FREEDOM DO WE
HAVE TO DIE WITH DIGNITY?

The U.S. Supreme Court Decides, 1997

> At the heart of liberty is the right to define one's own concept of existence, of meaning, of the universe, and of the mystery of human life.
> —Associate Justice Anthony Kennedy,
> *Planned Parenthood of Southeastern Pennsylvania v Casey,* 1992

> Opposition to and condemnation of suicide—and, therefore, of assisting suicide—are consistent and enduring themes of our philosophical, legal, and cultural heritages.
> —Chief Justice William Rehnquist,
> *Washington v Glucksberg,* 1997

There are two answers to the question of how a competent, terminally ill patient can legally hasten death with the assistance of a physician: (1) Push legislation creating a PAD bill. This path is the more arduous of the two, fraught with political, cultural, and medical pitfalls. Or pro-PAD advocates could (2) go into federal courts to challenge state laws that make it a crime for a physician to provide a terminally ill patient with a prescription that would end that person's life. In 1990, all states prohibited PAD and provided criminal penalties for doctors who engaged in PAD. The PAD advocates opted for the latter path. Taking that strategic tack revealed two very different mind-sets held by PAD supporters.

I. Two Kinds of PAD Advocates: The Aggressive, Dr. Jack Kevorkian, and the Conventional, Dr. Timothy Quill

There are, in this contentious debate, two types of advocates for death with dignity. There is the aggressive medical practitioner, typified by the late Dr. Jack Kevorkian, who actively sought out clients—not necessarily terminal— who wished to die in order the assist them in their quest. This medical practitioner is a "zealot"[1] committed to assisting a client to die, with no fear about arguing for euthanasia as a humane public policy.

The conventional doctor's approach to PAD is quite different. Dr. Timothy Quill represents this approach to PAD, an approach emulated by the vast number of pro-PAD doctors. It is a close doctor-patient relationship with substantive discussions regarding the treatment and the options available to the terminally ill patient. There is an essential interaction between doctor and patient; the practitioner is opposed to euthanasia while committed to legislation that decriminalizes physician-assisted death.

The overwhelming number of pro-PAD advocates supports the conventional approach. The aggressive advocates are anathema to the conventional group for a number of reasons. First and most important is the fact that euthanasia is the very essence of the anti-PAD forces opposition to PAD. For these adversaries, PAD legalization is the beginning of the slippery slope that leads to euthanasia. The conventional pro-PAD advocates, as will be seen, do everything in their power to distinguish their strategy from pro-PAD advocates who tie PAD to euthanasia. They treat such advocates—Derek Humphry[2] and Dr. Kevorkian being the two most associated with pushing euthanasia as public policy—as their enemy.

The conventional advocates also reject Dr. Kevorkian's relationship (more appropriately, the lack of any relationship) with what he called his clients. Perhaps because Kevorkian was a pathologist before he retired, there was never the typical doctor-patient interactions. He was providing a service to strangers who came to him to die. There were no clinical psychiatric examinations to determine whether the client was clinically depressed. Although all his clients were ill, many of them were not terminally ill. All of them just wanted to die. There was no counseling offered by Kevorkian to them. He advertized his service and provided the mechanism for the client to use to end his life.

a. The Aggressive PAD Advocate

As seen in Kevorkian's history, he literally ran newspaper advertisements offering a dignified death to those who wished to die. Unlike the vast majority of PAD medical advocates, Kevorkian urged the nation to accept euthanasia as a social policy for those competent, sick, but not necessarily terminal, patients who wished to die.

Euthanasia is an action that results in the immediate merciful killing by a doctor of a sick and suffering patient who has consented to this action. It is the deliberate and very humane ending of a patient's life to prevent further suffering.

The case for euthanasia rests on two fundamental principles: autonomy and mercy. The *autonomy* principle means that the doctor must respect a competent and informed patient's wishes and choices. The *mercy* principle means that a medical practitioner must relieve the pain or suffering of another person who requests such assistance because the patient physically cannot do it alone. The autonomous and competent patient has the liberty to seek to be free from agony or a worthless life.[3] Kevorkian supported euthanasia unequivocally. His task was not to counsel the patient regarding alternatives to death; it was to provide the terminal relief requested by the patient by either assisting the person or by actually killing him.

Although, in the United States, there was some public support for euthanasia in the early decades of the twentieth century; by 1945 it had become a term associated with the brutal activities of Adolf Hitler's Nazi Germany. Since then it has been soundly rejected by Americans, especially those in the medical community.

Euthanasia, however, became very visible to Americans in 1988. In that year, in an essay titled "It's Over, Debbie," published in the *Journal of the American Medical Association* (*JAMA*), an anonymous medical resident confessed that early one morning s/he administered a lethal injection to a young female patient suffering from terminal ovarian cancer. The admittedly very sleepy resident had never met the dying patient before the event. The medical resident was not her doctor and had had no discussions with the patient. The doctor instantaneously responded to her pleas for someone to do something to end her suffering and injected her with a fatal dose of morphine. The patient died almost immediately.[4]

The uproar in the medical community was instantaneous and loudly condemnatory of the doctor's action. It violated the sacred Hippocratic Oath, the ancient medical standard that instructs doctors to "do no harm"; to save lives, not intentionally end life.[5]

Clearly, however, the most visible public example of an aggressive medical practitioner that people the world over have *ever* seen, to date, were the actions of a retired Michigan medical pathologist, Dr. Jack Kevorkian. He was quickly labeled by the media (although colleagues labeled him decades earlier) as "Dr. Death." His actions—he claims to have *actively* assisted in the suicides of more than 130 sick clients and euthanized one patient—took place over a period of eight years, from 1990 to 1998.

While the anonymous doctor who killed Debbie evidently did the deed in an instant, in response to the plaintive pleas of the dying woman, "Dr. Death" was an active and vocal supporter of euthanasia since his medical school days.

Although Dr. Kevorkian began helping patients to die in 1990, it was something he planned well in advance of that watershed year. He regularly rejected the Hippocratic Oath's value. In response to that primary precept, Kevorkian wrote that "just as the oath never had any real meaning with regard to abortion, so too it's now irrelevant in the right-to-die debate."

It's time for a society obsessed with *planned birth* to consider diverting some of its attention and energy from an overriding concern with longevity of life at all costs to the snowballing need for a rational stance on *planned death*, i.e., the purposeful ending of human life by direct human action.[6]

These words shocked the medical community. He did not care about the hurt feelings of the medical community. He did anything to assault their values because of his belief that doctors must respond to requests by sick people to end their suffering. He set out, after his retirement in the 1980s, to find a humane way to assist patients who wanted to die. He focused his efforts on inventing a machine that would kill patients who wished to die because of their illness and their pain and their fear of becoming incompetent before they could commit suicide.

By 1986, using about thirty dollars worth of scrap parts, he had created his suicide machine, a gadget he called the Mercitron.[7] This was Kevorkian's contribution to a "planned death" for suffering patients. And, by 1989, it was ready to be used by fearful persons who were committed to exiting their pain-wracked lives while they still were still "alive."

Kevorkian began to publicize his Mercitron in the *Detroit Free Press* and in weekly newspapers across Michigan. One did not have to jump out of a window anymore, these ads and news stories stated.[8] One of these ads ran in the "Medical/Dental Counseling" section of the *Detroit Free Press*. It read: "Death Counseling / is someone in your family terminally ill? / Does he or she wish to die—and with dignity? / call physician consultant / ([Telephone Number])."[9]

With his quick-and-easy death machine, as one *Detroit Free Press* essay said, "all those oppressed by a fatal disease, a severe handicap, a crippling deformity" had to do was:

plug it into a wall socket, punch it into your arm, press a button, and five minutes later, you're dead. It's painless, portable, and legal. Kevorkian is certain it would work, if only someone would give it a whirl. Applications are being accepted.[10]

On June 4, 1990, Janet Atkins became the first of more than 130 ill and fearful clients to commit suicide with the assistance of Dr. Jack Kevorkian. Most deaths took place in Kevorkian's old, rusted, and battered 1968 Volkswagen van parked in Groveland Oaks Park, near the town of Holly, Michigan, forty miles north of Detroit.

On June 6, the *New York Times* ran its first story about the actions of Dr. Kevorkian. It was not the last time the national newspaper headlined stories about Dr. Death. This time the headline read: "Doctor Tells of First Death Using His Suicide Device." In a telephone interview with a *Times* reporter, Kevorkian explained what happened and why:

My ultimate aim is to make euthanasia a positive experience. I'm trying to knock the medical profession into accepting its responsibilities, and those responsibilities include assisting their patients with death.[11]

Kevorkian's action, wrote the reporter, "raises the specific legal question of what constitutes assisted suicide and the more general philosophic question of what role, if any, doctors should play in helping their seriously ill patients die."[12] My aim, he said years later, "was not to cause death, that's crazy. My aim was to end suffering."[13] Because of his highly publicized actions, he was tried four times by Michigan prosecutors between 1990 and 1998, He was acquitted by sympathetic juries three times; one trial ended in a mistrial.

His actions did not lead to changes in the medical profession's attitude about assisted suicide, though. In 1998 a frustrated Kevorkian took another action that led to a fifth trial.

In September 1998, Kevorkian took the critical, never-before-taken step (by him), of euthanizing a fifty-two-year old man, a former race car driver,[14] Thomas Youk, who was dying from ALS and could not turn on the Mercitron. Not only did Kevorkian give Youk a fatal injection of potassium chloride but he filmed the entire event and sent the tape to the CBS television show, *60 Minutes*. On November 22, 1998, the tape aired, with commentary provided by Kevorkian, interviewed by Mike Wallace.

Three days later, on November 25, 1998, he was charged by the state with first-degree murder—premeditated murder—and with the delivery of a "controlled substance" without a license. The tape of the *60 Minutes* segment was introduced by the prosecution as evidence of Kevorkian's guilt.

One of the prosecutors, John Skrzynski, argued that the defendant "used" Mr. Youk as part of his continuing campaign to rally public support for PAD and the concept of euthanasia. "The defendant chose to put us in this sad situation. This is not a case where the prosecutor went looking for Dr. Kevorkian," he said.[15]

A jury found him guilty, however, of second-degree murder; on April 13, 1999, Circuit Judge Jessica Cooper sentenced him to ten to twenty-five years in prison on the murder conviction and three to seven years for delivery of a controlled substance. She also denied bail to Kevorkian.[16]

He appealed his conviction to the Michigan Supreme Court and, twice, to the Supreme Court. In 2004 the U.S. Supreme Court denied *certiorari* a second time. In his effort to get the Justices of the U.S. Supreme Court to hear his appeal, in September 2000 Kevorkian sent a lengthy letter to the nine jurists. He wrote:

I respectfully implore your High Court to exercise its prerogative under the supreme authority of the Ninth Amendment[16] by validating as constitutionally protected the choice of suffering patients to request medical euthanasia and the choice of physicians to assess all aspects of that request and to honor it according to stringent guidelines. . . . As guardians of human rights, you and your colleagues have the authority, opportunity, and obligation to rid society of this lingering medieval malady [prohibiting *medical euthanasia*] by using the Ninth Amendment to guarantee this most precious and humane *right of choice* for all Americans.[17]

There was no answer. On June 1, 2007, he was paroled after promising not to offer his services to sick patients. For three years, Kevorkian traveled across the nation, giving lectures, primarily on college campuses. His message did not change: PAD must be de-criminalized because it is the only humane way of ending the plight of persons in great pain and with chronic suffering. He died in 2010.

b. The Conventional PAD Advocate

In 1991 an essay "Death and Dignity," published in a major medical journal, *NEJM*,[18] written by Dr. Timothy Quill, described how he assisted in the death of his patient "Diane." She was Quill's patient for over eight years and was suffering from acute leukemia. She asked Dr. Quill to write a prescription that would allow her to acquire enough sleeping pills to end her life when the pain became excruciating. After many discussions with her to try (unsuccessfully) to change her mind, including describing a treatment that, if she went through with it, gave Diane a 25 percent chance of survival, Quill acceded to his patient's request and gave her a prescription. Four months later, Diane killed herself. She was the proximate cause of her death; Quill indirectly assisted Diane.

This poignant story is the classic example of PAD as it should be administered, wrote Quill afterward. Unlike Dr. Kevorkian's actions, the doctor and the patient knew each other, had serious conversations about the options available to Diane. She was competent, was not clinically depressed, and fully informed about the different paths she could take. And, for both doctor and patient, PAD became Diane's final option.

Quill's compassionate interactions with Diane led to legal challenges to existing State anti-PAD statutes, in federal courts, by Quill and other doctors and dying patients in New York State and by other set of pro-PAD physicians and their dying patients in Washington State. Unlike Kevorkian, Quill and others were received more sympathetically by many in the medical community, and his approach to PAD was adopted by advocates in state and federal courts and in PAD-proposed laws in state legislatures.[19]

II. PAD Advocates Enter the Federal Courts, 1994–1995

In 1990 New York State's Penal Laws punished those who assisted in a suicide in two ways: promoting a suicide attempt and promoting a suicide. Section 125.15 (3) of the Penal Code stated: "A person is guilty of manslaughter in the second degree when . . . (3) He intentionally causes or aids another person to commit suicide. Manslaughter in the second degree is a class C felony." Section 120.30 of the same Penal Code stated that "a person is guilty of promoting a suicide attempt when he intentionally causes or aids another person to attempt suicide. Promoting a suicide attempt is a class E felony."

Washington State's anti-assisted suicide law was the same as the New York "promoting suicide" statute except for the punishment segment. Its Revised Code, Section 9A.36.060, read: "(1) A person is guilty of promoting a suicide attempt when he knowingly causes or aids another person to attempt suicide. (2) Promoting a suicide attempt is a class C felony."

By 1990 most states had very similar prohibitions against assisting suicide attempts. At least thirty-five states had passed statutes explicitly criminalizing assisted suicide. Other states criminalized assisted suicide through the states' common law of crimes legal precedents.[20] This was the reality the right-to-die supporters faced in their efforts to achieve their goal.

After pro-PAD advocates in Washington State lost their battle to legalize the PAD process through a voter referendum in 1991, they took the only road available to them: challenge the Washington statute prohibiting PAD in federal court. They hoped that federal courts would be open to either applying the common law of self-determination or extending the meaning of the liberty clause in the Fourteenth Amendment in this right to personal privacy area. Would the federal judges extend the liberty that, in 1973, allowed a woman to choose to have an abortion to a right of privacy to die with the assistance of a doctor?

The lawyers for the pro-PAD litigants were not sanguine about this legal reality. They faced a significant obstacle: the federal judiciary itself. By the early 1990s, the federal courts were heavily populated by conservative judges. For twelve years, the nominating presidents, Ronald Reagan, 1981–89, and George H. W. Bush, 1989–93, were Republicans who shared a very conservative Republican agenda. For them and for most Republicans, a primary domestic issue—and public policy—was protecting the sanctity of life, seen in their fierce opposition to abortion and to the 1973 abortion decision, *Roe v Wade*.

Presidents Reagan and Bush successfully appointed conservatives to the U.S. Supreme Court. By the time the PAD litigation entered the federal courts in 1994, they had appointed five new Republican Justices to the High Bench: Sandra Day O'Connor, 1981; Antonin Scalia, 1985; Anthony Kennedy, 1987; David Souter, 1991; and Clarence Thomas, 1992. They joined Chief Justice William Rehnquist, already on the Court since 1971 (and Chief Justice since 1986).

The clear hope of conservatives was that these six Republican jurists, all appointed by Republican presidents and, it was assumed by scholars who studied the Court, all opposed to the *Roe v Wade*[21] precedent, would overturn that very liberal precedent. Although it was a judgment expected by conservatives and liberals alike, the overturn of *Roe* did not take place.

Indeed, in the case of *Planned Parenthood of Southeastern Pennsylvania v Casey*,[22] a 1992 Term plurality decision of the U.S. Supreme Court, *Roe* was saved by a trio of the recently appointed Republican justices, Justices O'Connor, Kennedy, and Souter. They wrote a joint opinion, to the anger and dismay of the "originalist" conservative jurists sitting on the bench, that defended *Roe* (while significantly changing its constitutional parameters regarding a woman's self-determination and her constitutionally protected liberty to have an abortion versus the state's interest and power to intervene).

When, two years later, the petitions were filed in the federal courts by the opponents of the state anti-PAD laws, the *Casey* decision was one of two very recent precedents the lawyers drew upon to argue that state laws punishing PAD were unconstitutional. The other Court precedent was, of course, the Court's 1990 right-to-die case from Missouri, *Cruzan v Director, Missouri Department of Health*.

One knows the importance of the *Cruzan* decision in the general debate about the right to die. *Casey*, however, was a case that involved the constitutionality of a number of provisions in the Missouri abortion statute. The law severely limited a woman's fundamental right to an abortion by allowing the state to place burdens on women before they could undergo the procedure.

(An example of these "burdens" was the section in the statute that required a woman to notify her husband before she could have an abortion.)

The trio of justices, joined by the two dissenters, concluded (1) that abortion remained a "fundamental right" (which was the judgment made by seven Justices in *Roe*), and (2) that the spousal notification restriction was an "undue burden" placed on a woman by Missouri and was struck down by the Court.

The other four justices, Chief Justice Rehnquist, and Associate Justices Scalia, Thomas, and White, believed that *none* of the state restrictions were unconstitutional. Furthermore, they concluded, abortion was *not* a fundamental right of women protected by the Constitution.

Because there was no "opinion" of the Court in *Casey*, that is, it was not a decision joined by five or more of the justices, the plurality judgment written by Justices O'Connor, Souter, and Kennedy was not as substantive. However, the pro-PAD lawyers used *Casey* as precedent in their written briefs and oral arguments before the federal judges.

In *Casey* two sentences were used in the written briefs filed by them in *Compassion In Dying* and in *Quill*; in the *amici* briefs filed by dozens of interested groups, pro and con on the issue of assisted suicide; as well as in the oral arguments presented in all the federal courts. A person reading the two sentences from the *Casey* opinion well understands why they were in play from the very beginning of the litigation that began in 1995:

> Our law affords constitutional protection to personal decisions relating to marriage, procreation, contraception, family relationships, child rearing and education. . . . *These matters, involving the most intimate and personal choices a person may make in a lifetime, choices central to personal dignity and autonomy, are central to the liberty protected by the Fourteenth Amendment. At the heart of liberty is the right to define one's own concept of existence, of meaning, of the universe, and of the mystery of human life.* (my emphasis)

When the petitions for *certiorari* were filed in federal district court, first in Washington State in March 1994, followed months later by the filing in federal district court in New York, the PAD debate moved from medical and legal and religious journals into the judicial system.

The petitions filed in Washington and New York argued that the state anti-PAD laws violated a person's fundamental right to make decisions based on their liberty protected in the Fourteenth Amendment's Due Process Clause. Both sets also maintained that the laws criminalizing PAD violated the Fourteenth Amendment's Equal Protection Clause.

The briefs used the *Casey* and *Cruzan* opinions to buttress their position. They argued, using *Casey*, that (1) terminally ill, competent, and fully informed patients had a fundamental liberty, protected in the U.S. Constitution, to make the decision to die with the assistance of a physician. "At the heart of liberty," quoting from *Casey*, is a person's right "to define one's own concept of existence . . . and of the mystery of human life."

In addition, using the *Cruzan* opinion as a foundation point for their Equal Protection argument, the plaintiffs (the physicians and their terminally ill patients along with the Compassion in Dying pressure group's attorneys), maintained that (2) there was no substantive difference between assisting a terminal patient like Diane to die and withdrawing the feeding and hydration tube from Nancy Cruzan, thereby allowing her to die.

In both instances, the patient mercifully died. Any future medical action in both cases was *futile*. There was no bringing Nancy Cruzan back to even a minimal level of cognition and sensation; there was no real possibility of Diane recovering from her leukemia.

For Washington and New York to permit the withdrawal of a life-saving medical protocol from Nancy, leading to her death while criminalizing an action, PAD, that would have led Diane to the same end, was a violation of the Fourteenth Amendment's Equal Protection Clause. "Equals must be treated equally," is the belief embedded in the Equal Protection Clause; the two women were not treated equally, therefore both states—and all other states that criminalized PAD—violated the Fourteenth Amendment.

The first challenge to arrive in the federal court came from Washington State: Dr. Harold Glucksberg and a few of his colleagues; a group of three terminally ill patients (who had died by the time the case was heard in the federal appeals court); and the pro-PAD pressure group, Compassion in Dying. The case, *Compassion in Dying v Washington*,[23] was heard in the U.S. District Court for the Western District, Washington. The plaintiffs asked Judge Barbara J. Rothstein to rule Washington State's anti-PAD law unconstitutional. (Judge Rothstein was appointed to the U.S. District Court in 1980 by the Democratic president Jimmy Carter.)

To the chagrin of the state's lawyers, on May 3, 1994, the judge ruled in favor of Glucksberg on both Due Process and Equal Protection grounds. In her decision, announced in 1994, Judge Rothstein used both the *Casey* and *Cruzan* precedents to overturn the Washington statute.

The Supreme Court, in a bevy of opinions over the past decades, "had established that personal decisions . . . are constitutionally protected." Rothstein found "the reasoning in *Casey* highly instructive and almost prescriptive on the issue [of PAD]." Both the abortion decision and the decision to receive the assistance of a physician in dying, she adjudged, quoting *Casey*, "involve the most intimate and personal choices a person may make in a lifetime;" both constitute a "choice central to personal dignity and autonomy."

> This court concludes that the suffering of a terminally ill person cannot be deemed any less intimate or personal, or any less deserving of protection from unwarranted governmental interference, than that of a pregnant woman.

"This court also finds," Rothstein wrote, "*Cruzan* instructive." For her, as it was for the plaintiffs, "the question [is] whether a *constitutional distinction* can be drawn between refusal or withdrawal of medical treatment which results in death, and the situation in this case involving competent, terminally ill individuals who wish to hasten death by self-administering drugs prescribed by a physician. . . . The court concludes that a competent, terminally ill patient has a constitutionally guaranteed right under the Fourteenth Amendment to commit physician-assisted suicide." Washington State's statute constitutes an "undue burden" on terminally ill patients who wish to die.

Seven months later, in October 1994, the New York State prohibitions against PAD were challenged by Dr. Quill, a few of his colleagues, and three terminally ill patients, in the federal U.S. District Court for the Southern District, New York. They made the exact same arguments the Washington plaintiffs made: the statutes violated the Fourteenth Amendment's Due Process and Equal Protection Clauses.

The case[24] was heard by U.S. District Court Judge Thomas P. Griesa, who was appointed to the district court in 1972 by Republican President Richard M. Nixon. He rendered his decision on December 15, 1994.

Judge Griesa, however, reached the exact opposite conclusions. He rejected both Fourteenth Amendment claims made by Quill and the lawyers, "just as emphatically as Judge Rothstein had sustained them."[25] In so doing, he rejected the effort by plaintiffs to extend the *Cruzan* and *Carey* precedents to PAD.

For Griesa, a person's liberty to receive PAD was not a "subject so *fundamental* to personal liberty that government invasion is either entirely prohibited or sharply limited." He rejected their argument that the *Cruzan* and *Casey* precedents "are broad enough to establish that there is a fundamental right on the part of a terminally ill patient to decide to end his life."

The plaintiffs "reasoning," he wrote, "is too broad." Using an argument put forward by U.S. Supreme Court majorities in cases involving homosexual rights[26] and the constitutionality of the death penalty,[27] the federal judge said that there was absolutely "no historic recognition" that PAD was so rooted in the nation's values as to be considered a fundamental right.

> The majority of states have long imposed criminal penalties on one who aids another in committing suicide. [PAD] has never been given any kind of sanction in our legal history which would help establish it as a constitutional right. . . . The court holds that PAD does not involve a fundamental liberty interest protected by the Due Process Clause of the Fourteenth Amendment.

With equal dispatch, Griesa dismissed the plaintiffs' Equal Protection argument. He rejected their legal assertion that "refusal [or withdrawal] of treatment is *essentially the same thing* as committing suicide with the advice of a physician." And, if there are distinctions, and if the state has presented "reasonable and rational" arguments for its intervention in PAD, then there is no violation of the Fourteenth Amendment's Equal Protection Clause.

> It is hardly unreasonable or irrational for the State to recognize a difference between allowing nature to take its course . . . and intentionally using an artificial death-producing device. The State has obvious legitimate interests in preserving life, and in protecting vulnerable persons.

Washington State's Attorney General immediately appealed the Rothstein ruling to the U.S. Circuit Court of Appeals, Ninth Circuit (CA9). And in New York, Dr. Quill's lawyers immediately appealed the Griesa decision to the U.S. Court of Appeals, Second Circuit (CA2).

Most of the appeals from the federal trial courts—the U.S. District Courts—are heard by randomly selected three-judge panels in the circuit courts. A three-judge panel of the CA9 heard the state's appeal. In a 2:1 vote, written by Circuit Judge John T. Noonan Jr.,[28] who was appointed by Ronald Reagan in 1985, they overturned Judge Rothstein's analysis of the Fourteenth Amendment.[29]

> The conclusion of the district court . . . cannot be sustained. The language taken from *Casey*, on which the district court pitched its principal argument, should not be removed from the context in which it was uttered. [To do so] is to make an enormous leap to do violence to the context and to ignore the differences between the regulation of reproduction and the prevention of the promotion of killing a patient at his or her request.

After rejecting the Equal Protection views of Judge Rothstein, Noonan blasted the creativity of liberal judges who, he maintained, create new constitutional principles:

> Unless the federal judiciary is to be a floating constitutional convention, a federal court should not invent a constitutional right unknown to the past and antithetical to the defense of human life that has been a chief responsibility of our constitutional government.

When three-judge panel decisions are handed down, the loser usually asks the full circuit court sitting *en banc*, in this case, the then-twenty-four-member CA9, to review the three judge panel's decision. Most of these appeals are denied by the full court. Because of the importance of the PAD issue, eleven of the twenty-four circuit judges of the CA9 sat and reviewed the issue again.

Their request for an *en banc* review led to a CA9 overturn of the decision of the three-judge panel.[30] The majority opinion, written by Judge Stephen Reinhardt, appointed by Jimmy Carter in 1980, tackled the issue by answering the essential question raised by the plaintiffs:

> Is there a right to die? *Because we hold that there is*, we must then determine whether prohibiting physicians from prescribing life-ending medication for use by terminally ill patients who wish to die violates the patients' due pro-

cess rights. [After defining a person's liberty interest by examining the U.S. Supreme Court's abortion rights decisions, the majority concluded that the Supreme Court] has recognized that the Fourteenth Amendment affords constitutional protection to [intimate] personal decisions. . . . We believe that two relatively recent decisions of the Court, *Cruzan* and *Casey*, are fully persuasive, and leave little doubt as to the final result.

The judges, however, balanced a person's liberty interest in hastening death with some degree of "prohibitory and regulatory state action" that state governments possess. Although the protection of life is a prime responsibility of government, "the state's interest is *dramatically diminished* if the person it seeks to protect is terminally ill." In this sentence, the panel echoed the view of the New Jersey Supreme Court's *Quinlan* decision.

And while the state has a legitimate interest in preventing suicide, that interest, the majority concluded, "*is substantially diminished in the case of terminally ill, competent patients* who wish to die. . . . Not only is the state's interest in preventing such individuals from hastening their deaths of comparatively little weight, *but its insistence on frustrating their wishes seems cruel indeed*" (my emphasis).

The majority also concluded that the Equal Protection's "distinctions suggested by the state do not individually or collectively serve to distinguish the medical practices society currently accepts."

> In disconnecting a respirator a doctor is unquestionably taking an active role in bringing about a patient's death. . . . We see no ethical or constitutionally cognizable difference between a doctor's pulling the plug on a respirator and his prescribing drugs which will permit a terminally ill patient to end his own life. To the extent that a difference exists, we conclude that it is one of degree and not of kind.

In their concluding paragraphs, the majority addressed the critics of PAD, and especially their fear about sliding down the slippery slope toward involuntary euthanasia and a racist eugenics policy. To the opponents of PAD, "it will be only a matter of time before courts will sanction putting people to death, not because they are desperately ill and want to die, but because they are deemed to pose an unjustifiable burden on society. . . . The[se] nihilistic opponents of [PAD] conjure up a parade of horribles and insist that the only way to halt the downward spiral is to stop before it starts."

This "nihilistic argument can be offered against any constitutionally protected right or interest," stated the majority. However, courts in America have "never refused to recognize a substantive due process liberty or interest merely because there were difficulties in determining when and how to limit its exercise."

The CA9 concluded by holding "that a liberty interest exists in the choice of how and when one dies" and that the state prohibition against PAD "violates the Due Process Clause." After this dramatic turnabout decision of the CA9, the state had one final appeal route: the U.S. Supreme Court. It took that path.

Clearly expressed in these judicial opinions are the diametrically opposed views surrounding the right-to-die issue. The conservative judges on the CA9 saw the district court opinion as an example of liberal jurists giving their own views in the guise of finding precedent. For Noonan, there was no right of privacy nor was there a right to die rooted in the history of the nation. The Constitution's protections cannot be extended to provide a liberty to abort a fetus or receive physician assistance in dying: "unless the federal judiciary is to be a floating constitutional convention, a federal court should not invent a constitutional right unknown to the past and antithetical to the defense of human life that has been a chief responsibility of our constitutional government."

The liberal judges expressed a very different view of the expansiveness of the Due Process Clause. There is, they wrote, a right to die and the state cannot prohibit physicians from providing prescriptions for lethal amounts of medicine to terminally ill, competent patients. And, like their conservative brethren, the CA9 liberals cast aspersions on the attitudes of the opponents of PAD.

Back in New York, Dr. Quill and his lawyers appealed Judge Griesa's decision to the CA2. In a three-judge CA2 panel decision, Griesa's ruling that PAD *"does not involve a fundamental liberty interest* protected by the Due Process Clause of the Fourteenth Amendment"[31] was upheld, 3:0 by the panel.

In the decision, written by circuit judge Roger Miner, appointed in 1981 to the U.S. District Court, and then in 1985 appointed to the CA2, both times by Ronald Reagan, the panel concluded the trial judge's analysis of the Fourteenth Amendment "liberty interest" was correct. There was nothing rooted in the history or traditions of the nation which indicated that PAD was a "fundamental liberty" that all persons possessed. And, wrote Miner, the court is extremely "reluctant to undertake an expansive approach in this unchartered area."

However, that was not the end of the matter. The appeals court panel also *rejected* the argument made by New York's lawyers—and accepted by Griesa—that there was a significant distinction between "allowing nature to take its course [and] intentionally using an artificial death-producing device."

> It seems clear that New York does *not treat similarly circumstanced persons alike:* those in the final stages of terminal illness who are on life-support systems are allowed to hasten their deaths by directing the removal of such systems; but those who are similarly situated, except for the previous attachment of life-sustaining equipment, are not allowed to hasten death by self-administering prescribed drugs.

Furthermore, the panel concluded, the prohibition against assisting suicide is *not* rationally related to some legitimate state interest.

> What interest can the state possibly have in requiring the prolongation of a life that is all but ended? What concern prompts the state to interfere with a mentally competent patient's "right to define [his] own concept of existence, of meaning, of the universe and the mystery of life" [*Casey*] when the patient seeks to have drugs prescribed to end life during the final stages of a terminal illness?

"None," was the panel's answer to these questions: "The *greatly reduced* interest of the state in preserving life *compels* the answer to these questions: 'None.'" Both New York and Washington State's anti-PAD statutes violated the Equal Protection Clause of the Fourteenth Amendment and were, therefore, unconstitutional.

The next, and final, step for the losers in the cases, Washington State and New York State, was appeal to the U.S. Supreme Court. Lawyers for the two state governments filed petitions for writs of *certiorari* with the U.S. Supreme Court's clerk's office. On October 1, 1996, *certiorari* was granted by the Supreme Court. The nine justices would hear these controversial PAD cases.

It was a court, however, where a majority of the Justices had criticized and rejected the *Roe v Wade* precedent a number of times. A majority of them shared the views of the conservative lower federal court judges who had written harshly regarding the idea of federal judges giving the Constitution new meanings that were not rooted in America's social and legal history. The road ahead for the lawyers representing the pro-PAD advocates would be a very rough one.

III. The Cases in the U.S. Supreme Court: *Washington v Glucksberg* and *Vacco v Quill,* 1997

The Court in 1996 was a very closely divided judicial body—and would remain so until 2005 when Chief Justice Rehnquist died and Associate Justice Sandra Day O'Connor retired.[32] There were the four conservative jurists, Chief Justice William Rehnquist (Nixon appointee) and Associate Justices Anthony Kennedy (Reagan appointee), Antonin Scalia (Reagan appointee), and Clarence Thomas (George H. W. Bush appointee); the latter two were firm adherents of the "originalist" approach to understanding the meaning of the Constitution's words.

Arrayed across the ideological divide were the four moderate jurists: Associate Justices John P. Stevens (Gerald Ford appointee), David Souter (George H. W. Bush appointee), and the two Clinton appointees, Ruth B. Ginsburg and Steven Breyer. Between these two cohorts was the Court's generally recognized swing vote and the most powerful of the nine Justices because of that political reality, Associate Justice Sandra Day O'Connor (a Reagan appointee).

a. The Briefs in the Two Cases

The briefs on the merits were prepared by the physicians' lawyers in Washington and New York and the Attorneys General for both states. Essentially, the contents were very similar to the briefs filed in the lower courts. Each contained facts and legal precedents that bolstered their arguments about the constitutionality of the challenged anti-PAD statutes.

The *petitioners* were the losers in the CA2 and CA9, Washington and New York. The *respondents* were the proponents of PAD in the two cases. The task for the petitioners was to persuade the U.S. Supreme Court that the circuit courts erred and that their decisions should be overturned, *reversed*.

In the first case heard, *Washington et al., v Glucksberg et al.*, the state's lawyers noted that there were a number of substantive differences between "protected liberty interests in marriage, procreation, and the decision to bear a child," and the "alleged liberty interest" in PAD. The Supreme Court's earlier cases involved "activities that allow the individual a broader participation in life and society," while "a decision to terminate a life . . . has exactly the opposite effect once executed, life itself." Further, unlike the *Cruzan* fact situation, "assisted suicide *invites, rather than avoids, bodily intrusion.*"

The CA9 "disregarded" the differences between the abortion case facts and PAD facts. First, "the abortion decision does not implicate the life of a person. . . . Second, the abortion decision impacts women more profoundly than men, seriously implicating equal protection considerations that are absent in respect to assisted suicide. Finally, what is at stake in the abortion context is the decision whether to have a child. The Washington case involves death, which ultimately humans have little, if any, ability to control. Death is in fact the antithesis of liberty, neither can coexist with the other. Finding a liberty interest in the abortion context accords with reality; to do so in PAD does not."

The respondents brief countered these arguments. The brief interpreted the words in *Casey* in a very different manner. In *Casey*, they argued, the Supreme Court stated that "it is settled now, as it was when the Court heard arguments in *Roe v Wade*, that the Constitution places limits on a state's right to interfere with a person's most basic decisions about family and parenthood, as well as bodily integrity."

Casey held, the brief claimed, "that our society has historically afforded individuals the right to make personal decisions regarding their own bodies, medical care, and, fundamentally, the future course of their lives." In *Cruzan*, the nine jurists "acknowledged that the liberty to make this end-of-life decision is uniquely and 'deeply personal.'" Furthermore, they argued, "the Court made it clear that a state's interest in this area is limited to ensuring a voluntary decision—*in safeguarding personal liberty but not interfering with it.*" The liberty the patient had in *Cruzan*, the brief concluded, "applies at least as strongly to the choice to hasten impending death by consuming lethal medication."

Clearly, in these briefs the parties in the case were trying to persuade the justices of the merits of their respective arguments; one of the two arguments would succeed, the other would fail to persuade a majority of the nine members of the U.S. Supreme Court.

The briefs in the New York case, *Vacco v Quill*, did the same thing: present very similar arguments in the hope that they would convince the Justices to accept their reasoning and therefore rule in their favor. The New York State brief underscored, again, the substantive differences between dying "by the underlying disease or disorder" and dying "by some intervention unrelated to it." The respondents argued, as did their colleagues in *Washington*, that there was no substantive "distinction in 'causation' between 'natural death' and death by human 'intervention' to justify the line drawn by the state."

The Justices, in their separate chambers, read these four briefs, along with the decisions handed down in the lower federal courts. They also, with the help of their law clerks, read the many dozens of articles—in legal, and medical, and religious, and ethical journals—written about PAD.

They were also "helped" to find the answer to the tough questions raised in the PAD litigation by dozens of *amicus curiae* briefs filed by interested third parties who had some stake in the outcome of the legal dispute and who offered the Justices different perspectives on the PAD issue. There were forty-one *amicus* briefs filed in opposition to the argument that there is a constitutional right to PAD under the due process or equal protection theories. And there were nineteen additional briefs filed on behalf of the respondents, the physicians from Washington and New York who challenged the anti-PAD statutes in those states.[33]

During the oral argument in *Vacco*, Justice Ruth Ginsburg took note of the large number of briefs: "We're told [many things about PAD] in *this wealth of briefs*." And while this was an unusually large number of filings in a case before the U.S. Supreme Court, it was not the highest number filed in that Court. (That honor went to the *amici* who filed almost ninety briefs— many co-joined—in the 1989 Missouri abortion case before the U.S. Supreme Court, *Webster v Reproductive Health Services*.)

The authors of these *amici* briefs focused on their area of expertise—care providers, doctors, nurses, disability rights groups, hospice organizations, religious groups, survivors of the recently deceased plaintiffs in the two cases, governments, politicians, bioethicists, and civil rights organizations.

What the *amici* gave to the justices were their own particular take on the issue. The spokespersons for the medical and nursing associations directed the Justices to the "urgent necessity of extending to all patients" improved palliative care: "PAD is not the right answer to the problem of inadequate care."

The National Hospice Association's brief emphasized that the final stage of life "may be a time of profound opportunity for terminally-ill individuals and their families. . . . Given proper support, dying can become an important, valued *life* event." And the brief for the group representing disabled Americans, Not Dead Yet, tried to convince the justices that "assisted suicide is the most lethal form of discrimination against people with severe disabilities. [It is] the ultimate expression of society's fear and revulsion regarding disability."

The brief from the Jewish group, Agudath Israel of America, reflected their concern about another holocaust environment. "As representatives of a people whose numbers were decimated little more than half-century ago by a society that 'progressed' from its

"enlightened" practices of "mercy killing" to the mass slaughter of millions of human beings deemed physically or racially "inferior,'" Agudath Israel is particularly sensitive to the legal assignment of diminished levels of life protection based on diminished levels of life "quality."

The *amici* in support of PAD had the almost impossible task of trying to persuade the conservative majority on the Court that liberty and privacy arguments should be *extended* to enable terminally ill patients to kill themselves with the assistance of a physician or a nurse. This was a Court majority that had numerous times defended the sanctity of life in cases involving intimate family relationships.[34]

The ACLU brief pointed out to the Justices that "no person (physician or otherwise) has been meaningfully punished for aiding the terminally ill to end their suffering." For the civil liberties group, this was a clear sign that society had come around to the view that "it has no right to insist on the continued suffering of the terminally ill, and no right to punish those who honor the request of the terminally ill by assisting them in ending their agony."

The brief filed by thirty-six Religious Organizations pointed out that the common law ban on suicide and PAD is a relic of the past that violates the First Amendment:[35] "The common law's historic bans upon suicide are rooted in the incorporation of Roman Catholic canon law into the English common law."

And the brief filed by Surviving Family Members pointed out to the justices "the intense suffering their loved ones [experienced] in the weeks and months before their inevitable deaths."

> The statements [in the brief, written by family members of fifteen dead patients] dispel the myth that pills can always control all pain. Moreover, doctors sometimes refused to prescribe sufficient pain-killing medication because of their fear that it would be used to hasten death. . . . Additionally, as family members attest, a slow, deteriorating death often leads to loss of dignity and self-respect for the dying person.

All these briefs and articles were digested by the Justices in advance of the next step in the U.S. Supreme Court's decision-making process: oral arguments by the parties to the dispute in open court.

Sitting on the Court in 1997 were six members who had sharply reduced the scope of the 1973 *Roe v Wade* abortion decision. They were prepared, as early as the 1989 *Webster* case, to overturn the *Roe* precedent and would have, if not for the separate concurring vote of Justice O'Connor in *Webster*. The conservatives were categorically unwilling to extend the concept of *fundamental liberty* to any right that was not deeply *rooted* in the history and culture of the nation.

There were at least two members (Scalia and Thomas) who did not believe that "privacy" was a right protected in the Constitution *at all* and that, as Scalia wrote in his *Cruzan* opinion, the Court had no right to consider such questions. Furthermore, the two Clinton appointees, Justices Ginsburg and Breyer, were cautionary jurists and were certainly not ideological replacements for the outspoken—but deceased—Associate Justices William J. Brennan and Thurgood Marshall.

b. The Oral Arguments in Washington and Vacco

Oral argument is an important part of the U.S. Supreme Court's decision-making process. On many occasions an onlooker trying to discern the possible direction of the Court by listening to the argument feels much like the person trying to read tea leaves scattered at the bottom of a cup. This was certainly *not* the case when, on the morning of January 8, 1997, the Justices stepped out from the velvet curtains and took their seats to hear the lawyers discuss the issue of physician-assisted dying.

Less than three months after *certiorari* was granted, followed by an overwhelming number of briefs filed by the parties and the *amici*, the nine Justices were ready to discuss the issue raised in the litigation. The controversial question was: Did a competent, terminally ill patient have a fundamental right, constitutionally protected from state interference, to receive assistance from a physician in order to hasten death?

Oral argument serves another very important purpose: through the discussions—more than two hours were devoted to arguments in the two cases—the justices were able to gauge the attitudes, concerns, and beliefs of their colleagues on the Court. Using the lawyers before the bench as human conveyor belts, the Justices asked questions that effectively gave their colleagues messages regarding the issues that troubled them.

Finally, the oral argument stage in the Court's decision-making process is the very first time all nine jurists meet and listen to each other talk about the case.

Five lawyers addressed the nine Justices that morning. In the first argument, *Washington v Glucksberg*, three lawyers argued their positions: the state's Senior Assistant Attorney General, William L. Williams; the U. S. Solicitor General, referred to as "General," Walter Dellinger, next spoke for the nation. A Seattle lawyer, Kathryn L. Tucker, a lawyer with the pro-PAD national organization, represented the respondents in the litigation, Dr. Glucksberg, his medical colleagues, and the patients, spoke last.

Williams, representing Washington State, began his presentation by telling the Justices of the three major state interests in this type of case: protection of life, the prevention of abuse and undue influence, and the state's strong interest in the protection and regulation of the medical profession. (These were the three basic arguments other state governments presented in the *Cruzan* and *Schiavo* trials).

Justice Souter interrupted Williams to ask some questions about the state's "fear of abuse," associated with the slippery slope argument, raised in the two governments' written briefs and in the numerous *amici* briefs supporting Washington State and New York State. The concerned Justice spoke about the fears expressed that "the practice of [PAD] is going to sort of *gravitate down* to those who are not terminally ill, to those, in fact, who have not made any voluntary or knowing choice. And ultimately it's going to *gravitate out of PAD into euthanasia*" (my emphasis).

Souter continued voicing his concerns about what many *amici* discussed in their brief: the fear that PAD would be the start of trend that would lead to involuntary euthanasia. He asked how he "should weight or value the risk of abuse of PAD, of the slippery slope. The state's argument, he said, was plausible, but I don't know how realistic it is. . . . What empirical basis do I have for evaluating that [slippery slope] argument?" Williams could not answer Souter's questions.

Another concern of the justices, voiced first by Chief Justice Rehnquist, was the distinction between a *Cruzan*-type death and PAD. *Cruzan* involved a state standard—"clear and convincing evidence"—that had to be proved before a patient's life-maintaining medical devices could be removed. In the cases before the judges in 1997, the Court was facing no such evidentiary standard but an argument for an outright prohibition against any state action that would interfere with PAD. Unstated, but clearly announced, was Rehnquist's view that the two were not similar processes (the death of a person in a PVS and a terminally ill patient who wished to die) and therefore there was no equal protection problem. Other Justices then continued the discussion, telling their colleagues of their agreement with the Chief Justice.

General Dellinger then spoke with the justices. The Clinton administration's contention, in the written briefs, was that there was a limited liberty interest possessed by a person seeking assistance in hastening death, but that the Washington and New York anti-PAD laws were constitutionally valid. Before he could get into a summary of the federal government's position, Associate Justice O'Connor interrupted him.

She was confused and posed: "it's your brief that there is a liberty interest but nonetheless the law should be upheld." Wasn't there an inherent contradiction?

Dellinger's answer surprised the Court when he said that the government's defense of a liberty interest was not in PAD but regarding the original plaintiffs (who had died) who had been undergoing severe pain and suffering. Unfortunately, the state had the homicide statutes that prevented the dying patients from the means of relieving that pain and suffering.

Rehnquist asked Dellinger "what precisely is the liberty interest that you urge us to recognize?" The General answered by urging the Court to acknowledge that a person states a cognizable liberty interest when he or she alleges that a state is imposing severe pain and suffering or has adopted a rule, which prevents someone from the only means of relieving that pain and suffering. This is the narrow liberty interest of the government, Dellinger said.

In response to questions Justice O'Connor raised, Dellinger concluded that rooted in the history of the nation is the belief

> that a state may not compel a person to undergo unwanted medical treatment. [For the Solicitor General] the critical issue in these cases, as it was in *Cruzan*, was the state's overwhelming interest in affirming the value of life by prohibiting anyone from promoting or assisting a suicide.

No one disputes the constitutionality of those laws, he concluded. "The actual question before the court is whether the Constitution compels an exception to those laws here. *In our view, it does not.*" Dellinger noted that the 25 percent of patients who unnecessarily die in pain is a task for the medical profession, "but it's not a task that calls for the cheap and easy expedient of lethal medication rather than the more expensive pain palliative."

The final lawyer to face the justices was Kathryn Tucker, the lawyer for the physician respondents in the case. She tried to bring the Justices' attention back to the central point the doctors were making: that competent, dying patients "have the liberty to choose to cross that threshold in a humane and dignified manner. The Constitution prohibits the state to intrude in this private matter."

The Chief Justice interrupted her presentation. He asked whether the issue before the Court involved the patient's need for assistance from a physician to die. Tucker agreed with the Chief, saying that the dying patients "want a peaceful death, they want a humane death, and they want a dignified death. And, in order to access that kind of death they need the assistance of their physician. The physician is the gatekeeper for the medications that can bring that peaceful end to the suffering that for these patients is intolerable."

Justice Scalia then entered the discussion with a hypothetical: What if a doctor tells a patient that she will be in terrible pain for a decade. Shouldn't that patient have the right to choose PAD? Tucker responded by stating that the petition draws the line at terminally ill patients where the "dying process has begun and is underway."

Scalia then offered a classic "Scaliaism": "I hate to tell you, but the dying process of all of us has begun and is underway. It's just a matter of time. And it seems to me that the patient who has ten years of agony to look forward to has a more appealing case than the patient who is at the threshold of death."

Tucker disagreed with Scalia's view of the issue. However, before she finished, Justice Kennedy had an important question that he wanted her to answer: "Your argument basically is an autonomy argument, then."

Tucker jumped on the question because it gave her an opportunity to respond to Solicitor General Dellinger's argument:

> There is an interest in avoiding pain, but that was not the end of the matter. The second argument made involves a dying person's decisional autonomy, and the third is the interest of bodily integrity. Each of those separate interests is of constitutional dimension and each has bearing here.

Justice O'Connor then observed that if the Court accepted the respondent's position, the result would be that the federal courts would face "*a flow of cases* through the court system for heaven knows how long. [Death] is something that affects all of us."

Tucker's response was terse: the Court cannot leave the problem to the legislative process. "This court has *never* left to the legislative process the protection of vital liberties, and the liberty at issue in this case is certainly of a vital and substantive nature."

Justice Souter, who had been listening intently, then returned to the issue he raised initially: What empirical evidence is there that there will not be a gross misuse of the PAD, leading to involuntary euthanasia? There is none, he continued, and "isn't that a reason for saying we are not in a position either to [define the] liberty interest, although we may recognize there is one, or to weigh the countervailing claim of the states? And therefore, for substantive due process purposes, as an institution, we are not in a position to make the judgment that you want us to make. It would just be guesswork."

Tucker disagreed, arguing that there already existed, in federal case law, "a tremendous amount of guidance on how to weigh this liberty interest in the Court's precedents."

These segments from the highly focused *Washington* oral argument reflect many of the issues surrounding dying with dignity. Certainly the justices tried to place the central issue, the constitutional right of the dying patient to receive PAD, in their sights. In doing so they exhibited an extreme caution and a fear of the unintended consequences if they accepted such an extension of the meaning of liberty.

The oral arguments also reflect the wry sarcasm of Justice Scalia, the extreme caution of Justice Souter, and the general fear of unintended consequences—slippery slope, innocent people euthanized, a growing case load for the federal courts—should the Court affirm the lower federal appellate court decisions.

In the *Vacco v Quill* oral argument, which immediately followed the *Washington* arguments, New York's Attorney General, Dennis Vacco, presented the state's defense of its prohibition against PAD. General Dellinger spoke next to the Justices in this case. The Harvard Law School professor Laurence Tribe, who represented the respondents, Dr. Timothy Quill and his medical colleagues, spoke last.

In this case, the discussions focused on the relevance of the Fourteenth Amendment's Equal Protection clause. This issue reflected the constitutional difference between the two cases.

Vacco began his argument by telling the justices that the equal protection clause "was not implicated or offended" in the case. Withdrawing from life support was not the same fact and legal situation as a dying patient who seeks PAD.

Justice Ginsburg asked Vacco "to tell us why the CA2 was wrong. Vacco quickly responded. The patient who refuses life-saving medical treatment is exercising a fundamental right—in the common law and in the Constitution—to be left alone. The dying patient seeking the assistance of a doctor to end life is not asserting a fundamental right to have a third party—the physician—to help them die. "And we believe that these two acts are clearly distinguishable.

After Vacco's time expired, Dellinger again addressed the Justices. Justice Ginsburg asked him a question about an issue not raised in the first oral argument. "Could you deal with the argument," she began, "that's been made about winks *and nods*, that this issue *is a sham* because PAD goes on for anybody who is sophisticated enough to want it" (my emphasis). Dellinger replied that he could not address the argument Ginsburg alluded to.

However, Professor Tribe took over and immediately addressed the issue raised by Justice Ginsburg. For him, the "winks and nods" were real, "and relate to [a medical reality] that we all accept—the principle of the double effect."[36]

After further questioning about the distinctions between letting a person die of the underlying disease and PAD, Justice Kennedy observed that the distinction probably was "between allowing events to take their own course and third-person intervention." Tribe countered by returning to the "winks and nods" conversation he had with Justice Ginsburg. He added that when physicians act in accordance with the double-effect principle, "they're not going to talk to others about it because they might be prosecuted because of the lines that are drawn [in the state law]." And the practice, Tribe said, has for decades given "dangerous authority" to the medical profession. Ginsburg was shocked at this reality.

Chief Justice Rehnquist asked Tribe, "before your time expires, to tell us what you think the liberty interest is." His answer triggered a final set of comments by Justice Scalia that summarized that jurist's general views on the issue.

Tribe's answer to Rehnquist was direct: "liberty is the freedom, at this threshold at the end of life, not to be a creature of the state but to have some voice in the question of how much pain one is really going through." To which Scalia immediately said: "Why does the voice *just arrive* when death is imminent?" Tribe quickly retorted that, in life, there were "certain critical thresholds: birth, marriage, child-bearing. I think that death is one of those thresholds."

A bemused Scalia then asked where all these thresholds are found in the Constitution. Tribe uttered two words: "due process." Scalia, however, had the final comment: "this is a lovely philosophy. But you want us to frame a constitutional rule on the basis of that?"

The caution expressed by many of the Justices during the oral arguments was very telling. So was the concern of Justice Kennedy when he told Glucksberg's attorney: "You're asking us in effect to declare unconstitutional the laws in fifty states." And when Justice O'Connor voiced her concern about "the [increased] flow of cases through the court system for Heaven knows how long" if the Court invalidated the laws that prohibited PAD, the message the Justices seemed to convey to observers did not auger well for the PAD advocates.

Certainly, the fact that the Solicitor General's briefs sided with the states briefs was not a good sign because the Court majority generally (80 percent of the time) accepts his views of the case. And Court watchers and legal scholars did not believe that the justices granted *certiorari* in these hard cases "simply to concur with [the CA 2 and the CA9]."[37]

After these dramatic words spoken by the feisty Justice Scalia and the liberal Professor Tribe, the two cases were "submitted" to the Court for its judgment.

c. The Court Decides

After hearing oral argument, the Justices meet privately—in their Friday Conference—to begin the decision-making process. The Conference is the venue where the Justices try to find some kind of consensus on cases they heard in open court a few days earlier.

The Conference serves two important purposes. In these secret sessions, at least twenty during a Term of the Court, the justices determine which of the nearly ten thousand petitions received annually by the Court will form the agenda for the following Court Term. The second critically important action that takes place in the conference is the discussion and voting on the cases heard in oral argument earlier in the week.

The protocol for this activity is simple. The Chief Justice starts the discussion of the argued cases every time. In these PAD cases Rehnquist expressed his views on the constitutional issues, Due Process and Equal Protection, and after conveying his thoughts, announced his judgment regarding the lower federal appellate courts decisions in these PAD cases. It was a vote to reverse both the CA 9 and CA2 opinions.

After the Chief speaks, the Associate Justices in turn, from senior Associate Justice to junior of the eight, present their views and cast their "vote" on the disposition of the case or cases.

After all nine voice their views and their votes on the disposition of the case, the Chief tallies the result, announces the vote, and then, if the Chief is in the majority, announces that he will write the opinion or selects a Justice in the majority to write the opinion for the court. If the Chief is not in the majority, then the senior Associate Justice in the majority either writes the majority opinion or assigns the writing to one of the other justices.

In both *Washington* and *Vacco*, the tally in Conference was 9:0. All nine Justices voted to reverse the two lower federal appellate court decisions. Because of the importance of the issues raised in these cases, Chief Justice Rehnquist determined that he would write the majority opinions in both cases. Because both cases raised Due Process and Equal Protection issues, Rehnquist addressed the Due Process argument in the *Washington v Glucksberg* opinion and took up, very briefly, the Equal Protection arguments of the CA2 in the *Vacco v Quill* opinion.

This activity in Conference is just the beginning of the process of judicial decision making. The votes taken there are preliminary; a Justice can change position after reading the draft opinions circulated to the nine chambers. After weeks of back-and-forth dialogue between Rehnquist and his law clerks, as well as the writing of additional draft opinions by them, and after Rehnquist was satisfied with the legal product, the opinion was then circulated to the other eight chambers for comments and criticisms and suggestions for improvements.

After reading the early drafts of the Rehnquist opinions, five Justices decided to write separate concurring opinions in order to state their differences with the Chief regarding the issue of PAD.

Once Rehnquist's draft circulations were fully vetted by the other Justices, once all the modifications were made in them by the Chief, and once all the concurring opinions were drafted in chambers and then circulated among all the Justices, the decisions in *Washington v Glucksberg* and *Vacco v Quill* were ready to be announced in open court on Thursday, June 26, 1997.

It took the Court four months and eighteen days to find its collective mind on the issues raised in these two cases. There were an untold number of circulations in chambers and among the Justices before the opinion was completed and ready to be announced.[38]

While the vote was 9:0, that was a misleading statistic. Chief Justice Rehnquist's opinion had the full support of only three other Justices, Antonin Scalia, Clarence Thomas, and Anthony Kennedy. Sandra Day O'Connor, however, wrote a separate two-page concurring opinion *but* joined the Rehnquist opinion. With her "join," Rehnquist had the five votes needed to hand down an "opinion" of the Court. Had she not joined, Rehnquist's decision would be a "judgment" of the Court, because it lacked a majority of five. Clearly, the two PAD decisions of the Court reflected a serious "fracture among the justices concerning two points, one general and one technical."[39]

The *general* division in the Court was the *reasoning* behind the decisions' validation of the two states' anti-PAD laws. There were four other Justices who agreed with the final judgment of the Rehnquist opinion but, because they fundamentally *disagreed* with the Chief's reasoning that led to his decisions in the cases, did not join his opinion.

The four who wrote separately were Associate Justices John P. Stevens (an eight-page concurrence), David H. Souter (a fifteen-page concurrence), Steven Breyer (a two-page concurrence), and Ruth B. Ginsburg (whose concurrence was but a few sentences, stating that she concurred largely for the reasons expressed in Justice O'Connor's concurring opinion). Their concurrences clearly stated that each of them was "concurring in the judgment" only, not the reasons proffered by Rehnquist. Indeed, some of these concurring opinions were very critical of the majority opinion.

The technical split in the Court revolved around the reality that in both *Washington* and *Vacco*, all the terminally ill patients-plaintiffs died long before the cases arrived in the federal appeals courts and in the U.S. Supreme Court. Because of that fact, the cases became "facial challenges"[40] to the anti-PAD state laws, which meant that the doctors' lawyers in both cases "must establish that no set of circumstances exists under which the Act would be valid."[41] Such challenges, as Justice Stevens pointed out in his *Glucksberg* concurring opinion, "are the most difficult to mount successfully."

Had the patients-plaintiffs been alive when the Supreme Court announced the decisions, the cases would have been "as applied"[42] challenges to the state laws. Under this set of circumstances, the lawyers had to establish only that these anti-PAD Acts were invalid as applied to the living, terminally ill litigants. These *"as applied"* challenges "are judged according to a more easily met standard because the alleged violation is limited to a particular claim and does not have to be true of all applications of the law."[43]

The four concurring Justices disagreed with the more conservative jurists[44] on both points, but, because the cases were defined as facial challenges to the anti-PAD laws, they were left with only one choice: uphold the validity of the laws in these cases.

Chief Justice Rehnquist's opinion for the Court in *Washington v Glucksberg* has two major components. In the initial segment of the fifteen-page opinion, he focused on whether the statute "offends the Fourteenth Amendment's Due Process Clause. We hold that it does not."

He went on to point out that suicide and assisting suicide were never a part of "our Nation's history, legal traditions, and practices. In almost every state—indeed, in almost every western democracy—it is a crime to assist a suicide.

> [These state bans] are long-standing, deeply rooted, expressions of the States' commitment to the protection and preservation of all human life. . . . Opposition to and condemnation of suicide—and, therefore, of assisting suicide—are consistent and enduring themes of our philosophical, legal, and cultural heritages.

The second prong of Rehnquist's opinion examined—and rejected—the "respondents' constitutional claims." First, he reviewed the Court's precedents regarding the meaning of liberty in America's constitutional system, noting that the Due Process Clause, in addition to guaranteeing "fair process, also provides heightened protection against [substantive] government interference with certain fundamental rights and liberty interests." He enumerated the "long line of cases that, in addition to the specific freedoms protected by the Bill of Rights, that 'liberty' specially protected by the Due Process Clause."

Included in that list of rights were the right to marry, bear children, marital privacy, use of contraceptives, bodily integrity, and the right to have an abortion. "We have also assumed, and strongly suggested, that the Due Process Clause protects the traditional right to refuse unwanted lifesaving medical treatment."

> But we have always been reluctant to expand the concept of substantive due process because guideposts for responsible decision making in this unchartered area are scarce and open-ended. . . . We must exercise the utmost care whenever we are asked to break new ground in this field, lest the liberty protected by the Due Process Clause be subtly transformed into the policy preferences of the members of the Court.

And, for Rehnquist and his colleagues, the guideposts for such a Due Process analysis—"a restrained methodology," wrote Rehnquist—are found in the past decisions of the Court. First, there had to be a "careful description of the asserted fundamental liberty interest." In these cases, Rehnquist noted, the respondents provided such a description: A person has the right to choose a humane, dignified death with the assistance of a physician.

The second and final phase of the Court's "objective analysis" was to determine, specifically and "objectively," whether that carefully described liberty interest was "deeply rooted in this Nation's history and traditions." Did the right asserted by the respondents "have any place in our Nation's traditions?"

For Rehnquist, the answer was clear. All the evidence from America's history showed the opposite, that suicide and assisting a suicide were not part of the values "deeply rooted in this Nation's history and traditions." To affirm the federal appellate courts' decisions, Rehnquist wrote, "we would have to reverse centuries of legal doctrine and practice, and strike down the considered policy choice of almost every State."

Since this alleged right to die was never a fundamental liberty interest protected by the Due Process Clause, a state, if it wished, could ban assisted suicide as long as such a ban was "rationally related to legitimate government interests." After enumerating a number of legitimate state interests, including the "State's fear that permitting suicide will start down the path to voluntary and perhaps even involuntary euthanasia"—the infamous slippery slope,[45] Rehnquist concluded that the states met the "rational relationship" prerequisite. "This requirement is unquestionably met here."

> We therefore hold that Washington Revised Code does not violate the Fourteenth Amendment, either on its face or as applied to competent, terminally ill adults who wish to hasten their deaths by obtaining medication prescribed by their doctors.

The opinion ended with the following comments about the character of America's system of federalism: "Our holding permits this debate (about the morality, legality, and practicality of PAD) to continue, as it should in a democratic society."

Rehnquist's second opinion, *Vacco v Quill*, was a much shorter one than *Washington v Glucksberg*. In it, the Chief Justice addressed the question of whether "New York's prohibition on assisting suicide violates the Equal Protection Clause of the Fourteenth Amendment. We hold that it does not."

The Equal Protection Clause in the Fourteenth Amendment "creates no substantive rights. Instead," Rehnquist wrote, "it embodies a general rule that States must treat like cases alike but may treat unlike cases accordingly."

The New York statutes "neither infringe fundamental rights nor involve suspect classifications." Since assisting a patient to die was not a fundamental right (*Washington v Glucksberg*) nor was the competent, terminally ill patient cohort considered a "suspect class,"[46] there was no need for the justices to employ the toughest analysis, "strict scrutiny,"[47] to determine whether the state anti-PAD statutes were invalid. "These laws," concluded Rehnquist, "are therefore entitled to a strong presumption of validity."

> On their faces, neither New York's ban on assisted suicide nor its statutes permitting patients to refuse medical treatments treat anyone differently than anyone else or draw any distinctions between persons. Everyone, regardless of physical condition, is entitled, if competent, to refuse unwanted lifesaving medical treatment, no one is permitted to assist a suicide. Generally speaking, laws that apply evenhandedly to all "unquestionably comply" with the Equal Protection Clause.

Disagreeing with the CA2 majority, Rehnquist wrote that "we think the distinction between assisting suicide and withdrawing life-sustaining treatment, a distinction widely recognized and endorsed in the medical profession and in our legal traditions, is both important and logical; it is certainly rational."

The purpose of withdrawing life support from a competent patient, observed Rehnquist, is to "cease doing useless and futile or degrading things to the patient," and to allow the "underlying fatal disease or pathology" to cause the patient's death. However, "if a patient ingests lethal medication prescribed by a physician, he is killed by that medication." Finally, he concluded the opinion: "New York State has reaffirmed the line between 'killing' and 'letting die.' The judgment of the [CA2] is reversed."[48]

Justice O'Connor's important concurrence provided Rehnquist with the Court's needed fifth vote. However, she clearly displayed her concern about—and the limits of—her joining the majority opinion. She agreed with Rehnquist as to his opinion's conclusions regarding the facial challenges to the two states' anti-PAD bills; however, she also suggested that she may have decided differently if the Court faced an as applied challenge to the statutes.

If the patient-litigants had not died before the Court's decisions, O'Connor would have reached a different judgment.

It is interesting to speculate why she joined Rehnquist to give him a majority opinion and the other four Justices—with Justices Ginsburg and Breyer specifically joining most of her concurring opinion—essentially agreeing with her differences but writing concurrences *only* in the judgment. Of course, we will not know until she chooses to talk about the case or, much more likely, when we read about the dynamics of decision making in these two cases in the papers and files she will leave to the LOC or another archival library.

She opened her concurrence dramatically: "Death will be different for each of us." However, her concurrence addressed the source of her disagreement with Rehnquist. "There is no need [now] to address the question" raised by the respondents, O'Connor concluded. A dying patient in both states, she noted, who is experiencing great pain "has no legal barriers to obtaining medication, from qualified physicians, to alleviate that suffering, even to the point of causing unconsciousness and hastening death." This was acknowledgement by O'Connor of the reality of the double effect. Dying patients do receive lethal medication from their doctors to alleviate great pain, even though it may also kill the patient.

O'Connor concluded somewhat hopefully. When the time comes, she wrote,

> there is no reason to think the democratic process will not strike the proper balance between the interests of terminally ill, mentally competent patients who seek to end their suffering and the State's interests in protecting those who might seek to end life mistakenly or under pressure.

Justice Breyer concurred in both judgments. He wrote that New York's lawyers and briefs "articulated the state interests [that] justify the distinction between PAD and the withdrawal of life support. He wrote separately because he "did not agree, however, with the Court's formulation of the [respondents] claimed 'liberty' interest."

> The Court describes it as a "right to commit suicide with another's assistance." But I would not reject the respondents' claim without considering a different formulation, for which our legal tradition may provide greater support. That formulation would use words roughly like "a right to die

with dignity." But irrespective of the exact words used, at its core would lie personal control over the manner of death, professional medical assistance, and the avoidance of unnecessary and severe physical suffering—combined.

However, Breyer concluded, "I do not believe that this Court need or now should decide whether or not such a right is 'fundamental.' . . . Were the legal circumstances different, then the law's impact upon serious and otherwise unavoidable physical pain (accompanying death) would be more directly at issue. And, as Justice O'Connor suggests, the Court might have to revisit its conclusions in these cases."

Justice Stevens also concurred in the judgments reached by the Court in these two cases. However, some parts read like a partial dissent. For example, Stevens believed, contrary to the Rehnquist opinions, that *Cruzan* and *Casey* were appropriate to these PAD cases, as the respondents, the *amici*, and the lower federal courts argued in the briefs and in the CA2 and CA9 opinions. "I write separately to make it clear that there is also room for further debate about the limits that the Constitution places on the power of the states to punish the practice. . . . Today, the Court decides that [the two state laws are] not invalid 'on its face,' that is to say, in all or most cases in which it might be applied. That holding, however, does not foreclose the possibility that some applications of the statute might well be invalid."

Stevens believed that the "now-deceased plaintiffs in this action may in fact have had a *liberty interest even stronger* than Nancy Cruzan's because, not only were they terminally ill, they were suffering constant and severe pain."

Avoiding intolerable pain and the indignity of living one's final days incapacitated and in agony is certainly [here he quoted from *Casey*] "at the
heart of the liberty to define one's own concept of existence, of meaning, of
the universe, and of the mystery of human life."

For the senior Justice, "the liberty interest in this case differs from, and is stronger than, both the common-law right to refuse medical treatment and the unbridled interest in deciding whether to live or die. It is an interest in deciding how, rather than whether, a critical threshold shall be crossed."

Furthermore, Justice Stevens was, unlike the majority, "not persuaded" that there "will be a significant difference between the "intent of the physicians, the patients or the families in the two situations," that is, removing life support and PAD. "Some applications of these two states' statutes," he concluded, contrary to Rehnquist's reasoning, "may impose an intolerable intrusion on the patient's freedom."

Justice Souter's concurring judgment took a very different analytical path[49] but, finally, his analysis ended much the same way the Rehnquist opinion did: the anti-PAD statutes did not violate the Fourteenth Amendment: "The State's interests are sufficiently serious to defeat the present claim that its law is arbitrary or purposeless."

In the final analysis, what mattered for Souter was the possible correctness of the slippery slope argument against PAD. As was noted in viewing his questions in oral argument, Justice Souter was very concerned about the slippery slope argument made there and in the briefs filed by Washington and New York as well as the *amicus* briefs filed in support of the petitioners in the cases.

"The case for the slippery slope," he wrote in his concurrence, was "fairly made out" by the two States and the *amici*. If PAD was a part of the continuum of liberties protected by the Due Process Clause, there was no guarantee that PAD would not be followed by euthanasia, voluntary and then involuntary. "The day may come," he wrote, "when we can say with some assurance which side is right, but for now it is the substantiality of the factual disagreement, and the alternatives for resolving it, that matter. They are, for me, dispositive of the due process claim at this time."

The U.S. Supreme Court's majority opinion continued to preserve the law's distinction between the withdrawal of life support from a dying patient and PAD. Furthermore, all the justices wrote in support of the double effect and terminal sedation as viable alternatives to PAD.[50]

Terminal Sedation (TS), they observed, is a legitimate medical procedure—as the American Medical Association *amicus* brief noted and *all* the Justices quoted from in their opinions. However, as all the opinions also pointed out, TS is also a medical procedure that, after the terminally ill patient who has experienced "intolerable pain,[51] shortness of breath, delirium, or persistent vomiting is unconscious, assists the patient in dying.[52]

Although the Justices refused to conclude that a dying, competent person had a liberty interest in getting physician assistance in dying, ironically, some forms of PAD *do take place*, even if clandestinely. Indeed, one of the Justices pointed this reality out in his concurring opinion. Justice Stevens took "note that there is evidence that a significant number of physicians support the practice of hastening death in particular situations."[53]

Recent studies "have documented a secret practice of PAD in the United States." (my emphasis)

> In Washington State, 12 percent of physicians responding to a survey had received genuine requests for assisted suicide within the year studied. Twenty-four percent of requests were acceded to, and more than half of those patients died as a result. A study of Oregon physicians [undertaken before passage of Oregon's "Death with Dignity" statute in 1998] showed similar results. PAD is usually conducted covertly, without consultation, guidelines, or documentation.[54]

In sum, although a number of states have attempted to de-criminalize PAD,[55] over the years alternatives to PAD have come to the forefront; viable, non-criminalized options for dying patients and their physicians. Ironically, these alternatives—palliative care, hospice, and the double effect—are publicly supported by some major opponents of legitimatizing PAD, including the AMA and many religious groups, including the Roman Catholic Church.

These 1997 decisions of the nation's highest court quickly ended pro-PAD advocates' efforts to broaden the meaning of liberty in the Constitution. The advocates had to focus on the second path to legalizing PAD: the state legislative process. The next two chapters continue the story by examining the dynamics of these state political battles.

5

THE SECOND PATH TO PAD: PASSING LEGISLATION ALLOWING DEATH WITH DIGNITY

The Court should stay its hand to allow reasonable legislative consideration.
— Associate Justice David H. Souter[1]

The debate over the legalization of assisted-suicide will continue in the political process.
— Mark Chopko, U.S. Catholic Conference[2]

[Should] a religious group seek to impose its beliefs on the general public?
— Carol M. Ostrom[3]

Throughout the legal debates and the battles surrounding the controversial right-to-die issue, from *Quinlan* in 1976 through the 1997 cases from Washington State and New York State, the opposing forces were known. The large number of briefs filed on behalf of the two states in the 1997 cases represented the political, religious, and medical and nursing "establishments" in America: the United States (two briefs filed by the U.S. Solicitor General), the Roman Catholic Church (five briefs), the American Medical Association, and the American Nurses Association. Arrayed against these powerful forces were politically marginal organizations such as the Hemlock Society, the Grey Panthers, Compassion in Dying, and the American Medical Student Association.

I. The Opposition to PAD Legislation

The greatest concern of *all* opponents of legalizing PAD remains the slippery slope argument presented in numerous forums: in *amicus* briefs filed in the courts, in legislative chambers, in the press, in association meetings, in churches. Critics contend that PAD legislation will take civilized society down a slippery slope, leading to extensive abuses against the elderly, the infirm, minorities, the disabled, and other vulnerable groups, in the name of politics, ideology, finance, morality, and a host of other disingenuous reasons.

Beyond the slippery slope argument and the consequences it would bequeath to Americans, the men and women opposed to legalization of PAD argue that the signal alternatives to PAD are hospice and enhanced palliative care. Palliative care optimally reduces the severity of pain caused by illness. It relieves suffering; it does not cure the patient. Hospice is palliative care for the terminally ill patient provided at the last stage of the illness.

Increasingly in the United States, palliative care providers begin treatment earlier in a patient's illness, especially those with congestive heart failure, chronic obstructive lung disease, and cancer.[4] An August 2010 editorial in the *NEJM* encouraged the profession to shift its "long held paradigm that limits access to palliative care to patients who were predictably and clearly dying" to a new one: a "simultaneous care model that provides both palliative care and disease-specific therapies beginning at the time of diagnosis." The editorial concluded: "Perhaps unsurprisingly, reducing patients' misery may help them live longer."[5]

There are many organizations and groups opposed to PAD. However, the American Medical Association (AMA), the professional organization closest to the issue, has consistently been its strongest secular opponent. Representing less than a majority of physicians in the nation (about 40 percent of physicians are members), it has consistently rejected PAD[6] and euthanasia.[7] Its *Code of Medical Ethics* states that "both of these practices are 'fundamentally incompatible with the physician's role as a healer;' that they are 'difficult or impossible to control,' and possess serious societal risks."[8]

While there have been efforts at the twice-yearly AMA national meetings to pass resolutions reversing the AMA position on PAD, all have failed. The retention of the AMA policy "is in significant part attributable to the repeated mobilization of grassroots pro-lifers, and especially pro-life physicians, who have urged delegates not to betray the medical profession's long history of protecting vulnerable life."[9]

Some physicians opposed to PAD believe that "one cannot regulate the unregulatable."[10] Because PAD is an unregulatable protocol, the slippery slope argument inevitably presents itself in their criticism. After PAD is legalized, and if there is no practical way to regulate physician behavior, they believe there will be legitimatization of euthanasia, then PAD will be requested by surrogates for an unconscious but not a medically diagnosed incompetent *dying* patient, and so on down the hill.

Some of the most passionate critics of PAD are organizations that represent persons with disabilities, vulnerable individuals, the elderly, the uninsured, and members of minority groups.[11] Those above sixty years of age and minorities, according to critics of PAD, are especially wary and fearful of PAD as a public policy. "It is no accident that while polls show younger people favoring legalization [of PAD], it is opposed by most people over sixty. African Americans of all ages oppose it by two to one."[12]

Poll after poll suggests that ethnic minorities in the United States are "more concerned about the prospect of *legalized euthanasia* and its potential impact on them than are their white counterparts. . . . While 53 percent of whites sampled in Michigan could envision requesting assistance in suicide, only 22 percent of blacks could."[13]

Without any doubt, PAD advocates face one major political opponent, the Roman Catholic Church,[14] which "has played a *preeminent role* in the evolution of end-of-life decision-making policies."[15] The Roman Catholic Church is the largest religious denomination in the United States; almost 24 percent of Americans are Catholics.[16] And, in this area of public policy, it "has been a moral force to reckon with in medical-ethical debates over end-of-life decision making."[17]

While religious groups of all persuasions have general prohibitions against suicide and, for them, its correlate, PAD,[18] the Roman Catholic Church has used its financial strength to fight pitched battles against the PAD advocates in the courts, in the legislative assemblies, and in the political struggles surrounding initiatives and referenda that call for PAD.

Unlike other religious denominations actively opposed to PAD, the Roman Catholic Church is exceptional because of its vocal, long-standing involvement in the right-to-die debate at the level of both clinical specifics and theological generalities. In addition and unlike the other denominations, the Catholic Church has a sprawling complex of health care institutions that bring the Church into contact with clinical realities and real-life moral dilemmas on a regular basis. The Church also has a web of politically active state conferences that regularly issue specific statements on medical ethics for general consumption. In addition, the conferences lobby on specific legislative provisions in the state and federal capitols.[19]

Furthermore, the leaders of the Catholic anti-PAD movement have "recruited the fundamentalist [Protestant] Christian churches" to support their effort to defeat PAD initiatives. In the nation, the American Baptist Church "which counts 20 percent of the U.S. population among its followers, [and] is second only to the Catholic Church in size," along with the United Methodist Church (10 percent), and the Evangelical Lutheran Church (6 percent of the population), among other Protestant churches, have joined with the Catholic Church's leaders in opposing PAD.[20] These religious leaders—and a majority of their followers—see life as a sacred gift from God, one that must end only by the grace of God. One died a natural death. Death with the assistance of a physician was anathema to the believers.[21]

When the debate moved from the courts into the political arena, the imbalance of forces was starker. The supporters of physician assistance in dying faced an opposition that was financially better off as well as much more politically astute in the strategy and tactics of local and state politics. In the grassroots efforts to legalize PAD, it was the political amateur versus the political professional; it was the financially impoverished versus the establishment organizations' deep pockets. In 2011, the pros have beaten the amateurs in the game of local politics in every state but two.

II. State Politics: Initial Efforts to Legalize PAD through the Use of the Initiative and the Referendum Processes[22]

After *Glucksberg* and *Vacco*, the debates and the arguments over the right to die have continued unabated. However, political strategies and tactics, with financial support from religious groups, especially the Roman Catholic

Church, have replaced the shrillness of the protesters picketing against the right to die. In particular, as validated in *Glucksberg* and *Vacco*, states have the constitutional power (found in the Tenth Amendment to the U.S. Constitution) to prohibit PAD. Yet states also, through the local legislative processes, can *legitimatize* PAD through new legislation.

Political efforts to legitimatize PAD began in 1990 in a few states but accelerated after the two 1997 U.S. Supreme Court decisions that validated existing state laws banning PAD. State grassroots organizations began the movement to change these state laws. Some groups sought to lobby legislators to hold hearings on the subject of PAD; more groups sought to use the initiative and the referendum to change state law.

In the early 1990s, a single lobbying group, the controversial Hemlock Society[23] (since 2003 called Compassion and Choices), with its headquarters in Eugene, Oregon, played a significant role in bringing the issue of PAD before voters. It single-handedly was able to place "Death with Dignity" PAD *initiatives* on the ballots in three states, Washington, California, and Oregon.[24]

That small group based its strategy on the use of either the *initiative* or the *referendum*. The leaders were hopeful that through such efforts, PAD would become law. They based their expectation on the fact that, since *Quinlan*, many national public opinion polls showed that majorities supported some kind of physician assistance in dying.

Because twenty-seven states and the District of Columbia, have provisions for the *initiative petition* and its companion, the *referendum process,* the Hemlock strategy was to place the question of legitimatizing PAD directly on a state ballot, bypassing the state legislature.

However, the Hemlock Society, Compassion in Dying, and other small pro-PAD groups were outgunned by the political and financial strength of their opposition, especially the AMA and the Roman Catholic Church.[25]

Although polls showed public support for PAD "cuts across party, faith, and gender lines,"[26] the power of the well-organized, large, and financially well-off opposition groups defeated these early political efforts. The failure of the pro-PAD political efforts in great part was that in the face of strong opposition portrayed in political advertisements on television and in the media, they could not convert general public opinion support for PAD into the votes necessary to change public policy in the state.

Consequently, as one supporter of PAD said, there emerged the "back alley" of end-of-life care: *unregulated* PAD.[27] Physicians around the nation have reported, beginning in 1990, that they have received requests for assistance in dying from terminally ill patients. "A significant percentage of primary care physicians [18–24 percent] and an even larger percentage of oncologists [46–57 percent] in the United States report having been asked for their assistance in a patient's hastened death; *one quarter of them complied.*"[28]

Concerned about the unintended consequences surrounding "back alley" PAD,[29] supporters have continued to try to convince the public and legislators about the need for such an end-of-life option in the law. The initial effort occurred in 1990, in Washington State.

a. Washington State, 1990

In 1990, the state chapter of the Hemlock Society wrote a series of amendments to Washington State's 1979 Natural Death Act (it was the nation's second living-will law, and by 1994 all fifty states and the District of Columbia had passed similar legislation). Titled the Washington Initiative, in 1991, it became Ballot Initiative 119.

Initiative 119 was a far-reaching proposal that contained—albeit ambiguously—*both* euthanasia and PAD. The ballot question called for a yes-or-no vote on this question: "Shall adult patients who are in a medically terminal condition be permitted to request and receive from a physician aid-in-dying?" Aid-in-dying was defined in the initiative as a

medical service, provided in person by a physician, that will end the life of a conscious and mentally competent qualified patient in a dignified, painless, and humane manner, when requested voluntarily by the patient through a written directive.[30]

In the November 1991 election, Initiative 119 lost by a vote of 54 percent to 46 percent. Opponents of the bill successfully focused on the slippery slope argument: if passed, the law would give "unaccountable physicians more or less the right to kill." The opposition substituted a person's fear of dying in great pain and without much dignity with the fear of being killed by zealous medical professionals like Dr. Kevorkian.

In Washington, as in all the states that faced challenges to their anti-PAD laws, the Roman Catholic Church—with its political strategists who were well organized and well financed—was "the primary political opponent."[31] According to Hillyard and Dombrink, "in an apparently unprecedented action, the Catholic Church organized a major voter registration drive to swell the voting ranks before the general election."

> And in parishes across the state, inserts were stuffed into church bulletins, flyers were sent home with parochial school children, and clergy preached against the initiative. . . . Most significantly, by urging parishioners that it would take millions of dollars to educate the citizens of Washington, parish priests helped fund the opposition campaign by taking up special collections. The Washington State Catholic Conference "No on 119" committee donated $334,000; the Catholic Conference and archdioceses nationwide contributed more than $150,000; the Catholic Health Association donated another $50,000; the Sisters of Providence gave another $20,000. . . . Graham Johnson, executive director of the Public Disclosure Committee, said, "We cannot recall an organization of this kind taking such an active interest in this kind of campaign."[32]

In Washington, 65 percent of the money spent by the opposition, $746,000, came from the Roman Catholic Church. And, observed two scholars, this financial assistance "*understates* the total Catholic contribution in that the figure includes only what can be gleaned from public contribution and expenditure reports. . . . [It does] not reflect political contributions from individual Catholic donors who may be making contributions at the behest of their church or because they are Catholic."[33]

It wasn't until 1999 that pro-PAD supporters recovered from the defeat in 1991. In that year they slowly began to reorganize themselves to once again try to find a way to legalize physician assistance to terminally ill patients in order to hasten their death in a dignified fashion. (In 2009 they finally succeeded in getting the state to legitimatize PAD [see chap. 6].)

b. California, 1992

In November 1992, California voters faced an initiative drafted by the state's Hemlock Society (going by a new name, Californians Against Human Suffering). If passed, the California initiative would have allowed doctors to hasten death of patients by either writing a prescription for barbiturates or by practicing euthanasia, by personally administering a drug such as morphine to patients.

It contained, similar to Washington's ballot initiative, the phrase "physician aid-in-dying." The definition of that term was much clearer than the Washington definition:

> "Aid-in-dying" means a *medical procedure* that will terminate the life of the qualified patient in a painless, humane, dignified manner, *whether administered by the physician* at the patient's choice or direction or *whether the physician provides means to the patient* for self-administration.[34] (my emphasis)

Unlike Washington's failed effort, the California PAD leaders of the initiative were all volunteers, men and women who, without any media funds, worked desperately to get free media coverage for their effort. They also relied on passing out their literature in public places. Arrayed against these individuals were the two powerful organizations, the California affiliate of the AMA and the Roman Catholic Church. The Church organizations collected more than $2.2 million dollars to defeat the proposed bill. *Almost 80 percent of the total spent by the anti-PAD groups came from an assortment of Catholic groups* (in and out of California) to defeat the initiative.[35]

In one action, the National Conference of Catholic Bishops, a month before the election, designated Sunday, October 4, as "Respect for Life Sunday." Across the nation, leaflets were handed out to parishioners decrying PAD and especially the role of the Hemlock Society, "comparing its actions to the pro-abortion campaign of the 1960s," and collecting donations to defeat the proposition.

In November 1992 California voters defeated Proposition 191, the California Death with Dignity Act, by the same 54 to 46 margin that defeated Washington State's initiative one year earlier. Again, the slippery slope and the religious "sanctity of life" arguments proved successful in defeating the initiative. "With sufficient funds," said one analyst after the vote, "it is relatively easy to prevail over a defenseless grassroots campaign."[36]

In 1994 California's professional legal organization, the California Bar Association, formally approved PAD. More than 85 percent of the members concluded that medical doctors should prescribe medication to terminally ill, competent adults in great unremitting pain in order to hasten death.

This initial period of legislative activity to legalize PAD, the years from 1990 to 1992 marked a number of turning points in the efforts to change public policy through local political actions. Most important, after the defeat in California, the effort to include, in proposed PAD bills, euthanasia by lethal injection ended.

Simply put, introducing euthanasia into the political battles shifted the debate away from passive physician assistance (providing a prescription for a lethal amount of a drug) and concentrated on the feared aggressive physician assistance in hastening death. This shift immediately brought into the debates the actions of Dr. Jack Kevorkian, called "Dr. Death" in the media. Kevorkian's actions, at times actively assisting in the deaths of ill, but not terminal, patients, were in the headlines across the nation. The pathologist's actions fatally injured the pro-PAD movement's efforts in Washington and California.

Beginning with the 1992–1994 Oregon battles and thereafter, all pro-PAD challenges focused on the *passive assistance* of physicians in dying: lethal medications but taken by the dying patient. Also, beginning with Oregon's success in 1994, there was an end to the purely volunteer grassroots effort to change public policy.

These small state organizations were simply no match for the much more skilled, organized, and well-financed opponents of change. To combat the actions of the opponents of PAD, the pro-PAD supporters' tactics had to change.

After the *Glucksberg* and *Vacco* opinions were announced, the pro-PAD supporters took the Chief Justice's advice and, once more, entered the political process. However, their efforts made use of the traditional political process—introducing PAD bills in the state legislature in their states to change the law so that terminally ill patients could choose to die with some dignity.

III. Other State Efforts to Legalize PAD, 1997–2010

More than one dozen states, in addition to Washington and Oregon[37] have experienced some modest grassroots, organized political activities since *Glucksberg* and *Vacco* came down in 1997: Arizona,[38] California (again), Connecticut,[39] Hawaii, Maine, Michigan,[40] Vermont, and Wisconsin are some of the states that saw political battles fought over PAD.[41]

However, in every state to date, 2011,[42] all but two of the pro—PAD legislative efforts failed. In most states, either the initiative or referendum failed to gain a majority or the proposed PAD legislation never left the committee for a vote. And, as was the case in the early 1990s in California and Washington State, the financial support and the political acumen of the Roman Catholic Church's professionals, was the major factor in these defeats.

Reviewing the political battles that took place after 1997, one thing is clear: popular support is not enough. There is the absolute necessity of harnessing that support by organizing and raising money to counter the opposition's successful media strategy.

Viewing a number of these political battles raises our awareness of the uneven playing field as well as the lack of political skills and funding necessary for the supporters of PAD to achieve victory in state legislatures.

a. California, 1999–2008

As was the case with Washington State supporters of PAD, it was not until 1999 that the attempt to reintroduce legislation commenced. In that year, assemblywoman Dion Aroner, with the assistance of Compassion in Choices introduced a bill similar to the Oregon Death with Dignity Act (ODWDA). However, she pulled the bill after she saw that there was no support for it in the legislature that year.

Late in 2004, assemblypersons Patty Berg and Lloyd Levine announced that they intended to reintroduce a similar bill in the 2005 legislative session. In February 2005, they submitted the bill AB 654, the California Compassionate Choices Act. The state assembly's Committee on Ageing and Long-Term Care and the assembly Judiciary Committee held public hearings on the legislation in February 2005.

At the same time, the Field Poll of 503 California residents showed that 70 percent favored allowing PAD, while only 22 percent opposed such legislation. The poll also indicated that 63 percent of Protestants, 65 percent of Catholics, 83 percent of other religions, and 83 percent of those without a religious preference supported a PAD bill.[43]

Opposition to the proposed legislation immediately formed. The name of the coalition was Californians Against Assisted Suicide. In March 2005, the House of Delegates of the California Medical Association voted to "maintain current and long-standing policy against the practice of physician-assisted suicide, rather than vote to approve resolutions that would have changed that policy."[44]

However, in April 2005, the Assembly's Judiciary Committee voted 5:4 to approve AB 654. In May, the Assembly's Appropriations Committee voted favorably on the bill, 11:6. And in a parliamentary move, AB 654's provisions were substituted in a different bill, AB 651, already pending before the state senate.

In the meantime, California governor Arnold Schwarzenegger's position on such legislation was still "open-minded," according to one of the governor's senior aides. However, in July 2005, the supporters of the legislation, made a strategic decision to carry the proposed PAD legislation over to the second year of the legislative session, which began in January 2006.

The plan called for discussion of AB 651 in the state senate's Judiciary Committee in March 2006. Prior to that debate a few changes were made in the proposed legislation. A mental health evaluation became a mandatory procedure for a patient who was not in a hospice program. That same month, the initiators of the bill, assemblypersons Berg and Levine, stated in a press conference that they were "close" to acquiring the votes in the senate necessary for passage of the bill.

By March 2006, Governor Schwarzenegger announced that he believed that a state referendum, rather than the legislature, was the appropriate forum. He was, at this time, aware that the two Democrats vying to run for governor against Schwarzenegger supported the impending PAD legislation.[45]

Nevertheless, the legislative process continued in the state senate. In late June 2006, the Judiciary Committee held public hearings on the bill and hundreds of Californians testified for and against the proposed legislation. After the public hearings ended, the Judiciary Committee voted 2:3 against

AB 651. The chairperson of the committee, Democratic senator Joe Dunn, voted against it. Dunn, "generally one of the more progressive members of the legislature, announced his decision to vote against it after testimony was taken from hundreds of individuals who journeyed to Sacramento to speak on the measure."[46] With Dunn's switch, the bill died in committee.

Undeterred, assemblypersons Berg, Levine, and the speaker of the assembly Fabian Nunez introduced AB 374, the California Compassionate Choices Act, in February 2007. The bill was a copy of Oregon's successful Death with Dignity Act, approved in 1997. The Act allows mentally capable, terminally ill adults, with six months or less to live to legally obtain and use prescriptions to end their suffering. Twenty-four other assemblypersons co-authored the new bill. To pass, AB 374 needed forty-one votes in the Democrat-controlled, eighty-member assembly and twenty-one votes in the forty-member Democrat-controlled senate. In March 2007, the assembly's Judiciary Committee passed the bill in a partisan vote of 7:3.[47]

The anti-AB 374 lobbyists rallied to abolish, to kill, this legislation. The California Catholic Conference (CCC) was one of the major organizations that opposed passage of AB 374. It published daily fact sheets for Roman Catholic priests as well as for parishioners who were encouraged to lobby the legislators personally.

For example, in one of their "Backgrounders" on the proposed bill, the CCC reminded readers of the "Church Teaching" of Pope John Paul II, *Evangelium Vitae*, No. 66:

> To concur with the intention of another person to commit suicide and to help in carrying it out through so-called "assisted suicide" means to cooperate in, and at times to be the actual perpetrator of, an injustice which can never be excused, even if it is requested. True "compassion" leads to sharing another's pain; it does not kill the person whose suffering we cannot bear.[48]

The CCC's information sheet also provided "talking points" to the citizen-lobbyists visiting the state capitol to protest against AB 374:

> Legalizing physician-assisted suicide in California will increase the pressure to make the 'choice' for those who are uninsured, ill, disabled, old, or poor.

AB 374 offers a false 'choice,' because if those who are dying are offered comfort and compassion, they will not seek death, but will live their last days well.

Passing AB 374 would encourage suicides by people depressed by recent diagnoses.

It is especially remarkable that the Legislature is considering AB 374 at a time when millions of low-income Californians and their families do not have access even to basic health care.

Legalization of physician-assisted suicide offers a 'phony form of freedom' for those without adequate health insurance in California's competitive health care market.[49]

On March 25, 2007, the *Roman Catholic Blog* ran a Sunday special titled "Another Effort to Legalize A New Kind of Murder: The California 'Compassionate Choices' Act." Articles spoke of the efforts of "an eclectic coalition that includes physicians, nurses, hospice workers, advocates for low-income workers, a Latino civil rights organization, disability rights groups, as well as Catholic institutions (including the CCC) and pro-life advocates" to stop the passage of AB 374.

As Catholics we oppose euthanasia or assisted suicide because we believe that human life is a gift from God, that we are stewards—not owners—of that life, that we are made in God's image and that human life is sacred from conception to natural death. This, of course, informs and underlies our policy perspectives.

The *Blog* then listed talking points—similar to the CCC's talking points—that "we urge you to use when contacting your Assemblymember or Senator. . . . [We] have contact information for those of you who wish to call, FAX or visit their legislators in order to communicate your views. [We] also have facts, articles, essays, and statistics. We urge you to be 'faithful citizens' and participate in this important issue."[50]

The intense lobbying was extremely successful. The co-sponsors of the bill clearly received the message. After looking at the probable vote count, Berg and Levine saw that they did not have enough votes and decided not to send it to the floor of the assembly for a vote.[51]

In February 2008, Berg and Levine introduced another piece of legislation: AB 2747, the California Right to Know End-of-Life Options Act. Unlike earlier PAD proposals they introduced, this proposal did not mention physician assistance in dying *at all*. Instead, it called on:

> health care providers to provide patients with the opportunity to receive information and counseling regarding legal end-of-life options, following a diagnosis that a patient has a terminal illness or has less than one year to live. Those opinions would include hospice care, withholding or withdrawing life-sustaining treatment, voluntarily stopping eating and drinking, and "palliative sedation" (use of sedatives that make the patient unaware and unconscious during the progression of the disease leading to the patient's death).[52]

And, once again, the CCC flooded parishes with Backgrounders that provided Catholic lay persons with "facts" and "talking points" about the newest proposed end-of-life legislation. The Catholic pressure group called Berg's fourth bill "a stealth bill which creates a framework for the implementation of her 'Compassionate Choices Act,' should it ever become legal."

Particularly annoying to the CCC was that, among the medical options that would be mentioned to a terminal patient were voluntary stopping of eating and drinking (VSED) and palliative sedation. Because they were contrary to the Church's teaching about the naturalness of death and the sanctity of life. the organization claimed that:

> AB 2747 dangerously links cost considerations to life and death decisions. Presenting patients who have just received a "terminal diagnosis" with a list of options for end of life care that include VSED and palliative sedation would put incredible pressure on them to "choose to die"—especially those who are uninsured, ill, disabled, old or poor.[53]

Nevertheless, because the legislation did not include the PAD section, the bill passed in the assembly's Judiciary Committee and, in May 2008, passed in the full assembly by a vote of 42:34. In late May 2008 the bill arrived in the state senate and was referred to the Committees on Health and Judiciary.

Hearings took place in June 2008. In late August 2008, the senate voted 21:17 for the bill. The bill returned to the Assembly for its vote on the changes made by the senators. On August 28, the Assembly again voted 42:34 for the amended bill, and AB 2747 arrived at the governor's office on September 18, 2008, for Schwarzenegger's signature. He signed the bill into law on September 30, 2008.[54]

b. Hawaii, 2001–2007

In 1997, pro-PAD politicians saw the ballot initiative pass in Oregon. They included Governor Benjamin J. Cayetano of Hawaii. The Filipino-born Democratic governor wanted Hawaii to "become the health care center of the Pacific,"[55] and viewed the end-of-life issue as an important part of health care. In 1997 Cayetano and his brother were coping with their mother's severe back pain and her addiction to the pain killer Seconal. She would die in great pain in 2005. Cayetano knew firsthand of the suffering that a person in extreme pain lived with constantly.[56] That same year, he convened a blue ribbon committee on Living and Dying with Dignity. One year later, the panel recommended that Hawaii pass legislation similar to that passed in Oregon.

Cayetano immediately announced his support for the legislation. In January 2001, a bill was introduced in the Hawaii senate, SB 709, which allowed death with dignity by the request or advance written directive of a dying patient who had an "incurable medical condition that was expected to cause severe distress or render the patient incapable of rational existence." It went nowhere in that legislative session because there was little time for the bill's advocates to develop a strategy for getting legislative approval.

However, in 2002, in the Hawaii legislative assembly, there was another effort by pro-PAD organizations[57] to pass legislation to allow physician assistance to dying patients. The Hawaii HB 2487 called for the adoption of the Hawaii Death With Dignity Act, which was a close version of the Oregon DWD legislation. A second bill, HB 2491, would send to the voters a proposed amendment to Article One of Hawaii's Constitution that recognized the legislature's authority to authorize PAD legislation. The House Judiciary committee members voted 10:1 in favor of the bills and, on the floor of the House, the vote was 30:20, also in favor of the bill.[58]

The two bills went to the Senate Health Committee for further action. There, the chairperson, David Matsuura, a pro-life Democrat, refused to hold hearings on the two bills. Democratic senators, however, voted 15:10 to pull the Death with Dignity bill from the committee and vote up or down on the senate floor.

At this point, the Roman Catholic Church's professionals lobbied intensely and were able to change the votes of three senators. The groups participating in the anti-PAD lobbying effort included the Hawaii Right to Life, National Right to Life, the Respect Life Office of the Catholic Diocese of Hawaii, and the Hawaii Partnership for Appropriate Compassionate Care, as well as medical professionals and disability rights organizations.

The vote on the floor of the Senate, in May 2002, was 14:11 against passage of the bill.[59] The state came within two votes of becoming the second state to pass PAD legislation. However, the intervention of the Roman Catholic Church's top leader in the state—the night before the vote—proved to be the key factor that turned around the votes of three Catholic Democratic senators.[60]

However, in January 2003 the Hawaii Women's Coalition, drafted another death-with-dignity bill and Senator Colleen Hanabusa planned to introduce the bill in the senate. The pro-life opposition to the legislation, financially supported by the Roman Catholic Church's $40,000 contribution, launched a media campaign in the two weeks before the 2003 legislative session began. That effort led to Hanabusa's PAD bill, SB 391, and an identical bill, HB 862, introduced in the House, but both died in committee.

The proposed legislation was carried over to the 2004 legislative session where, on March 4, 2004, there was an "emotional" four-hour hearing before the House Judiciary Committee. Over 150 persons testified in that time. Disability rights spokespersons from organizations like "Not Dead Yet" tearfully spoke about their fear that PAD would lead to involuntary euthanasia of their members. Catholics and other religious leaders spoke strongly of the sanctity of life. Supporters of the legislation argued that citizens have the constitutional right to determine what happens to them: it is their life and their choice about how to live and die.

The Judiciary Committee voted 10:5 in favor of the bill and sent it to the House of Representatives for a final vote. However, less than one week later, House Democrats sent the bill back to committee.[61] They simply did not have the necessary votes to pass the bill.

Although the PAD bill returned in the Hawaii House of Representatives, and the House Health Committee held another poignant hearing on the proposed legislation, the committee voted against moving the bill out of committee, and it died once more. This happened again in 2006 (HB 2448) and in 2007 (HB 675 and SB 1995) with the same result. The bills never made it out of committee.

The anti-PAD political coalition in Hawaii, primarily the Roman Catholic Church's opposition, has been able since 1999 to kill all efforts to pass PAD legislation in that State. Since the narrow defeat of the PAD legislation in 2002, Hawaii has never even come close to getting legislation voted on.

Although Hawaii's death-with-dignity proposal has received the support of major newspapers,[62] the opposition has remained strong and financially able to muster effective media attacks on such legislation.

c. Maine, 2000

Hawaii's story was repeated in the state of Maine. In 1999 the National Hemlock Society funded a statewide effort petition drive to place a PAD question on the November 2000 ballot. The advocates created a grassroots organization that sponsored Question 1, a proposed bill modeled after the Oregon DWDA. In November 1999, Mainers for Death with Dignity submitted the requisite number of signatures to permit the state's voters to vote on their proposed Maine Death With Dignity Act on the November 2000 ballot. The referendum question: "Should a terminally ill adult who is of sound mind be allowed to ask for and receive a doctor's help to die?"[63]

Under Maine's Constitution, a referendum issue must first go to the Maine legislature for its action. If the legislators refuse to enact the legislation, it is referred to the voters. In February 2000, after hearings on the proposed legislation, the Judiciary Committee voted unanimously to send the proposal to the voters.

The introduction of Maine's referendum question brought out the usual opponents that rallied in California and Hawaii. The lead organization was the Maine Citizens Against the Dangers of Physician-Assisted Suicide. Included in the lead group were stakeholder groups such as the Maine Medical Association, the Maine Osteopathic Association, the Maine Home Care Alliance, Alpha One (representing disabled citizens), the Maine Hospice

Association, and the Roman Catholic Archdiocese of Maine, the director of Maine's Bureau of Health, and the Organization of Maine Nursing Executives. They faced, however, the reality of public opinion polls indicating that more than 70 percent of Maine citizens favored PAD.

The opposition, led by the Maine Citizens Against the Dangers of Physician-Assisted Suicide worked for ten months and spent more than two million dollars in the effort to defeat the referendum. The message they presented was a twofold one: the slippery slope consequence of PAD and the availability of palliative care and hospice. The opponents' slogan in the media barrage against the referendum was "No On One."

The Mainers for Death with Dignity sought the advice of the Hemlock Society and Oregon pro-PAD groups who led the successful effort in that state. The pro-PAD group also spent two million dollars during the lengthy pre-election campaign, almost all of the funds received from the Hemlock Society.

Although the vote was close, 49.5:51.5, the initiative in Maine failed, largely due to the successful efforts of the Roman Catholic Church's political strategists. The Catholic Church accounted for $1,289,000, or 74 percent of the total spent in Maine to defeat the initiative. The Church also provided videos and brochures charging that the proposed legislation was "filled with loopholes" and "fatally flawed." (Twenty-five percent of Maine's voters are Roman Catholics.)

The No On One supporters celebrated their come-from-behind victory. Their strategy addressed the fears of poor, minorities, and the disabled by condemning the proposed shifts of health care funds away from those groups to support PAD.

Videos prepared by the opponents aired on all Maine television stations because the media executives believed that they educated the public. For example, the critics pointed out in these television spots that the proposed PAD bill did not require a terminally ill patient to visit with a mental health professional in order to deal with depression. Furthermore, diabetes patients, because they had an "incurable" disease with an "irreversible condition," could participate in the PAD process even though they were not terminally ill.[64]

The following year, 2001, the anti-PAD No On One groups formed a new group, Maine Citizens for End of Life Care. They took the initiative in the continuing battle by proposing legislation to improve end-of-life care. Two bills arrived in the Maine legislature. One contained innovations to improve end-of-life care. The other bill would develop, implement, and fund Maine's first Medicaid hospice benefit. Together, the two bills contained five new protocols and funding arrangements to address end-of-life issues (excluding PAD):

1. Establish a Medicaid Hospice benefit, funded at 23% above the Medicare rate.
2. Mandate private insurers to cover hospice and increased the threshold of care from 6 to 12 months.
3. Establish a Maine Center for End of Life Care to educate, do research, and to coordinate improved end-of-life care.
4. Provide $50,000 in direct funding to all Maine hospice centers.
5. Develop and implement a study of professional entry-level and continuing education requirements related to end of life care for all licensed health care professionals.[65]

The bills cleared both houses of the legislature and Maine governor Angus King signed them in May 2001. PAD legislation has not been favorably received by the state legislature since 2001.

d. Vermont, 2003–2011

Vermont residents first saw the battles over PAD in February 2003, when two warring bills were introduced in the Vermont General Assembly. One, H 275, was a bill that would criminalize assisted suicide. The other, H 318, introduced by thirty-nine legislators, was a PAD proposal patterned after the Oregon statute.

Supporters of the PAD bill included the state chapter of the Hemlock Society, which was formed in the state in 2002, and Death With Dignity Vermont, formed in 2003. Their mission was identical to those of other state groups supporting PAD legislation:

[We] are advocacy organizations that seek to educate Vermonters about end-of-life options and to influence policy, regulations and practice that affect the terminally ill. [We] work to promote the best possible pain control, palliative and hospice care, and to enable terminally ill patients to choose the timing and manner of dying if even the best of care fails to prevent or alleviate unbearable suffering.[66]

Supporters of the PAD law in Vermont included former governors Madeleine Kunin and Phil Hoff, both Democrats, and Republican Barbara Snelling, the former lieutenant governor. For them, the bottom line in the PAD proposal was *control*: "Whether or not terminal medication is actually taken by an individual, the fact that he/she has control of his/her life is the comfort that is now lacking."[67]

The major opponents were the Roman Catholic Diocese of Vermont and the Vermont Alliance for Ethical Healthcare (VAEH), which was a physician-led organization.[68] The leader of the VAEH was Dr. Robert Orr, a physician affiliated with the Fannie Allen Health Center in northern Vermont. Orr had long been an opponent of the abortion rights movement and became an anti-PAD advocate when that issue arose to prominence in the 1990s.

Holding strong convictions about the sanctity of life he said publicly that "placing the biblical precept of the sanctity of individual human life [must be] at the top of our analytical assessment." Dr. Orr's leadership in opposing Vermont's proposed PAD legislation reflected his deep-seated view of the societal role of a health care provider:

[To] influence their families, colleagues, and patients toward a right relationship with Jesus Christ [and to] advance biblical principles in bioethics and health to the Church and society.[69]

The VAEH mission statement, however, did not reflect Orr's views directly. The statement spelled out the goals of the organization in a more secular manner: "The purpose of the VAEH is to promote the provision of excellent health care at the end of life in an ethical manner and to oppose efforts to legalize physician-assisted suicide or euthanasia in Vermont."

For 2500 years the medical profession has forbidden doctors from giving patients lethal drugs. Society has relied on this prohibition and has trusted physicians to be healers when that is possible, and to provide comfort when healing is no longer possible. In the last 30 years, hospice and palliative care organizations[70] within medicine and in the community have sought and promoted greater control over the physical, psychological, social and spiritual distresses that so often affect individuals approaching death and their families. *The common goal is life with dignity until natural death occurs.*[71] (my emphasis)

Since then, although the names of some of these groups have changed,[72] these organizations led the fight for and against PAD in Vermont.

Consistent with Vermont's "town meeting" ethic, these two factions began a series of public debates across the state in September 2003, a few months before the 2004 legislative session began. These debates were sponsored by the Vermont Medical Association, which took the position, in October 2003, that Vermont must not have legislation allowing doctors to hasten patients' deaths.

Assisted by the small size of the state (little more than 630,000 persons lived in Vermont in the first decade of the twenty-first century), the anti-PAD VAEH strategy for blocking legislation was to have their members contact and *stay in contact* with their representatives in the legislature. Further, they were encouraged to write letters to the editor to the regional newspapers, especially the *Montpelier Times-Argus* and the *Burlington Free Press* news dailies, and always turn out for the rallies and the public hearings held throughout the state.

In newsletters Dr. Robert Orr encouraged his followers to "write a letter to the editor," "contact your representative" in the legislature, and "send donations" to VAEH. And there were regular conferences held by the leaders of the anti-PAD movement in Vermont, especially with the Office of Communications at the Catholic Archdiocese.[73] (In addition, *both sides* hired lobbyists to "educate" the legislators on the issue.)

At the beginning of the 2004 legislative session, the chairs of the two Health and Welfare Committees, Sen. James Leddy and Rep. Thomas Koch, postponed all discussion of the bill until the 2005 legislative session. However, the Vermont lawmakers crafted a proposal that called for a comprehensive end-of-life policy for Vermont; Attorney General William Sorrell was tasked to prepare the study and to make it public by November 15, 2004, just before the 2005 legislative session began.

General Sorrell's January 2005 report recommended improved user-friendly advanced directives, a Bill of Rights for Hospital Patients, required pain management training for health care professionals, and guidelines on the relationship between the law and "aggressive treatment of pain."[74] However, it was silent on PAD legislation.

In February 2005, open hearings on the proposal began. Although eight of the eleven-person House Human Services Committee presented favorable comments about the bill, the chairperson of the committee, Ann Pugh, fearing defeat in the full assembly, did not call for a committee vote. The committee took no further action on the bill, and the legislation session ended in early June 2005. Such political non-action, by this time, was common in most state PAD battles.

In January 2007, a new PAD bill, H 044, entered the legislature. It focused on "patient choice, patient control," said Michael Sirotkin, a paid lobbyist for Death With Dignity.[75] For Dr. Orr, "[our] biggest concern is the expansion of the criteria and the abuses" that lead, inexorably, to euthanasia.[76]

The House Human Services Committee voted in favor of the proposed PAD legislation as did the House Judiciary Committee. On the floor of the House for a vote on the merits, it was defeated, 63 to 82.[77] It failed to gain approval because the opposition intensely lobbied their legislators.

Dr. Orr wrote a congratulatory letter to his organization's members the afternoon of victory day. "*This was a truly amazing vote!*"

> Just three weeks ago we were estimating that it would probably pass the House, but we thought we had enough votes to sustain a veto.[78] Slowly, over the past three weeks, the numbers have gradually shifted, so that by Monday of this week, we thought we might have enough votes to narrowly defeat the bill. The tide of change continued into this afternoon. And the result—a resounding rejection of this unneeded and dangerous bill.[79]

Vermont's political culture was similar to Oregon's, yet the legislators rejected the PAD bill. At bottom, in Vermont as in the other states that rejected PAD, emotions and gut feelings, fueled also by the opposition's fear-inducing messages, swayed the politicians.

Another major reason for the PAD bill's defeat was Republican Governor Jim Douglas's open opposition to it. However, in 2010, the state's citizens elected a new governor, an openly pro-PAD Democrat, Peter Shumlin. In 2010, as state senator, he co-sponsored S 144, "An Act Relating to Patient Choice and Control at the End of Life."

During his successful campaign, he reiterated his belief that a competent terminally ill patient has the right to choose to die with the help of a physician. In a televised interview, he said: "government should not get between a dying patient and her doctor."[80]

On February 17, 2011, HR H 274, Vermont Death with Dignity, entered the state House. In March 2011, S 103, identical to the House bill, entered the Senate. Supporters strongly believed that in 2011, Vermont would become the third state to pass a PAD bill.[81] However, the legislative session ended without any action on the bills. Pro-PAD legislators as well as the governor said that action will occur in 2012. However, the natural disasters the state faced after tropical storm Irene devastated Vermont in August 2011 have substantially changed the legislature's priorities for 2012.

IV. End-of-Life Policy Battles

As we have seen, in every PAD combat zone since 1990, the *primary* attack by opponents was the *slippery slope* argument. This was their chief strategy because, as a frustrated Justice David H. Souter said in his concurring opinion in *Glucksberg*, there simply is *no data* available to counter this frightening observation.

Beyond this dilemma, two fundamental realities emerge after reviewing the various battles over end-of-life policymaking in American states since 1990. First, the anti-PAD argument fueled of the fears of certain groups, especially the Roman Catholic Church, disabled persons and "all vulnerable Americans."[82] Indeed, opponents relied on fear to propel its slippery slope argument.

Organizations representing the disabled, for example, the National Spinal Cord Injury Association and Not Dead Yet instantly bought into the debate the notion that PAD will move to voluntary euthanasia, to involuntary euthanasia, and ultimately to some form of a eugenics policy that will target the disabled and other vulnerable persons.

Supporters of PAD decry the behavior of these spokespersons for the vulnerable. For Derek Humphry, the founder of the Hemlock Society, author of

Final Exit, and the leader of the successful Oregon initiative, these people are fear-mongers and their comments "win the red-herring prize of the year."[83]

The second reality that has emerged in these political battles is this: while the conflicts are fought locally, the political forces battling each other became, after 1997, segments of national alliances and have been active for many decades defending the sanctity of life.

Opponents of PAD regularly comment that decisions concerning the site of the next effort to pass PAD legislation are encouraged by the Death With Dignity National Center in Oregon, in conjunction with Compassion and Choices.

Likewise, supporters of PAD claim that the national leadership of the Roman Catholic Church in America as well as the AMA and a small number of national right-wing pro-life organizations such as Focus on the Family and the Family Research Council are the prime coordinators of the battles fought at the state levels.

In the twenty-first century, strategic forays into legislative politics have become the norm; paid lobbyists on both sides have become the point persons in the effort to pass—or to defeat—PAD legislation. What has emerged is a much greater integration of personnel, material, and funds in these clashes.[84]

As American society moves into the second decade of the new century, it is clear that the adversaries have become more sophisticated and strategic in their attempts to reach their goals. It is equally clear, looking at the debates and the politics surrounding the end-of-life controversy, that the issue remains a very "complex social and medical problem."[85]

One young scholar argued that there are six factors accounting for the success or failure of PAD initiatives in the states:

1. governor influence
2. interest group influence
3. the state's political culture
4. religion
5. age
6. gender.[86]

The politics of PAD initiatives in the states shows the impact of all of these factors. Since 1990 *all* efforts to pass legislation allowing physicians to provide assistance to terminally ill, dying patients have failed—except for the efforts in the states of Oregon and Washington.

These two battleground states exhibited, at different times, local and national actions involving initiatives, referenda, political personalities, legislative actions, judicial interventions, congressional efforts to destroy the Oregon PAD bill, and litigation in the federal courts, including the U.S. Supreme Court. The next chapter details the factors that accounted for these successful efforts to legitimatize PAD.

6

THE PIONEERING PAD STATES

Oregon and Washington

Even by the low standards of political campaigns, this (Oregon) battle over the right to die has not been pretty.
—Art Levine[1]

When the time comes when I no longer can keep busy, I want to control my exit.
—Washington governor Booth Gardner[2]

We put our pets to sleep when they're suffering and that's considered humane. And yet, if we want to do it to our loved ones, it's considered murder.
—Montana District Court Judge Dorothy McCarter[3]

In 1997, the U.S. Supreme Court rejected the constitutional argument that liberty extends to a person's right to die with the help of a physician. Even now, in 2011, there is little chance of pro-PAD advocates achieving success in the federal courts. However, use of state courts to legitimatize PAD is another matter. For example, in 2009 the Montana Supreme Court concluded that the state Constitution did not prohibit PAD.

The second path, legalization of PAD in state legislatures failed in more than a dozen states. This chapter focuses on the factors accounting for the two successful efforts to legitimatize PAD: Oregon's successful *efforts,* in 1994 and in 1997, to pass the nation's first end-of-life PAD legislation, the Oregon Death with Dignity Act (ODWDA) and the success in Washington State of an Oregon mirror-image Death with Dignity Act (WDWDA) in 2008.

Hardball politics surrounded passage of both PAD bills, but the opposition to PAD did not prevail. Why success in these two states? When will the efforts to rescind the bills end? If other states reopen the debate, can pro-PAD advocates succeed?

I. Passage of Measure 16: The Oregon Death with Dignity Act, November 8, 1994

In Oregon in the late 1980s, Derek Humphry, the founder of the Hemlock Society, began to work for legislation that would legalize PAD. It was not until 1994 that one of his efforts, Ballot Measure 16, made it onto the Oregon ballot.

The *Oregon Compassionate Choices* group, formed to support efforts to legitimatize PAD, began its work in 1993. These two organizations were the major actors in the successful effort to draft and then pass—by a 51 percent to 49 percent vote in November 1994—the Oregon Death with Dignity Act ballot initiative.

For the first time since PAD initiatives in 1990 entered the halls of American state legislatures, the Roman Catholic Church's financial support for the status quo in Oregon, $968,800 (59 percent of the total spent by the opposition), did not succeed in killing a PAD proposal.

One major difference between Oregon's successful Measure 16 and the defeated Washington Initiative 119 and California's Proposition 161, was that the Oregon proposal *explicitly prohibited euthanasia*: it was a reasonable "prescribing only" measure that barred any kind of lethal injection or other *direct action* on a dying patient by the physician. This difference was critical to the bill's success because it silenced the euthanasia threat to certain groups fostered by the opposition by exclusively endorsing the death-by-prescription model.

Furthermore, Oregon was the perfect state to get PAD legislation passed. The state has a history of political independence. Its history shows its uniqueness "both in terms of the long history of citizens using the initiative power as a tool of legal and social change and in terms of citizens' defiance toward both organized religion and outside political pressure."

Oregonians tend to be more open-minded to a wide variety of opinions. That climate is very important. Referring to the status of Oregon as a relatively secular place, [one historian] added, "Oregon has never been a strong church state." The fact that there has been no dominant religion has allowed a moral flexibility that a lot of states don't have.[4]

The state's political culture is one factor accounting for the success of the PAD advocates. Oregonians see themselves as "social progressives." They detest "religious pressure." Roman Catholics in Oregon, the largest religious group in the state, are only about 12 percent of the population. "Overall, Oregon, with a voting population of about 2 million voters, is 62 percent 'unchurched,' making it more secular than most states."[5]

The 1994 ODWDA[6] is worthwhile to examine because all other state pro-PAD advocates copied its essential provisions. There are four substantive sections in the bill. Section 1 contains the definitions of the bill's words and phrases. Included in the list are terms such as "counseling," "health care provider," "informed consent," and "terminal disease" ("which means an incurable and irreversible disease that has been medically confirmed and will, within reasonable medical judgment, produce death within six (6) months").

Section 2 contains the important guidelines for the "written request for medication to end one's life in a humane and dignified manner." Section 3, "Safeguards," addresses the responsibilities of the attending physician, the consulting physician, counseling referral, informed decision, family notification, written and oral requests, waiting periods, medical documentation requirements, residency requirements, reporting requirements, effect on construction of wills, insurance and annuity policies, and the construction of the ODWDA.

The key segment in Section 3 is the following paragraph:

> Nothing in the Act shall be construed to authorize a physician or any other person to end a patient's life by lethal injection, mercy killing, or active euthanasia. Actions taken in accordance with the Act shall not, for any purpose, constitute suicide, assisted suicide, mercy killing, or homicide, under the law.

Section 4, "Immunities and Liabilities," described the immunities for participants in the PAD process as well as the liabilities for any "person who without authorization of the patient willfully alters or forges a request for medication . . . or who coerces or exerts undue influence on a patient, or conceals or destroys a rescission of that request with the intent or effect of causing a patient's death shall be guilty of a Class A felony." This section addressed the fears of the opposition groups about the ease with which PAD can move to euthanasia.

In Oregon, *every* adult qualified resident has the option for a "humane and dignified death" if the patient presents a written request (witnessed by at least two individuals, one of whom cannot be related to the patient), can self-administer a lethal prescription of drugs, and can rescind the request at any time.

The patient must be qualified, that is, competent, have a medically confirmed (by the attending physician) terminal disease, and must make—voluntarily—an informed decision after an examination by another consulting physician. Under the law, the requesting patient must be determined not to suffer from any medical condition that would impair making an informed judgment. Once the patient's request is authorized, that person must wait fifteen days and then make a second, oral, request before the prescription may be written.

The opponents continued to speak about the act as the first of many actions on the slippery slope to euthanasia. Indeed, Derek Humphry helped them by insisting, during the months prior to the November 1994 ballot vote, that the ODWDA was the first step and that "when people become comfortable with this form of assisted dying, we may be able to go to the second step, which is euthanasia."[7]

So incensed and fearful of Humphry's militant polemics that the PAD leaders "asked him not to attend the deliberations between campaign strategists and wary community leaders."[8] Humphry reluctantly accepted their request. The payoff: the measure was passed by the voters, 51:49, in November 1994.

However, Oregon was years away from implementing the act. After Measure 16 narrowly passed, the opposition, within weeks, sought to block the ODWDA's implementation by challenging its constitutionality in federal court.

Simultaneously with the legal challenge, the Oregon Health Division (OHD) leadership took an important step. A working group began to write the administrative definitions of terms and the creation of rules and regulations needed for the reporting of the act's implementation. They needed the document ready for immediate use by the health care community once the litigation ended.

Strategically, the members of the group came from a variety of government offices (the OHD, the Oregon Senior and Disabled Services Division, and the Medical Examiner's Office) and private health care organizations, including the Oregon Hospice Association, the Oregon Nurses Association, the Oregon Association of Hospitals, the Oregon Health Care Association, and the Oregon Board of Pharmacy.[9]

In addition to this action, in January 1995, the Center for Ethics in Health Care at the Oregon Health Sciences University brought together another important group: the Task Force to Improve the Care of Terminally Ill Oregonians. This group brought together physicians, hospital administrators, members of the Oregon bar, the Oregon Board of Medical Examiners, the Oregon Board of Pharmacy, the OHD, the Oregon Hospice Association, the Oregon Nurses Association, the Oregon Psychiatric and Psychological Associations, and the Oregon State Pharmacists Association.

All these professional health care providers are involved in the care of dying patients, including those professionals who would provide lethal medical prescriptions to patients who requested such assistance.

These multifaceted public/private groups were effective because of the very breadth of their makeup. Although a number of the organizations opposed PAD (especially medical and hospice professionals), once it became law they were included in the critical discussions and decisions surrounding implementation of the law.

While court challenges to ODWDA and the legislative attempts to nullify the act were taking place, the two task forces continued to work on the creation of the administrative rules and procedures. In March 1998, the final product of the group was published: *The Oregon Death With Dignity Act: A Guidebook for Health Care Providers.* When the ODWDA's legal and political delaying battles ended, it became the administrative and monitoring framework for its implementation.

II. The Legal Challenge to the ODWDA, 1995–1997

Within one month of the act's passage, opposition groups, led by the Roman Catholic Church, waged a campaign in the federal courts to delay the implementation of the Oregon statute. In November 1994, fifteen days before the ODWDA was to take effect, a number of terminally ill adults and their physicians, along with representatives from a number of residential care facilities, brought a class action lawsuit in federal district court.

They sought to nullify the law because it violated the U.S. Constitution's Equal Protection Clause. Their claim: the law discriminated against disabled and depressed terminally ill Oregonians because the ODWDA did not protect them from coerced PAD the way it protected non-disabled, non-terminal Oregonians.

The latter cohort was, in the act, categorically unable to receive prescriptions for lethal medications. On the other hand, their petition maintained, depressed, gravely ill, or disabled patients could be coerced into dying under the ODWDA by those (their families, or their HMOs, or their physicians) who believed these vulnerable people would be better off dead.

The U.S. District Court Judge Michael R. Hogan heard the case, *Lee v State of Oregon*. Republican President George H. W. Bush appointed the judge, a Georgetown University Law Center graduate, to the federal bench, in 1991. He was the senior judge of the U.S. District Court when he heard the arguments in 1995, and his decision came down on August 3, 1995.

a. The U.S. District Court Decision, Lee v State of Oregon, 1995

The judge agreed that the plaintiffs had "standing to sue"[10] in federal court and that serious questions were presented by them about the ODWDA. Hogan concluded that, on balance, the fears and hardships faced by the disabled plaintiffs were greater than those faced by terminally ill patients who wished to have the assistance of a physician in dying. "The public interest in protecting vulnerable citizens from the irreparable harm of death," he concluded, was "greater" than the hardship to terminally ill patients who wanted PAD. According to Hogan, the ODWDA violated the Equal Protection Clause of the Fourteenth Amendment.

He immediately issued a temporary injunction blocking implementation of the ODWDA. Later, on August 3, 1995, Judge Hogan made the injunction permanent. The ODWDA violated the Constitution because "it provided insufficient safeguards to prevent an incompetent (i.e., depressed) terminally ill adult from committing suicide, thereby irrationally depriving terminally ill adults of safeguards against suicide provided to adults who are not terminally ill."[11] The county DA immediately appealed Hogan's ruling to the CA9.

b. *The CA9 Decision, February 27, 1997*

On March 6, 1997, a three-judge panel of the CA9 dismissed the U.S. District Court's injunction against the ODWDA. Judge Melvin Brunetti (appointed to the federal appellate court by Ronald Reagan in 1985), for the unanimous panel, wrote the majority opinion. It was a technical decision. "Because the federal courts do not have jurisdiction to entertain Plaintiffs' claims, we vacate and remand with instructions to dismiss Plaintiffs' complaint."

Brunetti wrote that "[judicial power] is not an unconditional authority to determine the constitutionality of legislative or executive acts." Standing is an important factor in determining whether the judicial power is applicable. "Standing addresses the question of *whether* the litigant is entitled to have the court decide the merits of the dispute."[12]

They were not entitled to federal judicial review because their claims were merely speculative and judicial power does not extend to litigation where "speculation and conjecture" abound. They also rejected the "class action" stipulation in the plaintiffs' brief: "If the litigant fails to establish standing, he may not seek relief on behalf of himself or any other member of the class."[13] The suit was vacated and remanded back to the district court. In October 1997 because the U.S. Supreme Court denied *certiorari* in the case , the CA9 ruling in *Lee v Oregon* stood.[14]

The opposition, however, was prepared for this defeat in the federal appellate courts. They had already placed in motion another effort to overturn the ODWDA: Ballot Measure 51. Only two days after the Supreme Court denied *cert* in *Lee*, in a "mail-in ballot procedure that [began October 16 and] concludes on November 4, Oregon voters will be asked to decide whether to repeal or retain the ODWDA that passed the first time by a margin of 51:49."[15]

III. The ODWDA Battles, 1997: Repeal Measure 51 Fails, 40:60

The opposition was able to persuade the Oregon legislature to place Measure 51 on the November 1997 election ballot. (Under state law, where the legislators proposed the initiative, there were no petitions for voters to sign to get the measure on the ballot.)

The legislative argument in support of Measure 51 reflected the concerns and fears of the opponents. The Joint Legislative Committee presented the argument for voting for Measure 51. It became part of the ballot process because the committee alleged that new information was uncovered since the 1994 vote "which casts doubt on the effectiveness of ballot Measure 16." The instructions on the ballot seemed clear. If the voters voted "YES" for Measure 51, the ODWDA died. In order to keep 1994s Measure 16, the voter must vote no on this measure.

The campaign saw the presentation, in ads, on television, on radio, of the same arguments for and against PAD. The opposition, however, led by the Roman Catholic Church, supporting Measure 51, went over the edge in their criticisms of PAD. (The Catholic Church's financial support for passage of Measure 51 was $1,677,700, or 73.6 percent of total spent to try to repeal the ODWDA.)

The right-to-die supporters "had little money for a big state-wide campaign" against their deep-pockets opponents. "Only a $250,000 donation from George Soros, a well-known philanthropist, and another $100,000 from Donald Pels, a New York businessman, allowed [the supporters] to mount their own television advertisements during the campaign's final three weeks."[16]

This new battle over the right to die was not pretty.[17] For example, the opponents of the ODWDA, "Yes on 51," ran a television "dramatization of a healthy-looking young man, 'Billy,' entering a waiting room and awaiting his doom."

Three weeks ago, Billy was told that he had less than six months to live. And in fifteen minutes, a doctor is going to give him a lethal prescription—*just to make sure*," the narrator intones. "But what Billy doesn't know is that he won't die right away. He'll choke on his own vomit, in painful convulsions, and linger for days." Even sadder, "Billy isn't terminal. His diagnosis was wrong.[18]

In another ad, run on many television stations, "the repeal proponents offered a new horror scenario":

The assisted-suicide law would spur teens to kill themselves in droves. A glossy four-page mailing, headlined "A deadly Message," argues that the law could make suicide the No. 1 killer of kids in Oregon by sending the message that suicide is socially acceptable, or even condoned: "Under Oregon's flawed suicide law, people will be killing themselves next door, or down the street—or maybe even in your own home."[19]

The supporters of the ODWDA were also playing to the fears of the voters. They tried to scare them about the role of the Roman Catholic Church:

"The Catholic Church is spending a fortune to repeal Measure 16," one TV ad warns. "They want to impose their views on the rest of us." A series of biting radio ads even sports the tag line "Paid for by Don't Let Them Shove Their Religion Down Your Throat Committee."[20]

And, in what one pollster called "one of the cleverest things done in Oregon politics in a long time," the Oregon Right to Die group "came up with a trick that would make Boss Tweed proud." [21] The pro-PAD group knew that polling studies showed that voters, when faced with a repeal measure where a yes vote is a rejection of the original law (1994's Measure 16), "and vice versa, as many as 25 percent accidentally vote against their own preferences."

They strategically designed their logo to mirror the repeal forces' logo. The opponents of the ODWDA had a "Yes on 51, Fatally Flawed!" bumper sticker with the number 16 in a red circle with a red bar across the number. The supporters of the original Measure 16 created a nearly identical "No on 51, Fatally Flawed" bumper sticker with the number 51 in a red circle with a red bar across the number.[22]

In the end, with the probability that some confused voters cast a wrong vote, Measure 51 was defeated: 40 percent for Measure 51 (445,830) *but* 60 percent against the Measure (666,275). "Advocates of PAD won an overwhelming victory in Oregon on Tuesday, and that victory may well represent the first step down a road that all of America could travel," wrote David J. Garrow in an op-ed piece in the *New York Times*.[23]

After this defeat, the "Groundhog Day" scenario continued. This time, the anti-PAD groups tried to have the 1970 federal Controlled Substances Act (CSA)[24] interpreted in a way that proscribed doctors from prescribing drugs to their dying patients. (That congressional legislation "controls the distribution of drugs by regulating those who are registered to prescribe and dispense them, and by assigning drugs to categories of risk or medical usefulness.")[25]

The opposition reasoned, correctly, that the types of drugs prescribed by physicians were likely to be those regulated under the law.[26] Their task was to convince national legislators and administrators of federal agencies that prescribing a lethal dose of a controlled drug in accordance with the ODWDA was not a "legitimate medical purpose."

IV. ODWDA Challenged in Washington, DC, by "Sanctity of Life" Republican Legislators, 1997–2001[27]

Immediately after the November 1997 defeat of Oregon's Measure 51, in Washington, DC, conservative U.S. Senate Republicans, spurred to action by the anti-PAD lobbyists, led by U.S. Senators Orrin Hatch (R-Utah) and John Ashcroft (R-Mo.) and Rep. Henry Hyde (R-Ill.), began congressional action to kill the act. In July 1997 they requested the U.S. Drug Enforcement Administration (DEA), in the Department of Justice, to apply the CSA to prohibit Oregon physicians from prescribing lethal medicine to their dying patients.

In their letter they sought the DEA's administrator's view "as to whether delivering, distributing, prescribing, filling a prescription, or administering a controlled substance with the deliberate attempt of assisting in a suicide would violate the CSA, notwithstanding the enactment of a state law such as Oregon's Measure 16 which rescinds state penalties against such prescriptions for patients with a life expectancy of less than six months."[28]

The DEA administrator answered the two congressional leaders on November 5, 1997. "Since receiving your inquiry, my staff has carefully reviewed a number of cases, briefs, law review articles and state laws relating to physician-assisted suicide [as well as] conducted a thorough review of prior administrative cases in which physicians have dispensed controlled substances for other than a 'legitimate medical purpose'":

> Based on that review, we are persuaded that delivering, dispensing, or pre-scribing a controlled substance with the intent of assisting a suicide would not be under any current definition a "legitimate medical purpose."[29]

In December 1997, the administrator ruled that Oregon physicians par-ticipating in the ODWDA were in violation of the CSA if they prescribed a controlled substance to a patient who wanted to hasten death.[30]

However, the Clinton administration's U.S. Attorney General Janet Reno agreed to review the entire matter, including the DEA interpretation of the CSA. In a June 5, 1998, letter to Representative Hyde and Senator Hatch, the Attorney General reversed the DEA position on the CSA (and the ODWDA).

The CSA's "relevant provisions," she noted in her letter, "provide criminal penalties for physicians who dispense controlled substances beyond 'the course of professional practice,' and provide for revocation of the DEA registration for physicians who have either engaged in such criminal conduct or in other 'conduct which may threaten the public health and safety.'"

The U.S. Department of Justice, she said, would not revoke registrations nor prosecute physicians who had assisted their patient's deaths in compliance with the protocols of the ODWDA. "There is no evidence," she wrote, "that Congress, in the CSA, intended to displace the states as the primary regulators of the medical profession, or to override a state's determination as to what constitutes 'legitimate medical practice.' [The CSA] does not authorize the DEA to prosecute, or to revoke DEA registration of, a physician who has assisted in a suicide in compliance with the Oregon law."[31]

a. The Lethal Drug Abuse and Prevention Act of 1998

Immediately following Attorney General Reno's ruling, Lori Hughes of the National Right to Life Committee condemned it:

> We think for this government, for this Justice Department to pull the safety net out from under the most vulnerable people in our society, people who are terminally ill, people with severe disabilities, we think it's unconscionable, and right now we call on Congress to act promptly to prevent any more tragic deaths in Oregon.[32]

Republicans opposed to the ODWDA then took to the bill-writing strategy. Another Groundhog Day appeared. Representative Hyde, the chairman of the House Judiciary Committee, introduced the Lethal Drug Abuse and Prevention Act of 1998.[33] It was an effort to overturn the ODWDA by adding language to the CSA directly aimed at the Oregon legislation.

The Senate version was supported by Senators Orrin Hatch, John Ashcroft (R-Mo.) and other conservative "sanctity of life" Republicans. They presented it as an amendment to the 1998 Omnibus Spending Bill. President Bill Clinton warned the Republicans that he would not sign the bill with that amendment attached, and Oregon's U.S. Senator Ron Wyden threatened to filibuster the legislation.

Ironically, President Clinton had no trouble one year earlier when he signed into law the Assisted Suicide Funding Restriction Act of 1997. That legislation banned the use of federal funds to pay for assisted suicide, euthanasia, or mercy killing.[34]

Dozens of health care organizations opposed the amendment and the American College of Physicians-American Society of Internal Medicine (ACP-ASIM) led the heavy lobbying in Congress against the bill. The president of that medical association, Harold C. Sox, wrote: "ideology inspired this bill and its chief sponsors didn't seem to understand our concerns about the harm it might cause. But we could also see its defeat as an uplifting civics lesson: Many legislators changed their minds when they realized that the bill could put their constituents at risk." Even the AMA opposed what was now labeled the Hyde/Nickles bill. The AMA believed "that expanding the DEA's authority in this matter would be an unacceptable federal intrusion over matters of state law regarding the practice of medicine."[35]

By the end of the legislative session, Senator Don Nickles (R-Okla.) withdrew the bill he had introduced. But he did not give up the plan, as was seen in his and other opponents' actions to overturn the ODWDA the following year.

b. The Pain Relief Promotion Act of 1999

In the 1999 version of Bill Murray's iconic film, the House of Representatives passed the Pain Relief Promotion Act, HR 2260, introduced by Congressman Hyde, If passed by both houses and signed by the president, it would have "amended the CSA to promote pain management and palliative care without permitting PAD and euthanasia."[36]

Senator Nickles introduced the identical bill in the Senate. Unlike the 1998 bill they introduced, this bill's first objective was the improvement of palliative care and pain relief. The second objective was the prohibition of PAD state legislation through amendments to the CSA.

In short, if passed, the law barred physicians from prescribing medications to their dying patients to assist them in hastening death but did not bar physicians from treating pain and suffering with the same medications even if it unintentionally killed the patient. "While it would not technically 'overturn' the Oregon law, the Hyde-Nickles bill would severely hamper the ability of patients to invoke it, since physicians would be unable to legally prescribe intentionally lethal doses of federally controlled substances."[37]

This time around, the AMA strongly supported Hyde/Nickles 2 and lobbied for its passage in the Senate. The bill was consistent with the organization's goal "to palliate pain without supporting assisted suicide."[38]

The National Conference of Catholic Bishops (NCCB), once again, supported Hyde/Nickles. Richard Doerflinger, the associate director for policy development at the NCCB, said: "Last year's bill gave priority to stating a new policy against assisted suicide, then explained that this policy does not forbid the legitimate use of controlled substances to control pain. [This year] the emphasis is reversed."[39]

Intense lobbying against the bill, led by the American Bar Association, the American Cancer Society, the American Nursing Association, and the American Pain Care Foundation appeared,[40] For example, the Nursing Association's opposed the bill primarily on the uncontrolled use of DEA discretion "in deciding whether a clinician prescribed with the intent to relieve pain or to aid suicide."[41] Newspaper editorials were published that were heavily against the proposed bill. Some politicians spoke out against the proposed bill. Ron Paul, a Republican Congressman (who ran in the 2008 and 2012 Republican primaries for the presidential nomination), said:

> I am strongly pro-life. . . . I disagree with the Oregon law. But I believe the approach here is a legitimate *slippery slope*. This bill should be opposed, I think it will backfire. If we can come here in the Congress and decide that the Oregon law is bad, what says we cannot go to Texas and get rid of the Texas law that protects life and prohibits euthanasia? That is the main problem with this bill.[42] (my emphasis)

President Bill Clinton, who was generally against PAD,[43] voiced reservations about the Pain Relief Promotion Act in press conferences. Because of the intense public lobbying against the bill, as well as the threat of a presidential veto, the bill failed to reach the floor of the U.S. Senate for an up-or-down vote before the 106th Congress adjourned.

V. The ODWDA Challenged by the George
W. Bush Administration, 2001–2005

Round and round went the sanctity-of-life national legislators in their efforts to eviscerate the ODWDA. This time, the action occurred in the White House. In December 2000, the Republican presidential candidate George W. Bush won a dramatically controversial presidential election, decided by a divided U.S. Supreme Court, over his Democratic opponent, Al Gore.[44] The president-elect presented a sanctity-of-life position in the run-up to the 2000 election, After his election, Bush selected the very conservative former U.S. Senator from Missouri, John Ashcroft, to be his administration's U.S. Attorney General.

On November 6, 2001, Ashcroft issued a directive on the subject of PAD. It was contained in a memorandum[45] to Asa Hutchinson, a former member of Congress and the new administrator of the DEA.

a. The "Ashcroft directive," November 6, 2001

Ashcroft's directive instructed DEA agents to investigate and prosecute physicians who prescribed federally controlled drugs with the sole intent to assist terminally ill patients to die. A White House Office of Legal Counsel opinion, "Whether PAD Serves a 'Legitimate Medical Purpose' Under the DEA's Regulations Implementing the CSA,"[46] provided the legal justifications for Ashcroft's action.[47]

Overturning his predecessor, Janet Reno, Ashcroft concluded that PAD was not a "legitimate medical purpose." Prescribing, dispensing, or administering federally controlled substances to assist a dying patient to hasten death "violates the CSA."

"This conclusion applies," asserted Ashcroft, "regardless of whether state law authorizes or permits such conduct by practitioners or others and regardless of the condition of the person whose suicide is assisted." He differentiated pain management, which "has long been recognized as a legitimate medical purpose justifying physicians' dispensing of controlled substances," from PAD. "There are important medical, ethical, and legal distinctions between intentionally causing a patient's death and providing sufficient dosages of pain medication necessary to eliminate or alleviate pain."

The reinstated DEA determination, he noted, "makes no changes in the current standards and practices of the DEA in any State other than Oregon." Ashcroft ordered the DEA to immediately enforce his determination.

For some in the medical community, the Ashcroft directive was paradoxical. While the AMA opposed PAD, the action of the federal government was "was motivated by ideology" and was "an unprecedented attempt by the federal government to usurp the authority of the states to regulate medical practice."[48]

The Ashcroft directive came down on November 6, 2001. The next day, the state of Oregon, along with a physician, a pharmacist, and some terminally ill state residents challenged his action in federal district court. Their brief urged the court to enjoin Ashcroft and other defendants from giving the Ashcroft directive any legal effect. They argued that the directive "exceeded Ashcroft's authority under the CSA. The law was intended to combat the illegal traffic in narcotics, not to regulate the practice of medicine, which is an area traditionally left to state control."[49]

Just two days later, U.S. District Judge Robert E. Jones, appointed by President Clinton in 2000, issued a temporary restraining order (TRO) against the federal government taking *any* action until after arguments were heard in his court in March and April 2002.

On April 17, 2002, Judge Jones ruled that the U.S. DOJ lacked the authority to overturn the ODWDA.[50] Frankly acknowledging the political and ideological dimensions of the litigation, Jones wrote that

> Attorney General John Ashcroft fired the first shot in the battle between the state of Oregon and the federal government over which government has the ultimate authority to decide what constitutes the legitimate practice of medicine, at least when Schedule II substances [morphine, phenobarbital, and secobarbital] regulated under the CSA are involved.[51]

For the judge, Ashcroft's interpretation of the CSA was a purely ideological one, one not based on the basic purpose of the act: to deter drug abuse and the illegal trafficking in drugs.

On September 23, 2002, Ashcroft appealed Judge Jones's ruling to the CA9. In the federal government's brief, Ashcroft argued that the case "presents challenges to an interpretive rule construing the CSA and its implementing regulations to prohibit the prescription of federally controlled substances for suicide."[52]

For Ashcroft the question was "whether the Attorney General has permissibly construed the CSA and its implementing regulations to prohibit the prescription of controlled substances for suicide." In the brief, Ashcroft noted that in enacting the CSA, "Congress found that the 'improper use of controlled substances' has a 'substantial and detrimental effect on the health and general welfare of the American people.'" The DEA, as the administrator and monitor of the use—and misuse—of controlled substances in America, could bar the use of the controlled substances when used to commit suicide. The ODWDA, in the eyes of the U.S. Attorney General, promoted a medical practice that serves no "legitimate medical purpose."

b. Ashcroft v Oregon; Gonzales v Oregon, 2005

On May 26, 2003, a few weeks after oral arguments took place in the federal appeals court, a three-judge panel of the CA9 ruled, 2:1, in favor of the state of Oregon and its law, the ODWDA. The ruling held that the Ashcroft directive was "unlawful and unenforceable."

Judge Richard C. Tallman, appointed in 1990 to the federal appeals court by Republican President George H. W. Bush, wrote the opinion. "We hold that the Ashcroft directive is unlawful and unenforceable because it violates the plain language of the CSA, contravenes Congress' express legislative intent and oversteps the bounds of the Attorney General's statutory authority."[53]

Although amendments to the CSA were added in 1984 that gave the U.S. Attorney General "new discretion" and "broader authority" to monitor and to act to prevent violations of the act—including the revocation of physician *registration*—it did not give the federal government the authority to trample state actions in the area of health care.[54]

The CA9 panel invalidated Ashcroft's Interpretive Rule. Reflecting the district court opinion, the Tallman opinion reasoned that, by making a medical procedure authorized under Oregon law a federal offense, the DEA altered the balance between the states and the federal government without the requisite clear statement that the CSA authorized the action. Further, the Ashcroft order could not be "squared with the plain language" of the CSA, "which targets only conventional drug abuse and excludes the Attorney General from medical policy decisions."[55] Ashcroft appealed the panel's ruling and requested an *en banc* CA9 rehearing of Oregon v Ashcroft. On August 11, 2004, the CA9 rejected his request.

c. The U.S. Supreme Court Decision, Gonzales v Oregon, 2005

On November 9, 2004, Ashcroft filed a petition for *certiorari* with the U.S. Supreme Court. Later that same day, Ashcroft announced his retirement from the office of Attorney General. In February 2005, the U.S. Supreme Court granted *certiorari* in the case of *Gonzales v Oregon*. (Alberto Gonzales became Attorney General in 2005, replacing Ashcroft.)

Oral arguments in the case took place on October 5, 2005. The question before the Justices was technically an administrative law query: "Whether the Attorney General has permissibly construed the CSA, and its implementing regulations to prohibit the distribution of federally controlled substances for the purpose of facilitating an individual's suicide, regardless of a state law purporting to authorize such distribution."

On January 17, 2006, the U.S. Supreme Court handed down its decision in *Gonzales v Oregon*. By a vote of 6:3, employing "a more critical eye," the Justices ruled that the U.S. Attorney General overstepped his authority in seeking to punish Oregon physicians who prescribed drugs to help terminally ill patients end their lives.

Associate Justice Anthony Kennedy wrote the majority opinion. He was joined by Associate Justices Sandra Day O'Connor, John P. Stevens, David H. Souter, Ruth Bader Ginsburg, and Stephen Breyer. Kennedy wrote that the federal government could regulate the writing of prescriptions through the CSA but only in relation to prohibiting doctors from engaging in illegal drug activity:

> Beyond this, the statute manifests no intent to regulate the practice of medicine generally. . . . The authority claimed by the Attorney General is both beyond his expertise and incongruous with the statutory purposes and design. . . . [When Congress passed the CSA], it did not have this far-reaching intent to alter the federal-state balance.

For the majority, Kennedy wrote that "the central issue in this case [is] *who* decides whether a particular activity is in 'the course of professional practice' or done for a 'legitimate medical purpose.'"[56] For the majority, the answer was very clear: "*not the Attorney General.*"[57] He "is *not authorized* to make a rule declaring illegitimate a medical standard of care and treatment of patients that is specifically authorized under state law."[58] The Attorney General's argument was not "sustainable."[59]

There were three dissenters: the Court's two conservative "originalists," Justices Clarence Thomas and Antonin Scalia, who wrote dissents in *Gonzales,* and the recently appointed Chief Justice John Roberts. (He joined Scalia's dissent, as did Justice Thomas.)

Justice Scalia's dissenting opinion was a lengthy, scathing critique of the majority's reasoning in what was, for Scalia, a fairly straightforward administrative law case. "The Court concludes," he began, "that the Attorney General lacked authority to declare assisted suicide illicit under the CSA because the CSA is concerned only with 'illicit drug dealing and trafficking.'"

He maintained that Ashcroft's interpretation of the CSA language "legitimate medical purpose" was "clearly valid, given the *substantial deference* we must accord it under *Auer v Robbins.*"[60]

Scalia's dissent concluded: "Even if that interpretation of the Regulation were incorrect, the Attorney General's independent interpretation of the statutory phrase 'public' and his implicit interpretation of the statutory phrase 'public health and safety' are entitled to deference under *Chevron U.S.A., Inc. v Natural Resources Defense Council,* 467 U.S. 837 (1984),[61] and they are valid under *Chevron.*"[62] Scalia "respectfully" dissented.

Justice Thomas's dissent was a much shorter critique. He pointed out that "a mere seven months ago," the Court, in *Gonzales v Raich,* reached a different conclusion regarding the scope of the CSA. That case involved a California law authorizing the possession of marijuana for medical usage that was invalidated under the CSA because it was a "comprehensive regulatory scheme specifically designed to regulate which controlled substances can be utilized for medicinal purposes, and in what manner."

The Supreme Court deferred to the judgment of the federal agency's understanding of the CSA. He noted that the earlier opinion "described the CSA as 'creating a comprehensive framework for regulating the production, distribution, and possession of controlled substances,' including those substances that 'have a useful and legitimate medical purpose,' in order to 'foster the beneficial use of those medications' and to 'prevent their misuse.'"[63]

But in *Gonzales v Oregon*: "The majority beats a hasty retreat from these conclusions."[64] The six-person majority simply rejected Ashcroft's "at least reasonable determination—and therefore entitled to deference—that administering controlled substances to facilitate a patient's death is not a 'legitimate medical purpose.'"

Concluding his dissent, Thomas said that "the Court's reliance upon the constitutional principles it rejected in *Raich* . . . is perplexing to say the least. Accordingly, I respectfully dissent."[65]

Interestingly, Justice Thomas *dissented* in *Reich* because he believed the CSA infringed states rights. But, a half year later, he dissented in *Gonzales*, a decision that *supported* a state's right to determine the parameters for a physician's behavior when caring for a patient. Justice Thomas's judicial behavior was somewhat "perplexing."

With the decision, the Supreme Court "removed an obstacle to state efforts to authorize physician-assisted suicide."[66] Many editorials praised the decision. The *New York Times*, for example, editorialized that the Court "smacked former Attorney General John Ashcroft and the Bush administration. . . . The decision was notable because it rejected Mr. Ashcroft's attempt to impose his religiously conservative ideology on a state whose voters had decided differently."[67]

Anti-PAD organizations were, obviously, angry after *Gonzales* came down. The *National Right to Life* organization voiced this rage in a press release:

> [*Gonzales*] is shocking. It sets a dangerous precedent for all vulnerable Americans, especially those with disabilities[68] and life or health-threatening illnesses. Drugs should be used to cure and relieve pain, never to kill.[69]

After the Supreme Court opinion came down, U.S. Senator Sam Brownback (R-Kan..) introduced the Assisted Suicide Prevention Act of 2006, which would prohibit physicians from prescribing federally controlled substances for the purpose of PAD. After Oregon Senator Ron Wyden (D-Ore..) announced that he would block the bill, Brownback withdrew the proposal.

Scott McClellan, President Bush's press secretary, said after the Court handed down the opinion: "We are disappointed at the decision. The President remains fully committed to building a culture of life, a culture of life that is built on valuing life at all stages."[70]

However, in November 2006, the midterm election saw the Republican Party lose control of both Houses of Congress to the Democrats. Any new congressional effort to amend the CSA or pass legislation to limit PAD ended when that happened. And, after Barack Obama was elected president in the November 2008 election, there was little probability that his Attorney General would act to restrict Oregon physicians from implementing the ODWDA.

VI. The ODWDA Data, 1998–2010

The first OHD report came out on February 17, 1999. It gave the data on all prescriptions filled under the ODWDA during 1998. For the first few years, the OHD's annual report was also published in the *NEJM* so that "the ODWDA should be subject to the scrutiny of peer review in the medical literature."[71]

Information was collected by OHD staff on the twenty-three patients who received a prescription for lethal medications and who died in 1998. (There were no prescriptions for lethal medications written in 1997.) Either the terminally ill patients died from taking the lethal dosage (fifteen) or from their underlying illness (six). Two patients were alive as of January 1, 1999.

The median age of the entire group was sixty-nine years. All of the patients were white and eleven were male. Twenty had been residents of the state for longer than six months. Four of the twenty-one received a psychological or psychiatric consultation, and all of those were determined to be "capable" of making informed choices under the ODWDA.

A fast-acting barbiturate, nine grams of secobarbital, was prescribed for nineteen of the twenty-one patients; one patient received another fast-acting medication, nine grams of phenobarbital, and one received one gram of secobarbital and one gram of morphine, an oral narcotic. Most of the cohort also received nonlethal medications (to prevent nausea and vomiting) taken with the lethal barbiturates.

The underlying illnesses that led to the terminal condition faced by the twenty-one patients were not surprising to medical professionals. Eighteen terminally ill patients (86%) had varieties of cancer, with twelve of them having lung, ovarian, or breast cancer. One patient was dying of Acquired Immune Deficiency Syndrome (AIDS). One was dying of congestive heart failure, and one other person was dying of Chronic Obstructive Pulmonary Disease (COPD).[72]

Finally, the *primary* reason for Oregonians choosing PAD is the importance of autonomy and personal control. Those who chose PAD were concerned about those two factors.[73] For physicians, autonomy was the "prominent characteristic" of their patients who chose PAD. These patients, the doctors wrote, had a "long-standing philosophy about controlling the manner in which they died."[74]

a. The Ten-Year Statistical Summary, March 2008

In 2008, the OHD provided the public with a statistical snapshot of the ODWDA'S first decade, 1998–2007. In that period, 341 terminally ill patients died after taking the lethal medications under the terms of the ODWDA.

Over the decade, the average age at time of ingestion was sixty-nine years, ranging from twenty-five to ninety-six years of age. Almost all of the patients (97.4%) were white and well educated: a majority of the cohort had some college education (23%), a baccalaureate degree (21%), or postbaccalaureate (20%) education. In addition, 82% of the group's underlying illness was terminal cancer, while another group of patients (7.6%) had amyotrophic lateral sclerosis (Lou Gehrig's disease) at the time of death.

Most of the patients (86%) were enrolled in hospice care; only three of the 341 patients (0.9%) had no health private or government insurance. The three major end-of-life concerns of the patients were: losing autonomy (89%), being less able to engage in activities making life enjoyable (87%), and loss of dignity (82%).

Complaints of unremitting pain fluctuated during the decade. In some years, 2003 and 2005, for example, nearly 50 percent of the patients who took the lethal doses said that their pain necessitated the request for a prescription. In other years, this reason accounted for 24–33 percent of the requests. Most of the patients (93.5%) died at home, while 5 percent died in a long-term care facility.

In 1998, there were twenty-four prescriptions written for terminally ill patients who chose death under the ODWDA. In the tenth year, there were eighty-five prescriptions written for dying patients. In 2000, twenty-two physicians wrote the lethal prescriptions. In 2007, forty-five doctors participated in the ODWDA.

Nearly all of the prescriptions (98.5%) the physicians wrote over the decade were for the fast-acting barbiturates, secobarbital and pentobarbital. In addition, over the decade, there were *no* referrals of physicians by the OHD to the Oregon Medical Board. If there were any physicians covertly prescribing lethal doses of medication for their patients, there was absolutely no evidence discovered by the OHD staff.[75]

It is clear, from an assessment of the report about the characteristics of the 341 patients who chose to die with the assistance of a physician, that they were generally well educated. They were also independent and decisive persons who valued their personal freedom and dignity. They believed it was their right, as autonomous and competent adults, to control the way they died.

b. The Continuing Attacks by the Opposition

The critics consistently condemned the reports, their findings, and the ODWDA, because they did not contain any information about the number of abuses committed by health care providers and how many PAD's went unreported.

However, the OHD's first report *did* address that dilemma. The agency "must" report *any* noncompliance with the ODWDA to the Oregon Board of Medical Examiners for further investigation. "Because of this obligation, we cannot detect or collect data on issues of noncompliance with any accuracy.[76] A 1995 anonymous survey of Oregon physicians found that 7 percent of surveyed physicians had provided prescriptions for lethal medications to patients prior to legalization. We do not know if covert PAS continued to be practiced in Oregon in 1998."[77]

Other critics believe, without any explanation, that the reports "signaled another step closer to the slippery slope."[78] They claimed that unremitting pain was not the major criterion for prescribing lethal medications for terminally ill patients; in fact, it was not even a criterion listed in the ODWDA. They saw that only about one-quarter of the 341 terminally ill patients gave "unremitting pain" as the reason for seeking PAD. Further angering the critics, nearly 100 percent of the patients listed *loss of autonomy* as a prime reason for seeking lethal medications. One angry critic wrote: "The Act does not require that the patient be experiencing any suffering whatever. It requires simply that the patient have a terminal illness which will produce death within six months."[79]

For them, the fact that loss of autonomy was an almost universal and seemingly self-evident reason for patients requesting PAD was a very clear sign of the beginning of the slide to euthanasia. For the spokespersons for disabled persons, the loss of autonomy explanation of the PAD cohort frightened them terribly. "Allowing assisted suicide based upon fear of needing help going to the toilet, bathing and performing other daily life activities will involve far more disabled and elderly people than terminally ill ones," wrote Wesley J. Smith. "Rather than alleviating concerns," he wrote, "the [OHD] study reveals that assisted suicide is bad medicine and even worse public policy."[80]

The Roman Catholic Church's hierarchy continued its criticism of the ODWDA after the annual reports appeared. Archbishop John Vlazny of Portland, Oregon, that "state's leading Catholic spokesman, said in a statement that the findings were a cause for 'sadness and shame' across the state. 'In allowing PAS to continue, the state of Oregon dismisses the value of human life,' the archbishop said."[81]

Others, however, were somewhat relieved after reviewing the data. "It's not the harbinger of destruction that people thought it was going to be," observed Reverend John F. Tuohey, a Roman Catholic priest. "It's being implemented thoughtfully and carefully." However, Tuohey continued, "it's still bad public policy. We'd rather people didn't choose it, but it challenges us to provide better care so that they won't choose it."[82]

Still other critics of the ODWDA, after reading the reports changed their views and joined the supporters of the legislation. Ann Jackson, the executive director of the Oregon Hospice Association (OHA), told reporters that although the OHA initially opposed passage of the ODWDA, Oregon hospices were, after 1999, working directly with Compassion and Choices of Oregon to assist terminally ill Oregonians.[83] In the dozen years since implementation of the ODWDA, "even some of the law's staunchest opponents say [that] the worst fears have never been realized."[84]

The ODWDA continues to provide a small number of strong-willed, terminally ill patients—primarily "well-off, well-educated white men"[85]—with the ability to end life on their own terms. "Give me liberty at my Death,"[86] sums up the characteristic attitude of the nearly five hundred terminally ill patients who chose to self-medicate themselves and die under their own terms and under their own control.

VII. Washington State's Passage of the Washington Death with Dignity Act (WDWDA), November 2008

In January 2006, proposed legislation entered the Washington State Senate; SB 6843 became the first attempt since the failed 1991 initiative to legitimatize physician assistance in dying. It was legislation, stated Sen. Pat Thibaudeau, patterned after the Oregon DWDA. Referred to the Senate Health and Long-Term Care Committee, the bill died in committee without a hearing.

One month later, the very popular former governor Booth Gardner, a Parkinson's disease sufferer since 1992, dropped a bombshell on Washingtonians when he announced that he would initiate a campaign for another ballot initiative. "When the day comes," he said at the time he announced his final campaign, "when I no longer can keep busy, and I'm a burden to my wife and kids, I want to be able to control my exit."[87]

In January 2008, seventeen years after the defeat of Initiative 119, and nearly two years after his surprise announcement, Gardner filed with the secretary of state the "Washington State Death with Dignity Initiative" (Initiative 1000), which mirrored the Oregon legislation.

In preparation for the political battles, by the summer of 2008, the bill's advocates raised almost $1.5 million. The opposition, the Coalition Against Assisted Suicide, included groups such as Not Dead Yet; the Roman Catholic Church; "people of faith;" hospice workers, and nurses.

In addition, while the Washington State Medical Association (WMA) strongly opposed the 1991 initiative and campaigned to defeat it, W. Hugh Maloney, the association's president in 2008 stated that the organization's nine thousand members were now "passionately split" and "very much in disarray" over the issue.

Ultimately, however, that organization, along with the Washington Hospice and Palliative Care Association, and other health groups, formally opposed Initiative 1000.[88] In the end, said Tom Curry, executive director of the WMA, "the fundamental rationale is that the Hippocratic Oath trumps I-1000. 'Do No Harm' is not compatible with the initiative."[89]

The major news dailies strongly endorsed the proposal. The *Seattle Times* wrote, on January 10, 2008, that "[Governor] Gardner's law will not affect many people. But those it does affect, and their families, will be thankful for its passage." For the organized Roman Catholic opposition, the issue was clear. The proposed WDWDA had nothing to do with personal choice at the end of life, said a spokesperson for the Church, Sister Sharon Park. The proposal "is a referendum on how the state views the dying." Assisted suicide, for Sister Park and the Church, was contrary to God's will and the sanctity of life. In France that week, Pope Benedict XVI once again told the faithful to accept death "at the hour chosen by God."[90] And in Seattle, the Roman Catholic Archdiocese called upon all local parishes to pass out envelopes to collect money from parishioners to oppose I-1000.[91]

The major criticism of the new initiative was, again, the slippery slope argument, especially the way it would adversely affect disabled persons. Their brochure argued that the initiative "shows no real safeguards to protect the vulnerable."

> Instead, Initiative 1000 pressures those without adequate insurance or financial means to think that they have no choice other than assisted suicide. It provides an incentive to health plans to cut costs by encouraging assisted suicide. And it places many Washingtonians at risk.[92]

Oregon's former governor Barbara Roberts (1991–95) countered this attack with an op-ed column in the *Seattle Post-Intelligencer* on September 15, 2008. Titled "I-1000 Is Not a slippery Slope," she argued that Oregon's decade of implementing the ODWDA clearly showed the absence of the slippery slope. "This proposed law is *not* a slippery slope that threatens those with disabilities of any kind."[93]

Washington's governor Chris Gregoire stated that while she was against such legislation, she would not actively campaign against it. In May 2008, a bipartisan group of Washington state legislators, comprising eleven Republicans and four Democrats, issued a joint statement that pleaded with voters not to sign the initiative petition.[94]

By July 2008, the supporters of I-1000 gathered over 300,000 signatures, more than the minimum of 224,800 signatures necessary to get the initiative on the ballot in November 2008. The initiative would permit terminally ill, competent adult Washington residents to request and self-administer lethal medication prescribed by a doctor.

The proposed bill virtually copied the ODWDA. It mandated that the patient "be free of depression and able to muster sound judgment;" request the prescription verbally and in writing after a fifteen-day waiting period; have two witnesses at his/her request (one of them not being an heir, related, or employed by the health care facility caring for the patient).[95]

When the initiative ballot became a reality, the Archdiocese of Seattle and the Catholic Health Association immediately gave $50,000 each to defeat it. However, by September 2008, the pro-1000 groups had raised $1.9 million to the anti-1000 forces' $509,000.[96] As one opponent of the initiative said of this unique development: "it (*Yes-I-1000*) is a Goliath to the opponents' David."[97]

There were two reasons for this unusual fact: (1) the personal involvement—on the side of the PAD bill—of the extremely popular former governor Booth Gardner, and (2) the positive impact of the Oregon death-with-dignity legislation. The data generated by a decade of the bill's implementation seemed to discount the opposition's criticism of PAD, especially the slippery slope argument.

The state of affairs in Washington State in the fall of 2008 was completely different from the situation in the months before the November 2001 initiative vote. (In the earlier political event, the pro-PAD forces, primarily grassroots volunteers without the necessary funds and political skills to combat their opponents, were defeated in that vote, 54:46.)

The campaign for and against Initiative 1000 was intense—and vitriolic. Like the Oregon experience, the advertisements on both sides were no-holds-barred ones, and about $3 million was spent for them: supporters spent $2 million while the opponents spent $1 million. Popular actors such as Martin Sheen appeared on television to urge a no vote on the initiative.[98]

Mistakes, made intentionally, abounded. Opponents told viewers and listeners that I-1000 "tells doctors it's OK to give a lethal drug overdose to a *seriously ill* patient." Not true. The WDWDA, if passed, would enable only *terminally ill* patients to receive the prescription for lethal drugs.

They also claimed that the proposed legislation "would allow doctors to give a lethal dose prescription even to a patient suffering from depression," and that "in Oregon, one in four getting the drugs suffer from depression." These statements were also not true.

Supporters of the initiative focused many of their ads on their major opponent: the Roman Catholic Church and its diocese in the state and across the nation. For example, a pro-1000 radio ad, aired days before the election, condemned a "small group" of "out-of-state[99] religious leaders [read Roman

Catholic]" for trying to "buy the election," impose their zealous religious beliefs on all Washingtonians, and defeat the proposed WDWDA.

Public opinion polls of Washington voters clearly indicated that the people polled strongly supported a person's right to seek physician assistance to hasten death. In the past, however, except for Oregon, such polling data was the kiss of death. There was a growing feeling on the part of supporters of the bill, however, that *this time* Washington State voters would support the initiative.

The opponents, moreover, were angry because of what they claimed I-1000 indirectly said to sick, disabled, and terminally ill people. Chris Carlson, the chair of the Coalition Against Assisted Suicide, was diagnosed with terminal carcinoid cancer. He maintained that the bill encouraged "people to prematurely give up hope, and I think that's wrong. I don't think the state should be encouraging people to give up hope."[100]

On the first Tuesday of November 2008, Washingtonians made their decision. There was a huge voter turnout: More than 84 percent of eligible citizens voted. By a vote of 518,506 to 399,775, 58 percent to 42 percent, Initiative 1000 passed.

For hospices in the state, "the crucial first step is to craft guidelines on how to handle a person who comes to them and says, 'You know, I'm really worried about how I'm going to die and I'm considering using the new law,'" said the executive director and CEO of the Washington Hospice Association. "Hospices need to be very clear about what to do when that conversation happens."[101]

The effective start-up date for the WDWDA was March 5, 2009. However, neither side in the Washington State end-of-life campaign put down their weapons. The opposition began planning for further attacks on the newly passed PAD legislation. "Clearly we know it's a bad law. We spoke out against I-1000," said Eileen Geller, the campaign coordinator for the Coalition Against Assisted Suicide, "because we think it's dangerous." She said that the law "puts low-income and vulnerable people at risk."[102] Once again, the opposition claimed that the WDWDA was "a first step toward, not only physician-assisted suicide, but ultimately *euthanasia*. And people shouldn't be blind to that."[103]

The pro-PAD supporters, too, planned their *next* moves. The leaders of the Death with Dignity National Center, met in November and December 2008 "to discuss which states to target next." Changing public policy in this controversial area, remained a difficult issue, "especially where law, medicine, and religion intersect."[104]

In March 2011, the Washington State Department of Health issued its initial report based on data on those who used the WDWDA in 2010. It included the information received regarding the patients who used the WDWDA in the ten months it was available in 2009.

Not surprisingly, the 2010 data indicates that the eighty-seven terminally ill Washingtonians who sought PAD shared the characteristics of Oregon patients. (The numbers of patients in each state who took the PAD option differed only because the populations of the two states were not similar: Washington's population in 2010 was more than 6.7 million; Oregon's was 3.8 million.)

Of the eighty-seven who filled prescriptions for the lethal dose, seventy-two participants died; fifty-one died from that action, another fifteen died without using the barbiturates, and for the remaining six patients who died, the ingestion status was unknown. For a director of Compassion and Choices of Washington, this data was significant. It illustrated the benefit of peace of mind, comfort, and control the law provides terminally ill patients.[105]

The Washington cohort's age ranged from fifty-two to ninety-nine years. Nearly 80 percent had cancer, while another 10 percent had neuro-degenerative diseases (including Lou Gehrig's Disease), and less than 12 percent had heart disease or other illnesses. Nearly 95 percent were Caucasian, 51 percent were married, and 62 percent had at least some college education. Ninety percent were concerned about the loss of autonomy, 64 percent said that loss of dignity led them to PAD, while 87 percent feared the loss of ability to participate in activities that made life enjoyable. Of the fifty-one who actually ingested the lethal medicine and died, 90 percent died at home and 84 percent were in hospice care when they took the medicine.[106]

VIII. The Montana Supreme Court's *Baxter* Decision, 2009, Allowing Doctor Assistance in Dying

Unlike Oregon and Washington, where the political referendum process led to passage of PAD Acts, the Montana path to PAD went through the state court system. A constitutional challenge by petitioners led to Montana being the first state in the nation to declare that PAD was a protected, fundamental right under the *state's constitution*.[107]

In October 2007, Robert Baxter, a seventy-five-year-old retired truck driver from Billings, Montana, petitioned the county district court in Helena to prohibit the state's homicide statutes from extending to a physician who aided a terminally ill patient to die. His complaint claimed that criminalizing assisted suicide violated the state constitution.

Specifically, the petition maintained that Article II, *Declaration of Rights*, Sections 3, 4, and 10, prohibited the state from arresting and trying doctors who assisted a dying patient to die with dignity. The state constitution underwent a substantive revision in 1972 "at the height of a privacy-rights movement that swept through this part of the West in the aftermath of the 1960s."[108] As a result, Article II was changed to provide Montana residents with enhanced rights. The three sections used by petitioners in the briefs and oral arguments were:

> Section 3, Inalienable Rights, added to a person's inalienable rights the following: "the right to a clean and healthful environment and the rights of pursuing life's basic necessities, enjoying and defending their lives and liberties, . . . and seeking their safety, health, and happiness in all lawful ways."
>
> Section 4, Individual Dignity, began with a sentence that became the lynchpin of the decision: "The dignity of the human being is inviolable." The section went on to protect persons from denial of the equal protection of the laws.
>
> Section 10 added the "Right of Privacy" guarantee to the constitution. "The right of individual privacy is essential to the well-being of a free society and shall not be infringed without the showing of a compelling state interest."

The petition asked the district court to establish a constitutional right to receive and provide assistance in dying to competent, terminally ill patients. Joining him in the petition as plaintiffs were four Montana board-certified physicians who treated terminally ill patients.

Baxter had suffered from lymphocytic leukemia, a terminal form of cancer, for many years. He received, during that time, multiple rounds of chemotherapy, which became a less and less effective treatment. His daughter said that her father "yearned for death,"[109] and wanted the option of assisted death when he could longer tolerate the pain.

Montana's attorney general argued that the state constitution conferred no right to assist in ending another person's life and that the state's homicide laws prohibit such action. Both the plaintiffs and the state asked the judge, Dorothy McCarter, to issue a summary judgment.

In December 2008, Judge McCarter issued a summary judgment in favor of the plaintiffs. She concluded that the constitutional rights of individual privacy (Article II, Section 10) and human dignity (Article II, Section 4), provide a dying patient with the liberty to choose to die with the assistance of a physician.

> This Court concludes that the right to personal autonomy included in the state constitutional right to privacy, and the right to determine "the most fundamental question of life" inherent in the state right to dignity, mandate that a competent, terminally ill patient has the right to choose to end his or her life.

She continued: "It is difficult to imagine a compelling state interest in preserving the life of an individual who is suffering pain and the indignity of the disease; . . . and for whom palliative care is inadequate to satisfy his personal desire to die with dignity."

Judge McCarter concluded by asserting that physicians are protected from liability under the homicide statutes. For a terminally ill patient to die with dignity requires "the assistance of his medical professional."[110]

The state's Department of Justice appealed the decision to the Montana Supreme Court and oral arguments took place on September 2, 2009. The judges received nearly two dozen *amicus* briefs arguing the merits of PAD.[111]

On December 31, 2009, the seven-person Supreme Court affirmed Judge McCarter's summary judgment, 5-2, but not on constitutional grounds.[112] While the state constitution did not guarantee a right to die with the assistance of a physician, there was "nothing in Montana Supreme Court precedent or Montana statutes indicating that physician aid in dying is against public policy."[113]

In its statutory analysis of the issue, the majority focused on the 1985 Montana Rights of the Terminally Ill Act. That law evidenced "legislative respect for a patient's autonomous right to decide if and how he will receive medical treatment at the end of his life." It explicitly shields physicians from liability for acting in accordance with a patient's end of life wishes, even if the physician must actively pull the plug on a patient's ventilator or withhold treatment that will keep him alive. There is no statutory indication that lesser end of life physician involvement, in which the patient himself commits the final act, is against public policy.

The decision, however, was silent on state regulation and oversight of PAD. That meant that the Montana legislators and the state's medical professionals were responsible for creating the regulations and reporting requirements. As Montana's legislature meets every other year, the *Baxter* decision remains in limbo. There was no way of knowing whether any dying patient received assistance in dying from her physician.

During 2010, advocates for both sides lobbied legislators for and against the Montana judicial decision. In February 2011, a number of bills came to the senate Judiciary Committee. One proposal, S167, mirroring Oregon's bill. The other bill, S116, if it became law, overturned the judicial decision by prohibiting PAD. After the hearings ended, the committee voted 7-5 to table both bills. The senate itself fully supported the committee's decision.[114]

Montana is at this time in a very ambivalent position. There does not yet exist a public law enumerating the standards and practices for a doctor to follow when assisting a terminally ill patient who wishes to die with dignity. Essentially, due to legislative inaction, the medical community is in limbo regarding PAD. To date, there has been no recorded event where a doctor in the state has provided a dying patient with a prescription for medication to end the person's life. In the absence of an authorized protocol for implementing PAD, such as the Oregon PAD guidelines, prudence seems to deter medical practitioners from taking any action regarding PAD.

IX. Now That There Are Three PAD States

After January 2010, the number of American states allowing PAD tripled. The first two successes were voter referenda that led to PAD statutes and regulations. The Montana story's limited success is due to a state Supreme Court decision that leaves regulatory and monitoring issues unresolved. So what comes next?

Will opponents in Oregon and Washington rally to overturn the ODWDA and the WDWDA? Will the Montana legislators overturn the Montana Supreme Court's decision or will they adopt the Oregon DWD statute?

Will other states pass PAD legislation? Will other state courts hand down decisions that follow the actions of the Montana courts? Or will a handful of terminally-ill patients, instead, become America's transplants by moving to these states to die with dignity?

Just what role *should* government play in this seminal moment in a person's life? Does a terminally ill person who is suffering have the *power* to determine his or her own final course of life?

The next chapter focuses on these central questions regarding the future of PAD in America.

7

> We think the citizens of all fifty states deserve death
> with dignity.
>
> —Barbara Coombs Lee[1]

In 2011, a terminally ill person who wants to choose death over life has a limited number of options available:

(1) withholding or withdrawing life-sustaining treatment;
(2) refusing life-support treatment;
(3) having the physician treating the pain increase the dosage of pain killing morphine, with the probability of the patient dying as a consequence;
(4) having a medical professional assist in the death of the terminally ill patient by providing a prescription for a fatal dose of medicine.

The first three options are not problematical. It is the last one, premised on an expansive interpretation of liberty, that has generally eluded its advocates in all but two states. (In 2011, Montana's situation is still indeterminate until further action is taken by legislators or by the state's public health professionals.)

The questions repeatedly raised in this book are important reflections of some basic American values and principles of governing. What has been the role of the judiciary in American politics? Can states pass "sanctity of life" laws that prohibit PAD? Are there viable alternatives to PAD for terminally ill patients who refuse to live without any realizable quality of life? At bottom, the fundamental question remains: Does a dying patient have the liberty—the power—to determine how she or he will die?

To answer these questions, one has to examine certain "givens" that have been present in all the battles over the right to die.

I. Summing Up the "Givens" in the PAD Story

There are a small number of so-called givens in the recounting of the efforts to introduce physician-assisted death into law in America. These ever-present realities pop up whenever the controversial issue is discussed. First, there are alternatives—the double effect reality, palliative care and hospice—to passage of a PAD bill. Opponents believe that PAD is an unnecessary and dangerous practice that will adversely affect the poor, the disabled, the elderly, and minorities in America. In the end, they contend that PAD will lead to voluntary and then involuntary euthanasia for members of these groups.

The second reality is the enormous power of the federal courts, especially the U.S. Supreme Court, in the PAD legal battles. Repeatedly, the profound differences between Democratic and Republican appointees appear in the death-with-dignity cases. These profound differences are over how a person's liberty interest found in the Constitution is interpreted by them and what the proper role of the judiciary is in our democratic republic.

Historically, because of the results of presidential elections, there has been an occasional pendulum shift in the Supreme Court majority's view of constitutional rights. For the past three decades, Supreme Court majorities refused to "invent" a constitutional right unknown in the nation's traditions and history. Until a different Court majority sits on the high bench, there is no possibility of overturning *Glucksberg* and *Quill*. Until that time, the Court rejects the idea that the Constitution is, as one conservative judge wrote, "a floating Constitutional convention."

The third certainty is the power of the "sanctity of life" PAD opponents that include the Roman Catholic Church and ideological political and religious groups. Constantly, and tirelessly, these groups battle all attempts—in the courts and in the halls of state legislatures and the Congress—to legalize PAD. For nearly four decades, they have campaigned against abortion rights and the right to die with the assistance of a physician. For them, the two issues are the core evils of the hated "culture of death."

The fourth given is the reality that in all the PAD battles, the politics is local. The factors that determine the outcome of these political struggles exist in the local and state community debating and voting on PAD legislation. These factors—cultural, demographic, religious, political—strongly affect the outcome of proposed PAD legislation.

a. There Are Alternatives to PAD

In the first decade of the twenty-first century, Americans facing a final, terminal illness and who wish to die in order to end their suffering can do so without a PAD law. They can get the death they want, "whether by surreptitiously gathering deadly doses of medication for possible later use, by seeking out doctors who they know will honor their requests to help end their lives or . . . by declining treatment to hasten death."[2]

Ironically, these practices of hastening death are so widespread that many doctors disapprove of efforts to legalize PAD. They argue that these public wars regarding PAD "bring unwanted attention to practices that are already common, if quiet."[3]

The two major substitutes to still-criminalized PAD are the "double effect" medical practice and enhanced palliative care in a hospice environment.[4] Interestingly, opponents of PAD consider that these substitutes "constitute adequate and appropriate options for hastening death, obviating the need for legalization of PAD."[5]

An additional benefit arising from the treatment of terminally ill patients in these ways has been the emergent acceptance, reflected in the dramatic growth of palliative care in the past two decades, of the use of sufficient pain medications to relieve pain in a great many dying patients. Until very recently, and still somewhat of a problem in the first decade of the twenty-first century, many medical practitioners were very wary about administering morphine and other narcotics to their dying patients. Incredulously, they argued that such medical action would turn their dying patients into morphine addicts.

Occasionally the double-effect protocol transmogrifies into a variant. It constitutes what Supreme Court Justice Ginsberg called "winks and nods" during the *Vacco* oral argument. It is a given that "sometimes a 'covert dialogue' takes place between doctor and patient that result in an unspoken agreement."

> We will give whatever it takes to relieve the suffering, and whether or not it crosses the line into intending to hasten death is something we don't talk about as a rule. In practice, she said, that means a doctor will tell a nurse, "Start the morphine and go ahead and be generous, if you know what I mean."[6]

Responding to these arguments, PAD advocates point to the reality that a few strong-willed dying patients receiving palliative care in a hospice still want to die by self-medicating themselves. They want to determine the manner of their final exit. And, they tenaciously assert, they have the constitutional liberty to do so. However, they possess that liberty if the U.S. Supreme Court says so.

b. The Power of the U.S. Supreme Court to Interpret the Constitution

Certainly, since the two conservative majority 1997 U.S. Supreme Court decisions, *Glucksberg* and *Quill*, rejected PAD as a substantive liberty interest found in the Constitution, that path to physician-assisted death is closed. It was not a surprising decision. Rather, "it was a necessary conclusion [for the conservative majority] since an overwhelming number of states forbid the practice."[7] For that reason, it would have been highly unlikely that the present Supreme Court majority would find PAD "implicit in the concept of ordered liberty." As the Court said in the PAD cases, the concept of physician-assisted death is totally absent in American history.

Very few times in our legal history has a Supreme Court majority decided cases that did not reflect the views of the majority of Americans. One notable period where this occurred came during the tenure of Chief Justice Earl Warren, 1953–69. During a great part of that era, Warren, joined by a majority of liberal Justices sitting on the bench with him,[8] labored to read the Constitution as expanding the rights and liberties of Americans. Unlike the two contemporary "originalist" Justices Scalia and Thomas, and, decades earlier, the dissents of Justice Hugo Black, Warren and his brethren maintained that the Constitution's protections must be broadly interpreted to respond to the reality of modern social life. In a number of substantive constitutional areas— criminal justice, free speech and press, the rights of Communists and other deviant groups, search and seizure, the right to counsel, the right of privacy, religious freedom, and civil rights—the Warren Court majority broadened the scope of the Constitution's words to protect millions of Americans.[9] In doing so, as has been shown, it expanded the idea of individual liberty.

For most of American history, however, U.S. Supreme Court majorities possessed a very different understanding of the role of the Court. These majorities were prudent defenders of American values. They were unwilling to assert their power in response to society's problems regarding, for example, slavery, racial segregation, the rights of labor, and the dilemmas fostered by an uncontrolled industrialization. Indeed, these majorities insisted that they did not have such "legislative" power to rewrite through interpretation the fundamental law.

Further making it difficult for PAD advocates to seek changes in the meaning of fundamental concepts such as liberty, the reality is that lower federal courts do not possess the power to define the Constitution's meaning. Their task is to make decisions in cases before them in light of the precedents established by the U.S. Supreme Court. As seen in *Glucksberg* and *Quill*, if a lower federal appeals court deviates from this established principle of law, the U.S. Supreme Court can and generally *will* overturn the judgment.

Consequently, the lower federal courts will *not* view sympathetically the legal, constitutional, and moral arguments that an adult, competent, terminally ill person has a liberty interest or a privacy right to choose to die with the passive assistance of a physician. Even if there is sympathy present in the lower court's judgment in such a case, the judges know what fate awaits such a decision when the contemporary Supreme Court grants *certiorari*.

The federal courts now and in the projected future will be of *no help* to supporters of PAD. The truth is that at all appellate levels of the federal judiciary, a majority of the judges are sitting because conservative, "sanctity of life" presidents from Ronald Reagan (1981–89) through George W. H. Bush (1989–93) and George W. Bush (2001–09) appointed them.

The appointment process reality is quite simple: presidents appoint *their kind* of man or woman. Democratic presidents will appoint Democratic judges; Republican presidents will appoint Republicans. Presidential goals are the same whether one is a Democrat or a Republican: stack the judiciary with men and women who share the views and values of the appointing president. The hope of the president is that when a policy of their administration is challenged because of its alleged unconstitutionality, the federal judges will validate the legislation.

Five of the nine sitting Justices of the U.S. Supreme Court are categorically opposed to the idea that PAD is a fundamental liberty interest that individuals possess in the United States. Until there is medical calamity or death that leads one of the members of this conservative quintet to leave the Court— accompanied by the presence in the White House *and* in the U.S. Senate of moderate Democrats—there will be no modification of this constitutional viewpoint.

Additionally, presently more than 62 percent of the federal appellate judges are essentially social conservatives appointed by the trio of Republican chief executives. There are 101 conservative Republican jurists sitting on the thirteen federal appeals courts (out of 164 sitting judges). Further, this group of conservative judges *is in the majority* in nine of the thirteen circuit courts. They are not about to construct "liberal" interpretations of the Due Process Clause![10]

President George W. Bush's administration "has transformed the nation's federal appeals courts, advancing a conservative legal revolution that began nearly three decades ago under President Ronald Reagan." During Bush's tenure, he appointed "more than a third of the federal judiciary expected to be serving when he leaves office, a lifetime tenured force that will influence society for decades and that represents one of his most enduring accomplishments."[11]

President Bush was just the latest president to pack the courts with his "kind" of judicial appointments. An angry woman's-rights leader exclaimed that Bush appointed "'extremists' who share an agenda of hostility to regulations and the rights of women, minorities and workers. 'George W. Bush has made great strides in cementing the ultraconservative hold on federal courts.'"[12]

c. The Enduring Vitality of the "Sanctity of Life" Proponents in the PAD Battles

Another given, seen in every clash of forces over the right to die, is the continuing and vigorous opposition of the "sanctity of life" organizations. Included in this group are the Roman Catholic Church, conservative family rights groups, and groups such as "Not Dead Yet" representing disabled persons. Whether the PAD battle is in courtrooms over the meaning of the Constitution's words or in legislative chambers, these groups organize to defend the right to life. They have acted whether the issue is abortion or the right to die or some other social issue that rejects the blessedness of a person's right to live until death comes naturally.

Over and over again they have successfully blocked the efforts of PAD lawyers and organizations to legitimatize PAD either by constitutional interpretation or legislation. Only in Oregon, Washington, and Montana have their efforts failed. However, rest assured that they will continue to introduce referenda or support legislation whose goal is to undo PAD in these states.

d. PAD Battles Reflect Congressman Tip O'Neal's Belief That "All Politics Is Local"[3]

In the 1997 right-to-die cases, and reaffirmed in the 2005 *Gonzales* decision, the U.S. Supreme Court majority left the ultimate decision regarding physician assistance in dying to the state democratic political processes. If people in a state want such a policy, then it will become law. And we know the results of these tough, no-holds-barred battles.

The key factor in convincing the electorate in a state where pro-PAD forces are gathering or regrouping for another effort at passing legislation is to work incessantly to overcome the vitriolic argument that such a law is the embodiment of the "culture of death." There must emerge a dialogue that transcends the culture of death argument proffered by PAD critics. There needs to be, instead, a focus on the concept of compassion.

Compassion reflects the ability to personalize and feel for the person who is dying and in great pain or without *any* quality of life. "Death," someone wrote, "is not the ultimate tragedy. The ultimate tragedy is depersonalization, dying in an alien and sterile arena."[14] And when the battles in the states focus on culture of life versus culture of death, there is an objectification of the dilemma. Trapped by "sanctity of life" haranguers, or the beliefs of Hemlock Society stalwarts, we tend to forget the plight of the individual who is dying but does not yet have the liberty to die under his own terms. However, until there is a backing off the vitriolic language used by both sides, there is, I fear, little hope of bypassing these slogans in the political and legal battles for physician assistance in dying.

Unless there is such a change in the dialogue, most states will continue to deny dying with dignity for the miniscule number of Americans who desire to move in that direction. These patients, presently, have no legitimate right, except in Oregon, Washington State, and—perhaps—Montana to get the physician assistance they need to die with dignity.

II. The Ever-Present Slippery Slope

While there have been many events that impacted the PAD debates, a dominant religious and philosophical argument (one examined by the very concerned Supreme Court Justice David Souter in *Glucksberg*) is the insidious danger of the slippery slope. It is an inevitable evil, PAD opponents maintain, realized when even the smallest change occurs in how we treat the terminally ill in America. However, as Erich H. Loewy has written:

> Many if not most of our activities can constitute slippery slopes. Having a glass of wine may lead to drunkenness, and eating a good dinner can be the first step on the road to gluttony. Slippery slopes are unavoidable. Rather than disallowing certain considerations or actions, the presence of the slippery slope merely counsels cautious action in making choices. Discretion, which makes actions safer, if not safe, and better, if not good, proceeds in a social context in which choices must be made.[15]

If slippery slopes are inevitable, a reality we live with, then the focus on PAD legislation must be on the preventive steps built into the law to avert movement from passive physician assistance in dying to active physician action in the death of terminally ill patients. Both Oregon and Washington State legislation include preventative methods that will thwart the slide to the feared euthanasia.

These two state laws also reflect the compassion of the voters of these states. They have enabled a very small handful of terminally ill patients to take a path to death that will liberate them. As one proponent in Seattle said in a poster, "give me liberty at my death."

Down the road in the twenty-first century, there will certainly be new U.S. Supreme Court Justices, new sets of lower court federal judges, and new litigation that focuses on questions raised by living, terminally ill patients. There may be a substantial change in the way Americans view death with dignity.

Until then, defenders of PAD must try, in local community after local community, to persuade voters that the key to all PAD legislation is compassion for the dying patient's wish to end life with a degree of respect—surrounded by family and friends.

And until that era arrives, the only reasonable and compassionate alternative is to transplant oneself to either Oregon or Washington State and use the compassionate care provided by their public health servants to those who wish to die with the assistance of a physician.

III. America's Transplants—But Only to Oregon, Washington State, and, Maybe, Montana

Until and unless other states pass similar legislation to assist their residents, there will be the sad reality of America's transplants, a few dying men and women who move to one of the states that allow terminally ill persons to end their lives on their own terms.

Tony Miller is an American transplant. He "was drawn [to Oregon by its law] that enables terminally ill patients to obtain lethal prescriptions once their life expectancy falls below six months."[16] Nearly a decade ago, he was teaching history. Then he was diagnosed with severe prostate cancer. After the diagnosis, he received medical treatment in Maryland. Then he transplanted himself to Oregon. He explained why:

> I am doing all I can to stay alive and prolong my life up to the point where my life becomes nothing but physical agony. It all depends on the level of pain. When it gets to the point when the medication is not working and life is grim—I will make my final decision. . . . With [Oregon's] Death with Dignity Act, I feel safe.[17]

There is no reason why, like Miller, persons in the United States cannot travel to Oregon, and Washington State, and perhaps, in the future, Montana, and choose to die with dignity and compassion. Actions in these states make such a decision possible.

In this area of constitutional law, different U.S. Supreme Court majorities over the past century and a half have said that all persons in the nation have the absolute liberty to travel without any restrictions placed on them by states and local communities. Whether the traveler was an "Okie" trying to escape the Depression by traveling with his family to California for a better life,[18] a traveler who moved to Connecticut and was denied welfare because she had not lived in the state for at least one year,[19] or was a Communist Party member denied a passport by the U.S. State Department,[20] the Supreme Court overturned these laws and regulations. In a 1966 civil rights case that dealt with Klansmen murdering a black army officer on a Georgia highway, the Court majority upheld the validity of the indictment. The Klansmen interfered with interstate travel, which was a privilege of national citizenship.[21] The fundamental reason for these decisions: the right to travel is a liberty protected by the Due Process Clauses in the Constitution.

There is nothing in the PAD laws that prevents someone from moving to Oregon or to Washington State in order to die. There is no minimum residency requirement. All one has to do is establish that one is *currently* a resident of the state.

How does a patient demonstrate residency? The patient must provide "adequate documentation," that is, a driver's license, a lease agreement of property ownership document that shows that the patient rents or owns property in the state, and the like. However, "it is up to the attending physician to determine whether or not the patient has adequately established residency."[22]

We do not know how many "Tony Millers" are transplants or will become transplants. We may never know because no such data exists. We do know that it can happen here much like Europeans transplant themselves to Switzerland to die with dignity.

Why is the Oregon and Washington State "transplant" necessary for a very small number of Americans? Because forty-eight states ban PAD, and the federal courts, especially the U.S. Supreme Court, are unwilling to interpret the U.S. Constitution to enable a very tiny number of dying Americans to do so on their own terms.

When will things change? We really do not know the answer to that. We only know that change has taken place, but it has occurred very slowly, almost molecularly, in our nation's social, legal, and cultural history. Whether the issue be slavery, or racial, religious, gender, or sexual preference discrimination, changes occurred in the way disadvantaged and discriminated groups have been treated. Until there is a change in the way Americans view the right of a few to choose to die with dignity, there will be American transplants.

◆   NOTES

NOTES TO THE INTRODUCTION

1. Dudley Clendinen, "The Good Short Life," *New York Times Sunday Review*, July 9, 2011.

2. Ibid.

3. See Mark Landler, "Assisted Suicide of Healthy 79-Year-Old Renews German Debate on Right to Die," *New York Times*, July 3, 2008, A8. Also, Susan Donaldson James, "Tourists Trek to Mexico for 'Death in a Bottle,'" *ABC News*, July 31, 2008, www.abc.com. In addition, see "The Suicide Tourist, *PBS Frontline*, March 2, 2010, at www.pbs.org.

4. Paul Bartlett is a Tucson lawyer who participated in a right-to-die symposium in the winter of 2007. He spoke about medical breakthroughs that led to kidney and liver transplants, followed by successful heart transplants. "And now," he said, "we have the 'Oregon transplants.'"

5. For a story about one Oregon transplant, see Hal Bernton, "Washington's Initiative 1000 is Modeled on Oregon's Death with Dignity Act," *Seattle Times*, October 13, 2008, A1.

6. See *Roe v Wade*, 410 U.S. 113 (1973).

7. See *Loving v Virginia*, 388 U.S. 1 (1967). In 2011, six states and the District of Columbia allow marriage between same-sex couples. The latest state to pass such legislation is New York State. Given the liberty to travel, many same-sex couples have traveled to these states in order to marry.

8. 73 U.S. 35 (1868).

9. *Edwards v California*, 314 U.S. 160 (1941).

10. In this time period, there was a total increase of 126 percent: from 658 hospitals to nearly 1,500. See Roxanne Nelson, "Palliative Care Programs Continue to Increase in American Hospitals," *Medscape Medical News*, April 10, 2010, www.news@medscape.net.

11. A word about the use of the term "physician-assisted death (PAD)": The supporters of the policy of allowing a physician to assist a terminally ill patient to die do not refer to that practice as "suicide." I agree with mental health specialists that "'suicide' and the choice made by a dying patient to hasten impending death in a peaceful and dignified manner *are* starkly different. The American Psychological Association has recognized that the "reasoning on which a terminally ill person (whose judgments are not impaired by mental disorders) bases a decision to end his or her life is fundamentally different from

the reasoning a clinically depressed person uses to justify suicide." Throughout the book, there will appear the phrase "physician-assisted death (PAD)" rather than the older phrase, used by opponents, "physician-assisted suicide (PAS)." Quoted in Kathryn L. Tucker, "In the Laboratory of the States," 106 *Michigan Law Review* 1593, 1595, June 2008.

12. Margaret P. Battin, *The Least Worst Death: Essays in Bioethics on the End of Life*, New York: Oxford University Press, 1994.

13. COPD is *chronic obstructive pulmonary disease.* The lungs are damaged, due primarily to cigarette smoking, making it very hard and painful to breathe. The airways—the tubes—that carry air in and out of the lungs become obstructed.

14. In Greek mythology, drinking from the River Lethe caused complete forgetfulness and then death.

15. See John Schwartz and James Eslin, "In Oregon, Choosing Death Over Suffering," *New York Times*, June 1, 2004, A1.

16. Both amendments have the identical language: "nor [shall any person] be deprived of life, liberty, or property, without due process of law."

17. 381 U.S. 479 (1965).

18. According to the Free Legal Dictionary, penumbras are "the rights guaranteed by implication in a constitution." *www.thefreedictionary.com/penumbras.*

19. Griswold at 487.

20. Ibid., 500.

21. Ibid., 520.

22. 405 U.S. 438 (1972).

23. Chief Justice Warren Burger dissented. He maintained that the statute reflected a legitimate health bill.

24. 405 U.S. 453.

25. 410 U.S. 113 (1973).

26. PVS is a clinical-medical diagnosis that because the patient's brain has been deprived of oxygen for more than six minutes, the person is without any cognitive facilities. While there are primitive physiological behavior patterns, the person is nearly brain dead—without cognition and sensations and, in a majority of cases, blind—and it is impossible to have *any* medical improvement in the indeterminate future.

27. See *In Re: Guardians of Schiavo*, No 90-2908 GD-003 (Florida 2d District Circuit Court, 2000), and *Jeb Bush v Schiavo*, No. SC04-925, September 2004.

28. Congress, on March 20, 2005, passed the "For Relief of Parents of Theresa Marie Schiavo" Statute, and President George W. Bush, on March 21, 2005, signed the bill into law.

29. In 2001, the new administration of Republican President George W. Bush began an effort to eviscerate the Oregon law by interpreting the 1970 Controlled Substance Act in a manner that would prevent Oregon doctors from prescribing lethal medicines for a few of their terminally ill patients. In 2005, in the case of *Gonzales v Oregon,* the U.S. Supreme Court rejected that effort.

NOTES TO CHAPTER I

1. Quote in Claire Danosian Dunavan, "Looking Squarely at Death, and Finding Clarity," *New York Times*, August 19, 2008, D5.

2. Quoted in www.aarp.org.

3. Sherwin B. Nuland, *How We Die: Reflections on Life's Final Chapter*, New York: Vintage, 1995, 42, has written that "the experience of dying does not belong to the heart alone. It is a process in which every tissue of the body partakes, each by its own means and at its own pace. The operative word here is *process*, not *act*, *moment*, or any other term connoting a flyspeck of time when the spirit departs."

4. Leslie Ivan, *The Way We Die: Brain Death, Vegetative State, Euthanasia and other End-of-Life Dilemmas*, Groseto, Italy: Pari Publishing, 2007, 25.

5. There are over thirty trillion cells in human beings. In a healthy adult, more than "two hundred billion cells die and are born every day." Ibid., 26.

6. Memorandum, *Diagnosis of Death in U.K.*, Conference of Medical Royal Colleges and Their Faculties in the United Kingdom, January 15, 1979, 1 *British Medical Journal* 332, February 3, 1979. See also Canadian Neurocritical Care Group, "Guidelines for the Diagnosis of Brain Death," 26 *Canadian Journal of Neurological Science* 64–66, 1999; National Conference of Commissioners on Uniform State of Laws, Uniform Determination of Death Act, U.S.A. in Ivan, *The Way We Die*, 225.

7. Ivan, *The Way We Die*, 34.

8. Ibid., 45.

9. Ibid., 42.

10. Brain death is the *total* absence of all brain activity, and it is irreversible. Unlike other organs in the body, there is still no scientific or medical technology that can "restart" or "replace" the brain as we have been able to restart breathing and the heart, and replace kidneys, eyes, and even the heart.

11. The cerebral cortex is the "thinking, feeling part of the brain." It requires a "constant, uninterrupted supply of blood, glucose, and oxygen to function. . . . If it is deprived of its blood or oxygen supply for as little as *four to six* minutes, extensive and irreversible damage can result. Once such deprivation takes place, that part of the brain is dead, and over time, will begin to shrivel." William H. Colby, *Long Goodbye*, Carlsbad, CA: Hay House, 2002, 18.

12. Memo, *Diagnosis of Death*, 54. In 1980, reflecting these new developments, the National Conference of Commissioners on Uniform State Laws, with the cooperation of the American Medical Association and the American Bar Association promulgated the Uniform Determination of Death Act: An individual who has sustained either (1) irreversible circulatory and respiratory functions, or (2) irreversible cessation of all functions of the *entire* brain, including the brain stem, is dead. A determination of death must be made in accordance with accepted medical standards. All fifty states and the District of Columbia have adopted this standard.

See Marcia Angell, "After Quinlan: The Dilemma of the Persistent Vegetative State," 330 *NEJM* 21, 1524–1525, 1524, May 26, 1994.

13. Roy Porter, *The Greatest Benefit to Mankind: The Medical History of Humanity*. New York: W.W. Norton, 1997, 628, 718.

14. Dunavan, "Looking at Death," D5.

15. Porter, *Greatest Benefit*, 306–307

16. Ibid., 320.

17. Ibid., 672.

18. David Cutler, Angus Deaton, and Adriana Lleras-Muney, "The Determinants of Mortality," December 2005. Paper presented in NIA-sponsored workshop on the *Determinants of Mortality*, Princeton, NJ, July 16, 2004, 3.

19. Colby, *Long Goodbye*, 31.

20. John Hartwig, "Medicalization and Death," presentation at 2006 annual conference of the American Psychological Association, 8, at http://www.apa.udel.edu/apa/publications/newsletters/MedicineNL/v06n1.htm.

21. Rabies, 1885; plague, 1897; diphtheria, 1923; pertussis, 1926; tuberculosis, 1927; tetanus, 1927; yellow fever, 1937; polio, 1955/1962; measles, 1964; mumps, 1967; rubella, 1970, and hepatitis B, 1981, were some of the major vaccinations developed. Cutler, "Determinants," 9.

22. Ibid., 5.

23. Ibid., 7–8. In the United States, in 2010, the principal federal health agency is the Public Health Services (PHS) division of the U.S. Department of Health and Human Services.

24. *Health, United States, 2006*, U.S. Department of Health and Human Services, CDC, National Center for Health Statistics, Washington, DC, 2006, 3.

25. Margaret Pabst Battin, *The Least Worst Death: Essays in Bioethics on the End of Life*, New York: Oxford University Press, 1994, 9. "With longer life expectancy comes increased prevalence of chronic diseases and conditions that are associated with aging. Some diseases, including diabetes and hypertension, produce cumulative damage if not properly treated, while others, such as emphysema and some types of cancer, develop slowly or after long periods of environmental exposure." *Health, United States, 2006*, U.S. Department of Health and Human Services, CDC, National Center for Health Statistics, Washington, DC, 2006, 3.

26. Jane Gross, "How Many of Us Expect To Die?" The New Old Age, Caring and Coping, *New York Times*, July 8, 2008, at www.newyorktimes.com/newoldage.

27. Ibid. See also Joanne Lynn, *Sick to Death and Not Going to Take It Anymore: Reforming Health Care for the Last Years of Life*, Berkeley, CA: University of California Press, 2004, 45–53 passim.

28. Gross, "How Many of Us?"

29. John Hartwig, "Medicalization and Death," presentation at 2006 annual conference of the American Psychological Association, 8, at http://www.apa.udel.edu/apa/publications/newsletters/MedicineNL/vo6n1.htm.

30. Almost half of all accidents were car accidents (42,437 deaths).

31. *Current State of Foodborne Illness*, a presentation by Arthur P. Liang, MD, MPH, Director, Food Safety Office, National Center For Infectious Diseases, Centers for Disease Control and Prevention, 2002, at http://www.fsis.usda.gov/Orlando 2002/presentations/aliang_text.htm.

32. *Health, United States, 2006*, U.S. Department of Health and Human Services, CDC, National Center for Health Statistics, Washington, DC, 2006, 7. See also Gross, "How Many of Us?"

33. Cutler, "Changes," 20–21.

34. Louise Harmon, *Fragments on the Deathwatch*, Boston, MA: Beacon Press, 1998, 8–9.

35. Of that percentage, approximately 20 percent of deaths occur in intensive care units (ICUs) of America's hospitals. The majority of these deaths involve withholding or withdrawing life-sustaining therapies. J. Randall Curtis and Robert Burt, "Point: The Ethics of Unilateral 'Do Not Resuscitate' Orders," 132 *Chest* 748–751, 2007, 748. See also Donald Cook, et. al., "Withdrawal of Mechanical Ventilation in Anticipation of Death in the ICU," 349 *NEJM* 1123, 2003.

36. Ibid., 7.

37. Cutler, "Determinants," 14–15.

38. David M. Cutler and Ellen Meara, "Changes in the Age Distribution of Mortality Over the 20th Century," Paper presented to the *U.S. National Institutes on Aging*, September 2001, 2, 4.

39. *Oxford English Dictionary*, Additions Series, vol. 3, 1997.

40. Porter, *Greatest Benefit*, 677.

41. Hartwig, "Medicalization and Death," 12.

42. Ronald Cranford, "Diagnosing the Permanent Vegetative State," *American Medical Association (AMA) Virtual Mentor*, 2005, at www.ama-assn.org/ama/pub/category/12720.html.

43. An EEG is a noninvasive test that monitors electrical signals taking place in a patient's brain.

44. Cranford, "Diagnosing."

45. Carol M. Ostrom, "Doctors Divided on Assisted Suicide," *Seattle Times*, October 1, 2008, A1.

46. Note, "Death and Dying: Medicalization of Dying," *Medicine Encyclopedia*, 1. http://medicine.jrank.org/pages/417/.

47. Douglas N. Walton, *Ethics of Withdrawal of Life-Support Systems: Case Studies in Decision-Making in Intensive Care*, New York: Praeger, 1987, 53.

48. Byron Jennett, *The Vegetative State: Medical Facts, Ethical and Legal Dimensions*, New York: Cambridge University Press, 2002, 81.

49. Note, "Death and Dying," 2–3. Recall also the very last scene in the moving, provocative film *Wit*, starring Emma Thompson. She portrayed a dying cancer patient. After cardiac and respiratory arrest, emergency personnel tried to resuscitate her but were stopped by a sympathetic doctor who had been relentlessly treating her cancer for almost a year.

50. Karen Ann Quinlan, discussed in chapter 2, was a twenty-one-year-old woman who was in a PVS for many years. She was on life support while in this state, and her parents wished to withdraw the apparatus in order to allow her die.

51. Julia Duane Quinlan, *My Joy, My Sorrow*, Cincinnati, OH: St. Anthony Messenger Press, 2005), 76.

NOTES TO CHAPTER 2

1. Ian Dowbiggin, *A Merciful End: The Euthanasia Movement in America*, New York: Oxford University Press, 2003, 147.

2. English common law developed the notion that a competent person can refuse medical treatment, even though such a decision can lead to death. This common law principle became embedded in colonial and post-Revolution American common law and, subsequently, in state statutes.

3. See Melvin I. Urofsky, *Letting Go: Death, Dying, and the Law*, New York: Scribner's Sons, 1994, xiii.

4. Article One, Section 8, Clause 17.

5. U.S. Constitution, Tenth Amendment, adopted, 1791. The Civil War Amendments, Thirteenth Amendment (1865), Fourteenth Amendment (1868), and Fifteenth Amendment (1870), provided constitutional restraints on certain "state actions."

6. *Metropolitan Life Insurance Company v Massachusetts*, 471 U.S. 724 (1985), 756.

7. Donald R. Steinberg, "Limits to Death with Dignity," 1 *Harvard Journal of Law and Technology* 129, Spring, 1988, 133. Although the "state's interest in the preservation of life is stronger in the case of a non-terminal patient, [the state] generally will not prevail." 143.

8. Quoted in Steinberg, "Limits to Death with Dignity," 141.

9. *People v Kevorkian*, 527 *N.W. 2nd* 739, 1990.

10. Susan M. Wolf, "Physician-Assisted Suicide, Abortion, and Treatment Refusal," in *Potentially Vulnerable Patients*, 174.

11. *Bouvia v Superior Court*, 179 *Cal App. 3rd* 1127; 225 *Cal Reporter*, 297 (1986). Interestingly, Elizabeth Bouvia chose not to end her life. A decade later, she appeared on a television talk show during which she discussed the circumstances surrounding her original decision and why she changed her mind. See also *Bartling v Superior Court*, 163 *Cal App. 3rd* 186; 209 *Cal Reporter* 220, 1984, involving removal of respirator from the body of a non-terminally ill patient. The Court stated that if a patient's right to self-determination was "to have

meaning, that right must be *paramount* to the interests of the patient's hospitals and doctors" (my emphasis).

12. Steinberg, "Limits To Death with Dignity," 129.

13. *Superintendent of Belchertown State School v Saikowicz*, 373 *Mass* 728, 370 *N.E. 2nd* 417 (1977), 424.

14. *Union Pacific v Botsford*, 141 U.S. 250 (1891), 251.

15. *Dicta* is a Latin term meaning "Expressions in an opinion of the Court which are not necessary to support the decision; language unnecessary to a decision; ruling on an issue not raised." William S. Anderson, ed., *Ballentine's Law Dictionary*, 3rd ed., Rochester, NY: Lawyer's Cooperative Publishing Company, 1969, 346.

16. *Cruzan v Director, Missouri Department of Health*, 497 U.S. 261 (1990), 278. He cited decisions where a person's liberty interest meant the right to decline vaccinations and forcible body searches.

17. *Cruzan*, 287. On this point, the dissenters in *Cruzan* agreed with their colleagues. Justice William J. Brennan's dissent stated that a competent person has a "*fundamental* right to be free of unwanted treatment," while Justice John P. Stevens wrote that what was at stake "was highly invasive treatment . . . [and that a competent patient had the right to be] free from physically invasive procedures."

18. Susan M. Wolf, "Physician Assisted Suicide, Abortion, and Treatment Refusal," in *Potentially Vulnerable Patients*, 172.

19. In *Cruzan*, Justice William J. Brennan took "judicial notice" of the fact that "Out of 100,000 patients who, like Nancy Cruzan, have fallen into PVSs in the past 20 years due to loss of oxygen to the brain [*anoxia*], there have been only three even partial recoveries documented in the medical literature. The longest any person has been in a PVS and recovered was 22 months." *Cruzan*, Brennan dissenting, 307, n. 8.

20. In the law there are four types of guardians: (1) limited (surrogate for medical decisions); (2) plenary (with authority to make *all* decisions for the patient); (3) general (whose authority derives from a state's guardianship statute); and (4) *guardian ad litem* (a special guardian appointed by the court to represent the incompetent patient's "best interests" in the litigation before the court). Sharon F. DiPaolo, "Getting Through the Door: Threshold Procedural Considerations in Right-To-Die Litigation," 6 *Franklin Pierce Law Review* Winter 1997, at www.piercelaw.edu/risk/vol6/winter/dipaolo.html

21. See Quinlan, *My Joy, My Sorrow*, 37–38.

22. Ibid., 39.

23. Annette E. Clark, "The Right to Die: The Broken Road From *Quinlan* to *Schiavo*," 37 *Loyola University Chicago Law Review* 383, 2006, 384.

24. Quinlan, *My Joy, My Sorrow*, 41, 43–44.

25. Quoted in Clark, "The Right to Die," 385.

26. Ibid.
27. Equity is a respected group of rights and procedures to provide fairness, unhampered by the narrow strictures of the old common law or other technical requirements of the law. In essence, courts do the fair thing by court orders such as correction of property lines, taking possession of assets, imposing a lien, dividing assets, or injunctive relief (ordering a person to do something) to prevent irreparable damage. The rules of equity arose in England when the strict limitations of common law would not solve all problems, so the king set up courts of chancery (equity) to provide remedies through the royal power. http://.forum.free dictionary.com.
28. This quote and all subsequent quotes from the chancery court petition and opinion are found in the opinion of the New Jersey Supreme Court, *In Re Quinlan, An Alleged Incompetent, 348 A. 2nd* 801 (NJ Superior Court, 1975), *modified and remanded* 355 A. 2nd 647 (NJ, 1976), at 653.
29. Quinlan, *My Joy, My Sorrow,* 45–46. What particularly irked the parents and Karen's brother and sister was the name the press tagged on her: the "Sleeping Beauty."
30. *In Re Quinlan,* 348 A. 2nd at 816.
31. Ibid., 819.
32. Ibid., 819–820, 826.
33. *Parens patriae* is a ancient legal doctrine meaning "that all orphans, dependent children, and incompetent persons, are within the special protection, and under the control, of the state." Anderson, *Ballentine's Law Dictionary*, 911.
34. Clark, "The Right to Die," 386.
35. *In Re Quinlan,* 355 A.2nd 647 (NJ, 1976), 647.
36. Ibid., 652.
37. At this point, the Court inserted n. 2, which quoted testimony presented by a neurologist, Dr. Julius Korein, during the earlier trial in chancery court: "The technology [to keep a patient alive] has now reached a point where you can in fact start to replace *anything* outside of the brain to maintain something that is irreversibly damaged" (my emphasis). Ibid. .
38. Ibid., 652.
39. Ibid., 661–662.
40. Ibid., 662.
41. Ibid. 662.
42. Ibid.., 663–664.
43. Ibid.., 664.
44. Quinlan, *My Joy, My Sorrow,* 53–54.
45. In 1994 Karen's brain autopsy report appeared in a medical journal. Pathologists found that lesions in her brain were consistent with *hypoxia-ischemia* (deprivation of oxygen) following a cardiopulmonary arrest. There was excessively severe damage in the thalamus, due to the lack of oxygen to her brain, compared with

the main cerebral cortex, supporting the view that the thalamus is needed for awareness, perception, and judgment. See H.C. Kinney et al., "Neuropathological Findings in the Brain of Karen Ann Quinlan—The Role of the Thalamus in the Persistent Vegetative State," 330 *NEJM* 21, 1469–1475, 1994.

46. Quoted in Quinlan, *My Joy, My Sorrow,* 106.

47. Clark, "The Right to Die," 392.

48. 497 U.S. 261 (1990).

49. At the time of her one-car accident, she was a twenty-seven-year old, twice-married woman and, on the hospital records, the name entered was Nancy Davis, wife of Paul Davis. During her lengthy stay in hospitals, and before litigation began, her husband divorced her (January 1984), and the records were changed to her maiden name: Nancy Beth Cruzan.

50. *Cruzan v Director,* 497 at 266.

51. Colby, *Long Goodbye,* 17.

52. Ibid., 18.

53. *Cruzan v Director,* at 266.

54. A flat EEG reading is a clear indicator of brain death. If Nancy's EEGs were flat, she would have been declared "brain dead," and all medical apparatus used to assist her would have been turned off and withdrawn. Hers, however, was "nearly flat"; she wasn't brain dead and would never be declared brain dead during the time she remained on the feeding tube from 1983 to 1990.

55. Quoted in Colby, *Long Goodbye,* 50.

56. *Pro bono publico* is a Latin term meaning "for the public good." Law firms, primarily large firms with many associates working in the firm, provide free legal counsel for those who cannot afford a lawyer.

57. Colby rejected this strategy. The right to privacy, he wrote, "wasn't a great foundation for a lawsuit in the state of Missouri. [That phrase] had become code words for abortion. In the summer of 1987, strong pro-life forces were at work in Missouri, fighting to stop abortion and limit the right to privacy wherever it appeared." Colby, *Long Goodbye,* 72.

58. Ibid., 58–59.

59. Ibid., 92.

60. Ibid., 232.

61. Colby writes about the politics of the appellate process. The appeal to the Missouri Supreme Court had been worked out even before Judge Teel announced his decision. Teel was contacted by the Chief Justice of the Court and told to instruct the state to immediately appeal to the Court and bypass any appeal to the intermediate state appellate court. Ibid., 235–242 passim.

62. Ibid., 257.

63. *Cruzan v Harmon,* 760 *S.W. 2nd* 416, 416–417 (Missouri, *en banc,* 1988).

64. Ibid., 419–420.

65. Ibid., 424–426.

66. *Cruzan v Director, Missouri Department of Health*, 492 U.S. 917 (granting *certiorari*).

67. *Certiorari*, a petition to the U.S. Supreme Court asking the justices to review a final decision of a state supreme court or a federal court of appeals, is generally denied by them. Most petitions to the Court (99 percent) are *certiorari* petitions. Granting or denying such petitions is a totally discretionary action of the Court; four Justices must vote to grant *certiorari* during discussions in the secret Conference Sessions. Rule 10 of the U.S. Supreme Court describes this power: "Review on a writ of *certiorari* is not a matter of right, but of judicial discretion. A petition for a writ of *certiorari* will be granted only for compelling reasons." Historically, very few *cert* petitions (less than 1 percent of the total received by the Court) are granted annually. See, generally, Howard Ball and Phillip J. Cooper, *The U.S. Supreme Court: From the Inside Out*, Englewood Cliffs, NJ: Prentice-Hall, 1992.

68. *Cruzan v Director, Missouri Department of Health*, 497 U.S. 261 (1990).

69. Colby, *Long Goodbye*, 289.

70. See, generally, Lincoln Caplan, *The Tenth Justice: The Solicitor General and the Rule of Law*, New York: Vintage, 1988, for an excellent examination of the very special role of the Solicitor General's office in the workings of the U.S. Supreme Court.

71. *Cruzan v Director, Missouri Department of Health*, Brief for the United States as Amicus Curiae Supporting Respondents, 6. www.usdoj.gov/osg/briefs/1989/sg890451.txt.

72. This view expressed by the Solicitor General is essentially the "originalist" argument for interpreting the words of the U.S. Constitution. Expressed by judicial and political conservatives, including Justices Anthony Scalia and Clarence Thomas, it means that jurists must be bound by the *original meaning and intent of the men* who wrote the U.S. Constitution and its amendments.

73. *Cruzan v Director*, 7.

74. Ibid., 3, 11.

75. Ibid., 14–17 passim.

76. *Cruzan, by her parents and co-guardians, Cruzan, et ux. v Director, Missouri Department of Health*, 497 U.S. 261 (1990), 278. All quotes that follow in the text are from the Supreme Court's opinions in *Cruzan*.

77. Ibid., 280.

78. Ibid., 285–286.

79. *Cruzan*, O'Connor concurring, 291.

80. *Cruzan*, Scalia concurring, 295.

81. Ibid., 299.

82. *Cruzan*, Justice Brennan dissenting, 305.

83. Ibid., 303–305.

84. Ibid., 325.

85. Ibid., 330.

86. *Cruzan*, Stevens dissenting, 345–346.

87. Ibid., 349.

88. *Cruzan*, Brennan dissenting, 305.

89. Jonathan D. Moreno, ed., *Arguing Euthanasia: The Controversy Over Mercy Killing, Assisted Suicide, and the "Right to Die,"* New York: Simon and Schuster, 1995, 19.

90. Quoted in Colby, *Long Goodbye*, 361.

91. Ashcroft became a U.S. Senator after ending his term as governor in 1992. He lost his seat when he ran for reelection in 1998. However, after George W. Bush's contested 2000 presidential election against the Democratic Party candidate, Al Gore, Ashcroft was appointed and confirmed as the U.S. Attorney General in 2001.

92. Quoted in Colby, *Long Goodbye*, 364.

93. *Rasmussen by Mitchell v Fleming*, 154 Arizona 207; 741 P.2d 674, 1987, at 217.

94. *In Re Daniel Joseph Fiori, an Adjudged Incompetent*, 543 Pa 592; 6783 A.2d 905 (1995).

95. Ibid., 597.

96. Ibid., 599.

97. *So. 2d* 4 (Florida, 1990) See also *Corbett v D'Alessandro*, 487 So. 2d 368 (Florida, 1986).

98. Ibid., 8.

99. Ibid., 9. This right of self-determination, the court stated, includes the right to make *all* choices about medical treatment. Finally, the court said: "We conclude that this right is not lost or diminished by virtue of physical or mental incapacity or incompetence." The legally appointed guardian was authorized to exercise this right for her, "but must do so in a manner that reflects the choice that the patient, if competent, would have made." The state's general interest in the preservation of life was insufficient to outweigh the patient's right to forego treatment. Ibid., 13–14.

100. *In Re Guardianship and Protective Placement of L.W.*, 167 Wisc. 2d 53, 482 N.W. 2d 60, 1992, 65.

101. Ibid., 77–78.

102. *In Re Guardianship and Protective Placement of Edna M.F. v Howard Eisenberg*, 95-2719, 1997, www. lw.bna.com/lw/19970/952719.htm.

103. Strict scrutiny is when an American court "assumes that [the challenged governmental action] is unconstitutional and the government has the burden of demonstrating its compelling interest." Kermit L. Hall, ed., *The Oxford Companion to the Supreme Court of the United States*, New York: Oxford University Press, 1992, 845.

NOTES TO CHAPTER 3

1. Marisa Martin, "*In Re Schiavo*: The Saga Continues," 1, at www.law.uh.edu/healthlaw/perspectives/Death/040229Schiavo.html.

2. Richard S. Myers, "Reflections on the Terri Schindler-Schiavo Controversy," in J. Koterski, ed., *Life and Learning XIV: The Proceedings of the Fourteenth University Faculty For Life Conference*, Washington, DC: UFL, 2005, 27.

3. *In Re Schiavo*, 789 *So. 2d* 248 (Florida, 2001).

4. On April 23, 2001, U.S. Supreme Court Justice Anthony Kennedy refused to carry over the case for a review by the full Court.

5. See, for example, John A. Robertson, "Schiavo and Its (In)Significance," *University of Texas Public Law Research* (March, 2005), paper no. 72, at www.ssrn.com/abstract=692901.

6. Wolfson, "Foreword," A.L. Caplan et al., *The Case of Terri Schiavo: Ethics at the End of Life*, Amherst, NY: Prometheus Books, 2006, 14–15.

7. Ibid.

8. In 2001, a Florida intermediate appellate court wrote, of the Schindlers: "No one questions the sincerity of their prayers for the divine miracle that now is Theresa's only hope to gain any level of normal existence." *In Re: Guardianship of Theresa Marie Schiavo, Robert Schindler and Mary Schindler v Michael Schiavo, as Guardian of the person of Theresa Marie Schiavo*, District Court of Appeal of Florida, Second District, Case No. 2D00-1269, 4. That same appellate court opinion also noted that Terri "did not regularly attend mass or have a religious advisor who could assist the court in weighing her religious attitudes about life-support methods" (8).

9. Kathy Cerminara and Kenneth Goodman. "Schiavo Case Resources: Key events in the case of Theresa Marie Schiavo, *University of Miami Ethics Programs*, July 25, 2008, 2, at www6.miami.edu/ethics/schiavo/terri_schiavo_timeline.html.

10. The Geer Orders were issued on April 1, 2001, October 3, 2003, and finally, on March 18, 2005. Terri Schiavo died on March 31, 2005.

11. Geer, *Order*, 9.

12. Ibid.

13. *In Re: Guardianship of Theresa Marie Schiavo, Robert Schindler and Mary Schindler v Michael Schiavo, as Guardian of the person of Theresa Marie Schiavo*, District Court of Appeal of Florida, Second District, Case No. 2D00-1269, 2, 9.

14. *In Re Schiavo*, 789 *So. 2d* 248 (Florida, 2001), Case No. SC01-559.

15. *In Re Schiavo, Schindler v Schiavo, Petition to Remove Guardian and to Appoint Successor Guardian*, November 15, 2002, 5, 6.

16. *In Re Schiavo*, Pinellas County, Florida Circuit Court, September 17, 2003, *Order*, 2.

17. *In Re Schiavo*, Civil Action No. 8:03-CV-1860-T-26-TGW.

18. *In Re Schiavo, Memorandum of Amicus Curiae Jeb Bush, Governor of the State of Florida, in Support of Plaintiff's Motion for Preliminary Injunction*, October 7, 2003, 1.

19. Bill No HB-35 –E, Chamber Action, October 21, 2003, 1.

20. Florida Governor's Office, *Executive Order Number 3-201*, October 21, 2003, 1.

21. *Michael Schiavo v Jeb Bush and Charlie Crist, Petitioner's Brief*, DCA, Civil Case No. 03-008212-CI-20, 1.
22. *Respondent's Brief*, 2.
23. *Schiavo v Bush*, Sixth Judicial Circuit, May 5, 2004, 6.
24. *Bush v Schiavo, Amicus Curiae Brief in Support of Michael Schiavo, Supreme Court of Florida*, July 27, 2004.
25. Ibid., 3, 8, 14.
26. One observer of the oral argument noted that the "justices appeared concerned that 'Terri's Law' granted Governor Bush unfettered powers. 'The act does not even require the governor to take into account the patient's wishes,' said Chief Justice Barbara Pariente. . . . 'There is a role [in this dispute] for the Legislature. There is a role for the governor,' said Ken Connor, an attorney representing Bush." William R. Levesque, "Justices Skeptical of Bush Team's Defense of 'Terri's Law,'" *St. Petersburg Times*, September 1, 2004, 1.
27. *Jeb Bush v Michael Schiavo*, Supreme Court of Florida, Case No. SC04-925, September 23, 2004, 1–2.
28. 109th Cong., 1st sess., HR 1151, "To Amend Title 28, United States Code, to provide the protection of Habeas Corpus for certain incapacitated persons whose life is in jeopardy, and for other purposes," modified March 16, 2005, as HR 1332.
29. 151 *Congressional Record*, No 33, House of Representatives, Representative Joe Pitts, "Bill Saving Terri Schiavo," Thursday, March 17, 2005, at H1625.
30. A private bill "provides benefits to specified individuals. Individuals sometimes request relief through private legislation when administrative or legal remedies are exhausted. . . . If a private bill is passed in identical form by both Houses of Congress and is signed by the President, it becomes a private law." www.senate.gov.
31. Ibid., 2, 3.
32. The White House, *Statement by the President*, March 21, 2005, at www.white-house.gov.
33. *Theresa Schiavo v Michael Schiavo et al.*, "Statement of Interest of the United States, U.S. District Court, Middle District of Florida, Tampa Division, Civ A No. 8:05-CV-530-T-27TBM, 5.
34. *Schiavo v Schiavo*, U.S. District Court, Middle District, Florida, *Order*, 3. "Plaintiffs have asserted five constitutional and statutory claims. To obtain temporary injunctive relief, they must show a *substantial likelihood of success* on at least one claim. . . . This court appreciates the gravity of the consequences of denying injunctive relief. [However,] this court is constrained to apply the law to the issues before it. As plaintiffs have not established a substantial likelihood of success on the merits, Plaintiffs' Motion for TRO must be DENIED." 5, 12–13.
35. State of Florida, County of Duval, *Affidavit*, William Polk Cheshire Jr., March 23, 2005, 3. For example, Cheshire wrote, "*although Terri did not demonstrate*

during our 90-minute visit compelling evidence of verbalization, conscious aware-ness, or volitional behavior, yet the visitor has the *distinct sense* of the presence of a living human being who seems *at some level* to be aware of some things around her," 6 (my emphasis).

36. Ibid., 6.

37. Editorial, "Theresa Marie Schiavo," *New York Times*, April 1, 2005, A23.

38. The Harris Poll, No. 29, April 15, 2005, "The Terri Schiavo Case: Paradoxi-cally Most U.S. Adults Approve of How Both Her Husband and Her Parents Behaved," at www.harrisinteractive.com.

39. MSNBC.com. "Even in Death, Acrimony Over Schiavo," June 21, 2005, at www. msnbc.msn.com. Ten days later, they informed the governor that there was no evi-dence of wrongdoing by Michael. "While some questions may remain following the autopsy, the likelihood of finding evidence that criminal acts were responsible for her collapse is not one of them. . . . We strongly recommend that the inquiry be closed and no further action be taken." On July 7, 2005, the governor dropped any further investigations into Terri Schiavo's 1990 cardiac arrest.

40. In September 2005, after the death of Chief Justice William H. Rehnquist, Presi-dent Bush re-nominated Roberts to fill the Rehnquist center seat on the U.S. Supreme Court. Robert Alito, another conservative U.S Court of Appeals judge, was then nominated to fill the seat vacated when Justice O'Connor retired.

41. Quoted in Sheryl Gay Stolberg, "Nominee Is Pressed on End-of-Life Care," *New York Times*, August 10, 2005, A1.

42. Mike Allen, "Counsel to GOP Senator Wrote Memo on Schiavo," *Washington Post*, April 7, 2005, 1.

43. Ibid.

44. MSNBC.com, April 26, 2007, at www.MSNBC.com.

45. Didion, "The Case of Theresa Schiavo." 10. The majority of Americans, however, "saw a gross example of legislative opportunism, a clear example of the power of the religious right too influence legislation." Ibid.

46. Cal Thomas, "St. Theresa Schiavo," *Jewish World Review*, April 1, 2005, at www. jewishworldreview.com.

47. Quoted in Allen, "Counsel to GOP Senator Wrote Memo on Schiavo," 1.

48. Colby, *Long Goodbye*, 381–383.

49. The researchers examined over 1,000 articles and more than 400 letters in the *New York Times,* the *Washington Post,* the *Tampa Tribune,* and the *St. Petersburg Times.* In *Neurology*, September 23, 2005, at www.physorg.com.

50. Ibid.

51. Ibid., 401.

52. Sylvia A. Law, "A Political and Constitutional Context," in Timothy E. Quill and Margaret P. Battin, eds., *Physician-Assisted Dying: The Case for Palliative Care and Patient Choice*, Baltimore, MD: The Johns Hopkins University Press, 2004, 302.

53. In 1991, the Washington Initiative, Ballot Initiative 119, was rejected by a vote of 54:46. In 1992 California voters defeated Proposition 191, the California Death with Dignity Act, by the same 54:46 margin. If passed, the California initiative would have allowed doctors to hasten death by either passively (writing a prescription for barbiturates) or actively (administering a drug such as morphine) assisting in the suicide of a terminally ill, tormented patient.

NOTES TO CHAPTER 4

1. Mike Wallace said of Kevorkian: "I've learned that the conventional wisdom about him was wrong. Fanatic? No. Zealot? Yes." Mike Wallace, "A Note on Dr. Kevorkian and Timothy McVeigh," 48 *New York Review of Books* 11, July 5, 2001, at www.newyorkreviewofbooks.com.
2. Humphry established the Hemlock Society in 1980. He repeatedly asserted that PAD legislation was only the first step and that "when people become comfortable with this form of assisted dying, we may be able to go to the second step, which is euthanasia."
3. Battin, *Least Worst Death*, 101–103. Battin also discusses another principle, *justice*, which is fulfilled when a physician terminates a *non-competent* patient in a PVS. See also Margaret P. Battin and Timothy E. Quill, "The Argument over Physician-Assisted Dying," in *Physician-Assisted Dying*, 5–8.
4. Anonymous, "It's over, Debbie," 259 *JAMA* 272, 1988.
5. The oath in part, states: "I will give no deadly medicine to anyone if asked, nor suggest any such counsel."
6. Jack Kevorkian, *Prescription: Medicide—The Goodness of Planned Death,* Buffalo, NY: Prometheus Books, 1991, 160.
7. According to a news report, the Mercitron killed in the following manner. Kevorkian would "insert an intravenous tube into the arm of the patient, [and] drip saline solution through it. Then the patient would push a button that stopped the saline and replaced it with *thiopental,* which caused unconsciousness. After a minute, the machine switched solutions again, to *potassium chloride,* which stopped the heart and brought death in minutes." Lisa Belkin, "Doctor Tells of First Death Using His Suicide Device," *New York Times,* June 6, 1990, A1.
8. Kevorkian, Prescription, 195–196.
9. Note, "The Mercitron," *Detroit Free Press Magazine,* March 18, 1992, 24.
10. Ibid.
11. Belkin, "Doctor Tells of First Death," A1.
12. Ibid.
13. Jack Kevorkian, speech, University of Florida, January 17, 2008, at www.vitabeat.com.
14. James Vicini, "Kevorkian Murder Conviction Upheld [*sic*] by U.S. Supreme Court," *CareCure Forums,* October 7, 2002, at www.sci.rutgers.edu.

15. Quoted in Dirk Johnson, "Kevorkian Sentenced to 10 to 25 Years in Prison," *New York Times*, April 14, 1999, A1.

16. Quoted in ibid.

17. Letter is reprinted in "A Letter From Dr. Kevorkian," *New York Review of Books,* July 5, 2001.

18. Timothy E. Quill, "Death and Dignity: A Case for Individualized Decision Making," 324 *NEJM* 691–694, 1991, at 691. In 1994 Quill's book, *Death and Dignity: Making Choices and Taking Charge* (New York: Norton), was published. It was an expansion of the ideas he wrote about in the *NEJM* article.

19. In all PAD proposed legislation, the advocates urged the policy for implementation by terminally ill patients only.

20. AP, "Assisted Suicide Laws State By State," at www.infonet.com. The reason for these anti-PAD state statutes goes back hundreds of years. At one time, in England and the colonies, suicide was a criminal offence. In the nineteenth century, suicide was decriminalized. However, criminal punishment statutes remained for those who aided a suicidal person to kill herself.

21. N.E.H. Hull and Peter Charles Hoffer, *Roe v Wade: The Abortion Rights Controversy in American History*, Lawrence: University Press of Kansas, 2001.

22. 505 U.S. 833 (1992).

23. 850 F. Supp. 1454 (W.D. Wash., 1994).

24. *Quill et al. v Koppell et al.*, 870 F. Supp (S.D.N.Y., 1994).

25. Susan M. Behuniak and Arthur G. Svenson, *Physician Assisted Suicide: The Anatomy of a Constitutional Law Issue*, Lanham, MD: Rowman and Littlefield, 2002, 63.

26. *Bowers v Hardwick*, 1986.

27. *McCleskey v Kemp*, 1989.

28. Circuit Judge Noonan, a devout Catholic, has written a number of books on intimate and personal issues. In 1968 he wrote *Contraception*, and in 1970 he wrote *The Morality of Abortion*.

29. *Compassion in Dying et al. v Washington et al.*, 49 F. 3d 586 (CA9, 1995).

30. *Compassion in Dying et al. v Washington et al.*, 79 F. 3d 790 (CA9, 1996).

31. *Quill et al. v Vacco et al.*, 80 F.3d. 716 (CA2, 1996). Since the 1994 trial, New York State elected a new attorney general, Dennis Vacco, and his name was put in as the defendant in the state's appeal to the CA2.

32. When the two vacancies occurred in 2005, there had been absolutely no change in personnel on the Court since Justice Steven Breyer took his seat on the High Bench in 1994. These two vacancies gave a very conservative Republican president, George W. Bush, the opportunity to bring onto the Court two bright and very conservative replacements: Chief Justice John Roberts (who filled Rehnquist's center seat) and Associate Justice Robert Alito (who replaced Sandra Day O'Connor).

33. See Richard E. Coleson, "The *Glucksberg* and *Quill Amicus Curiae* Briefs," 13 *Issues in Law and Medicine* 3, Summer 1997.

34. See Howard Ball, *The Supreme Court in the Intimate Lives of Americans*, New York: NYU Press, 2002, 2004.

35. The First Amendment states, in part, that "Congress [and the states] shall make no law respecting an establishment of religion."

36. Double effect is a process employed by doctors across the world. When a patient is dying and in great pain, the physician will order an enhanced quantity of morphine or some other barbiturate to end the pain, even though, in so doing, the patient may die because of the overdose. The primary goal is the relief of pain.

37. Jenifer Mattos, "Court Skeptical About Assisted Suicide," *Time*, January 8, 1997.

38. Scholars will get all the insight about these secret deliberations and writings once one of the sitting justices' papers are made available to the public in the LOC or another library. To date, only Chief Justice Rehnquist, of the nine who participated, has died, although the final disposition of his papers (1972–2005) is not yet known. Associate Justice Sandra Day O'Connor has retired but her papers have not been made available at this time.

39. Behuniak and Svenson, *Physician-Assisted Suicide*, 134.

40. A *facial challenge* is an argument, claim, or lawsuit that a law or government policy always operates in violation of the U.S. Constitution or a state constitution.

41. *United States v Salerno*, 481 U.S. 739, 745 (1987).

42. An *as-applied* challenge alleges that the statute may be, in part, unconstitutional, in redress of specific and particular injury.

43. Behuniak and Svenson, *Physician-Assisted Suicide*, 134.

44. Justice O'Connor's important concurrence, as will be seen, agreed with Rehnquist that there was no generalized right to assist a person to commit suicide. However, she believed that the important question of "whether a mentally competent person who is experiencing great suffering has a cognizable interest in controlling the circumstances of his or her imminent death" was not decided in these decisions of the Court because all the patients/plaintiffs who raised the question died.

45. In n. 23 of *Washington v Glucksberg*, Rehnquist cited a number of *amicus* briefs that were used by him when he drafted this segment of the opinion, including the Brief for the United States, Brief for Not Dead Yet, Brief for Bioethics Professors, Brief for the New York Task Force on Bioethics, and the AMA *amicus* brief.

46. Since the 1920s, U.S. Supreme Court majorities have ruled, in Equal Protection litigation, that if a challenge to a statute is brought by a suspect class, alleging that the law is an "invidious" discrimination based on the suspect cohort's race, or ethnicity, or religion, then the legal presumption is that the challenged statute is unconstitutional. The burden falls on the government, whether federal or state, to show that the statute is not a form of discriminatory behavior directed against that suspect class.

47. "Strict scrutiny" analysis of a challenged "state action" occurs when the state's discrimination is based on a person's race, or color, or religion, or national origin *or* when its actions infringe upon a known *fundamental right*. In such cases, the government, *not the petitioner*, carries the very difficult burden of proof to justify the constitutionality of its actions.

48. At this point in the opinion, Rehnquist spoke about the *legitimate intent* of a physician who provides *terminal sedation* to a terminally ill, competent patient. "When a doctor provides aggressive palliative care, in some cases, *painkilling drugs may hasten a patient's death*, but the physician's *purpose and intent* is, *or maybe*, only to ease his patient's pain. A doctor who assists a suicide, however, must, necessarily and indubitably, *intend primarily* that the patient be made dead." *Vacco v Quill.*

49. Souter's methodical path was to determine whether substantive due process recognized limits to the state's authority to restrain the unenumerated liberty interest a dying person has to hasten death that respondents claimed in their challenges. Was that right an aspect of "ordered liberty," was it a part of "a continuum of rights to be free from arbitrary impositions and purposeless restraints" (Souter quoting from *Poe v Ullman*, 1961, Harlan, dissenting).

50. David Orentlicher, "The Supreme Court and Physician-Assisted Suicide: Rejecting Assisted Suicide but Embracing Euthanasia," 337 *NEMJ* 1233–1239, October 23, 1997. Terminal Sedation (TS) is a heavy sedation that places the patient "in a sleep-like state in the last days of life to prevent the patient from experiencing severe pain" (1234).

51. The pain is probably caused "by cancer that has metastasized to the spine, intestinal obstruction, and headache due to massive intracerebral edema." Ibid., at 1235.

52. See Anemona Hartocollis, "Hard Choice for a Comfortable Death: Drug-Induced Sleep," *New York Times*, December 27, 2009, A1. It was a story that examined TS in the hospice unit at a hospital in Valley Stream, New York. "People were sleeping, but not like babies. It was the sleep before—and sometimes until—death."

53. *Washington v Glucksberg, Vacco v Quill*, Stevens concurring in the judgments; in Brock, n. 11, Stevens uses the results of medical studies described in Brock, n. 105, below.

54. Dan W. Brock, "PAD as a Last-Resort Option at the end of Life," in Battin and Quill, *Physician-Assisted Dying*," 134–135. See for example A.L. Beck, et al., "PAD and Euthanasia in Washington State: Patient Requests and Physician Responses," 275 *JAMA* 919–925, 1996; and M.A. Lee et al., "Legalizing Assisted Suiide: Views of Physicians in Oregon," 334 *NEJM* 310–315, 1996.

55. As chapter 5 shows, efforts to legitimatize PAD have continued in a number of states. Most of these grassroots organizations' hard work has fallen fate to the intense lobbying of anti-PAD groups, including the major medical and nursing associations, disability support groups, the Catholic Church, and other vicissitudes of the political process.

NOTES TO CHAPTER 5

1. *Washington v Glucksberg,* 521 U.S. at 789 (Souter concurring).

2. Quoted in Joan Biskupic, "Unanimous Decision Points to Tradition of Valuing Life," *Washington Post,* June 27, 1997, A01.

3. Carol M. Ostrum, "Initiative 1000 Would Let Patients Get Help Ending Their Lives," *Seattle Times,* September 21, 2008, A1.

4. See Jennifer S. Termel et al., "Early Palliative Care for Patients with Metastatic Non-Small-Cell Lung Cancer," 363 *NEJM* 733–742, August 19, 2010. The researchers found that "early palliative care led to significant improvements in both quality of life and mood. . . . [They] had less aggressive care at the end of life but longer survival."

5. Editorial, "Palliative Care—A New Paradigm," 363 *NEJM,* August 19, 2010.

6. In the *Code,* Opinion E-2.211 defines PAD as a practice that "occurs when a physician *facilitates a patient's death by providing the necessary means* and/or information to enable the patient to perform the life-ending act."

7. In the *Code,* Opinion E-2.211, euthanasia is defined as "the *administration* of a lethal agent by another person to a patient for the purpose of relieving the patient's intolerable and incurable suffering."

8. Mark A. Levine, "Sedation to Unconsciousness in End-of-Life Care," *Report of the Council on Ethical and Judicial Affairs, AMA,* CEJA Report 5-A-08, 2. See also *AMA Code of Medical Ethics,* Chicago: AMA, 2006, at www.ama-assn. org.

9. Burker J. Balch, J.D., Director of the National Right to Life Committee Department of Medical Ethics," www. nrlc.org.

10. Ibid.

11. See Felicia Cohn and Joanne Lynn, "Vulnerable People: Practical Rejoinders to Claims in Favor of Assisted Suicide," in Kathleen Foley and Herbert Hendin, editors, *The Case Against Assisted Suicide: For the Right to End-of-Life Care,* Baltimore, MD: Johns Hopkins Press, 2004, 238ff.

12. Foley and Hendin, "Introduction," in *The Case Against Assisted Suicide,* 13.

13. Neil M. Gorsuch, *The Future of Assisted Suicide and Euthanasia,* Princeton, NJ: Princeton University Press, 2006, p. 126.

14. Eli D. Stutsman, "Political Strategy and Legal Change," in Battin and Quill, *Physician-Assisted Dying,* 259.

15. James M. Hoefler, *Managing Death: The First Guide for Patients, Family Members, and Care Providers on Forgoing Treatment at the End of Life,* Boulder, CO: Westview Press, 1997, 62.

16. In the United States, 23.9 percent of Americans are Roman Catholic; followed by 10.8 percent who are Evangelical Baptists (although the total Evangelical Protestant Church membership in America is 26.3 percent, including, in addition to the Baptists, Methodists, Lutherans, Presbyterians, and Pentecostals,

and Mainline Protestant Church membership is 18.1 percent). Pew Forum on
Religion and Public Life/U.S. Religious Landscape Survey, "Religious Composition of the U.S.," September 2008, at www.pewforum.com

17. Ibid.

18. See Melvin Urofsky, *Lethal Judgments: Assisted Suicide and American Law*,
Lawrence, KS.: University Press of Kansas, 2000, 17–22.

19. Hoefler, *Managing Death.*, 66.

20. Ibid., 67–69.

21. See, for example, website of *Religious Coalition for Reproductive Choice*, www.
rcrc.org.

22. Generally, the *initiative* and the *referendum* are examples of direct democracy.
For some states, they are rights written into state constitutions They are political
processes that allow citizens in a state to vote *directly* on particular pieces of
legislation. The *initiative* allows citizens to propose or initiate a statute or
constitutional amendment. A *referendum* process allows citizens to refer a statute
already passed by the legislature to the ballot so that voters could either enact or
repeal the bill. See www.ballotpedia.org.

23. The Hemlock Society was founded in 1980. Its twofold mission was to (a)
provide information to dying persons who were considering hastening their
ends; and (b) to pass legislation permitting physician-assisted death with
accompanying guidelines to prevent abuse. It was the first such death-assistance
organization in America.

24. George J. Annas, "Death By Prescription," 331 *NEJM* 18, 1240–1243, November
3, 1994, at 1240.

25. Eli T. Stutsman, "Political Strategy and Legal Change," in Battin and Quill,
Physician-Assisted Dying, 246.

26. Ibid.

27. Kathryn L. Tucker, "In the Laboratory of the States: The Progress of *Glucksberg's*
Invitation to States to Address End-of-Life Choice," 106 *Michigan Law Review*
1593, June 2008, at 1609ff.

28. Ibid., 1609–1610.

29. "For example," wrote Tucker, "there is a much higher chance of an extended
time until death after consuming lethal medications under covert practice.
Moreover, the stress and anxiety for the patient and family is much higher when
no physician can legally be involved to counsel the patient and family and
provide the prescription for medications." Ibid., 1610.

30. Ibid., 1241.

31. Stutsman, "Political Strategy," 258.

32. Daniel Hillyard and John Dombrink, *Dying Right: The Death With Dignity
Movement*, New York: Routledge, 2001, 47–48.

33. Ibid., 259.

34. Tucker, "In the Laboratory," at 1243.

35. Included in this cohort were numerous Catholic Health Care facilities and the California State Council of the Knights of Columbus, *Not included* in the final financial tally were the small donations from millions of Catholic parishioners. These donations "were instead mixed in with other anonymous donations under $100." Hillyard and Dombrink, *Dying Right*, 59–60.
36. Stutsman, "Political Strategy," 251.
37. Chapter 6 focuses on the events in Oregon, from 1994 to 1997, that led to passage of the Oregon Death with Dignity Act (ODWDA) and to efforts by Republicans in Washington, DC, from 1998 to 2005, to dismember the ODWDA.
38. Every year since 2003, Representative Linda Lopez has introduced legislation similar to the Oregon Death with Dignity Act. Her latest effort, HB 2387, was introduced in January 2008. The bill died in committee, without the chairperson ever calling for a public hearing on the PAD bill. The chairperson of the House Health Committee, Representative Doug Quelland, continued to block any hearings on the bill.
39. Republican Senator Andrew Roraback introduced a bill that would allow individuals accused of assisting a patient to die to be eligible for a special form of probation, known as "accelerated rehabilitation (AR)." This is a program that gives persons charged with a crime or motor vehicle violation—for the first time—a second chance. The person is placed on probation for up to two years. If probation is completed satisfactorily, the charges are dismissed. Roraback's bill would allow first-time offenders to have their criminal records expunged after a probation period ends. If passed, it would replace PA 98-208, which excluded people charged with a number of crimes from being eligible for AR, such as those charged with second-degree manslaughter (which includes causing or aiding a person to commit suicide). The Judiciary Committee in both houses agreed to consider the bill in committee in 2007. However, the bill failed due to lobbying by the Catholic Church.
40. In 1998 Proposal B was introduced. It was a "prescribing only" PAD, modeled after the Oregon legislation. Financial support from the Roman Catholic Church for anti-PAD actions was $2,173,330, or 38 percent of the total spent by opponents of the legislation. The grassroots supporters of the bill were no match for the professionals lined up to defeat the bill. Scholars believe that even if Dr. Kevorkian's actions had not appeared in the national media, Proposition B, which lost by an overwhelming margin, 29:71, would still have failed. Stutsman, "Political Strategy and Legal Change," 252–253.
41. Two legislators, Sen. Fred Risser and Rep. Frank Boyle, have tried sixteen times, since 1997, to have a Wisconsin Death with Dignity bill (SB151 and AB 298) acted on by the legislature. For ten years, however, no bill they introduced has gotten to the vote stage in either the state assembly or the state senate. For only the second time, however, in January 2008, the senate version did have a public hearing—but no further action was taken.

42. In addition to the ten states mentioned, the following eight states saw PAD actions introduced and defeated in the legislative branch: Maryland (2009); Massachusetts (2010); Montana (2009, PAD ban bill introduced in 2010); New Hampshire (2010); New Mexico (2010); New York (2010); Pennsylvania (2009); Wyoming, PAD ban bill (2009), See "Living with Dying," *Death with Dignity National Center*, August 2011. www.ddnc.com. See Also Kevin O'Reilly, "Oregon Still Stands Alone: Ten Years of Physician-Assisted Suicide," *American Medical News*, May 12, 2008, at www.amednews.com.

43. Valerie Vollmar, ed., *Recent Developments in Physician-Assisted Death*, October 2005, at www.willamette.edu.

44. Ibid.

45. Vollmar, *Recent Developments*, October 2006, at www.willamette.edu.

46. Frank D. Russo, "'California Compassionate Choices Act' Modeled on Oregon Law, Dies in Committee," *California Progress Report: The Daily Briefing for Politics, Policy, and Progressive Action*, Sacramento, CA.: June 27, 2006, 1. (It was noted in the Russo piece that Dunn "consulted with his Bishop before the vote.")

47. Vollmar, *Recent Developments*, February 2007, at www.willamette.edu.

48. CCC, "No on AB 374: California Compassionate Choices Act," Catholic Lobby Day, 2007, at www.cacatholic.org.

49. Ibid.

50. Thomistic@ccatholic.org.

51. Vollmar, *Recent Developments*, February 2008, at www.willamette.edu.

52. Ibid.

53. CCC, "No on AB 2747: End of Life Care," Catholic Lobby Day, 2008, at www.cacatholic.org.

54. The act is the first in the nation to provide terminally ill patients with a full disclosure of, and counseling about, all available end-of-life care options accepted in law and medicine. When requested, information about hospice care, refusal or withdrawing of life-prolonging treatments, voluntary stopping eating and drinking (VSED), palliative care and palliative sedation are discussed with the patient. The act also requires that health care providers who do not wish to comply with a particular patient's request must refer or transfer the patient to another provider. The law went into effect for Californians on January 1, 2009. See www.compassionandchoicesca.org.

55. Quoted in "Hawaii Becomes First State to Approve Medical Marijuana Bill," *New York Times*, June 15, 2000. www.nyt.com.

56. See Benjamin J. Cayetano, "Mom," *Honolulu Magazine*, December 2006, www.honolulumagazine.com.

57. These groups included the Hawaii Advocates for Consumer Rights; American Civil Liberties Union; First Unitarian Church of Honolulu; Free Thinkers Maui; Hemlock Society Hawai'i ; Humanists Hawai'i; the Kokua Council of

Seniors; members of Hawaii's medical and legal communities; several highly
regarded members of the Hawai'i League of Women Voters; the Drug Policy
Forum of Hawai'i, and the Governor's Blue Ribbon Panel on Living and Dying
with Dignity.

58. www.capitol.hawaii.gov/session2002/status/HB2487.asp.

59. See L. Benoit's account of the switch of the three senators in "State Senate Re-
jects Physician-Assisted Suicide Bill on Final Day of Session," *Hawaii Catholic
Herald*, May 10, 2002, 1. See also www.capitol.hawaii.gov/session2002/status/
HB2487.asp.

60. Stutsman, "Political Strategy and Legal Change," 253–254. "In the dark of night
on May 1, 2002, the former Chair of the Democratic Party of Hawai'i, Catholic
Deacon Richard Port Killed *Death With Dignity* in Hawai'i." Deacon Port ac-
complished this deed by carrying a letter from Hawaii's Roman Catholic bishop
Francis X. DiLorenzo around to the Catholic Members of the State Legislature
the night before the final Senate vote—causing three critical votes to change and
the 2002 Death With Dignity legislation to fail. The bill had already passed the
full House. Convinced by Port, who used the shameful excuse that "the legislation would compromise the 2002 elections," the then Democratic Party chair,
Lorraine Akiba accompanied and aided Port's clandestine mission. The bishop's
letter, stated in part that:

> No one should underestimate the weight of the moral issue the state Senate
> now faces. Not only Catholic moral teaching, but the founding principles
> of our nation, recognize the unalienable right to life as the first and most
> fundamental right bestowed on us by our Creator. We have always held that
> with regard to the value and dignity of human life, each person—and each
> citizen of our nation and our fine state—is the equal of any other. With one
> vote, our Senate could carve out a very disturbing exception to that principle,
> by declaring that one vulnerable class of our citizens can legally be "assisted" to
> their deaths by lethal drug overdose.
>
> We should not fall victim to the easy euphemism that by so doing, the
> legislature would only be granting these citizens their "freedom of choice."
> Presumably we would continue to respond to suicidal "choices" made by all
> other citizens by seeking to prevent those suicides and address the real prob-
> lems underlying such a despairing choice. No, our state government would be
> making its own policy decision that the lives of certain sick or disabled citizens
> are not as worth living, not as worth protecting, as the lives of all others. We
> would be making our own "choice" as a society that some people's suicides
> are objectively better or more valid than others. And we would be making
> that dismissive policy decision, in advance, about an entire class of vulnerable
> patients who generally are not seeking aid in suicide or legislation like this.

"Who Killed Death With Dignity?" www.compassionatechoiceshawaii.org.

61. Vollmar, *Recent Developments*, June 2004, at www.willamette.edu.

62. See, for example, stories and editorials in the *Honolulu Star Bulletin*, March 18, 2007, and the *Honolulu Advertiser*, March 4, 2007.

63. Vollmar, *Recent Developments*, June 2000, at www.willamette.edu.

64. See "Come From Behind Victory Against Maine Assisting Suicide Referendum Elates Anti-Euthanasia Forces, www.nlrc.org.

65. www.nightingdalealliance.org.

66. *Mission Statement*, Patient Choices at End of Life—Vermont, at www.patien-tchoices.com.

67. Ibid.

68. Within months, other organizations voiced their opposition to PAD legislation. These included the Vermont State Nurses Association, the Vermont Coalition for Disability rights, the Vermont Chapter of the American Cancer Society, and the Hospice and Palliative Care Association of Vermont. Vollmar, *Recent Developments*, March 2004, at www.willamette.edu.

69. Quoted in Jean Szilva, MD, "Patients' Rights First; Doctors' Second," *Burlington Free Press* (Vermont), October 14, 2008, 5A.

70. Even supporters of PAD legislation in Vermont admit that palliative care and hospice are not adequate in Vermont. Dick Walters, the president of Death With Dignity—Vermont, stated that "according to national statistics, Vermont appears in the bottom tier of hospice penetration (22%) which is much lower than the national average (36%) and we are improving that more slowly than most states." Letter to the editor, "Vermont Deserves Credit for Debate," *Bennington Banner*, April 6, 2007.

71. Mission Statement for VAEH, at www. vaeh.org.

72. The national Hemlock Society became Death With Dignity, and then, in 2004, it became End-of Life Choices. That organization then merged with another national pro-PAD group, Compassion in Dying, to form a new combined nation-wide organization, Compassion and Choice, with chapters located in many states. This new organization, with the National Death With Dignity organization, are the two major national pro-PAD organizations that plan strategy and tactics for the numerous state battles fought since 1997.

73. "We will be sending DVD copies [of a sixty-minute film] to all Vermont legislators, the media, and others. This was done," wrote Dr. Orr, in *Newsletter 35*, October 16, 2005, "with the generous help of the film crew from the Office of Communications at the Catholic Diocese."

74. Vollmar, *Recent Developments*, February 2005, at www.willamette.edu.

75. Quoted in John Schwartz and James Estrin, "In Vermont, a Bid to Legalize Physician-Assisted Suicide," *New York Times*, March 30, 2005, A01.

76. Quoted in Ibid.

77. Vollmar, *Recent Developments*, October 2007, at www.willamette.edu.

78. Vermont's then-governor, Republican Jim Douglas, was opposed to *any* PAD legislation and threatened to veto any PAD bill that came to his desk.

79. Bob Orr, *VAEH Newsletter 44*, March 21, 2007. "Do you know who caused this shift? You did. By your many letters to the editor, by your phone calls, e-mails, and personal contacts with your Representatives, and by your generous donations."

80. Interview posted, December 7, 2010, on Death with Dignity National Center (DWDNC), www.dwdnc.org. See also Andy Bromage, "With a New Governor in Power, Will Vermonters Finally Win their 'Right to Die'?" *Seven Days*, January 12, 2011. http://www.7dvt.com. In December 2010, Shumlin met with the DWDNC executive director, Peg Sandeen.

81. "They have reason to believe right-to-die legislation could win passage this year, despite anticipated opposition from medical professionals, religious groups and disability rights advocates who warn that PAD is a slippery slope." Ibid.

82. The National Right to Life (NRTL), "NRTL Responds to Ruling on Gonzales v Oregon, January 17, 2006, at www.nrlc.org/press_releases_new/Release011706.html.

83. Letters, "Death in the Family," *New York Times Sunday Magazine*, December 9, 2007, 18.

84. Bob Orr, President, VAEH, *VAEH Newsletter 45*, February 6, 2008. In *Newsletter 28*, January 6, 2005, Orr wrote: "We continue to be in contact with our counterparts in Oregon, Hawaii, and California." The fear expressed by Dr. Orr in this and other newsletters was that "if a second state steps in line with Oregon, others will likely follow. We must do our utmost to prevent this from happening in Vermont."

85. Foley, "Compassionate Care, Not Assisted Suicide," 295.

86. Nikki Crutchfield, *To Succeed or Not to Succeed: How Do Political Influences, Culture, and Demographics Affect the Passing of Physician-Assisted Suicide Initiatives?* PhD diss., Auburn University, December 15, 2008. www.etdhelp@auburn.edu.

NOTES TO CHAPTER 6

1. Art Levine, "In Oregon, A Political Campaign to Die For," *U.S. News and World Report*, November 10, 1997, 56.

2. Quoted in Carol M. Ostrum, "Initiative 1000 Would Let Patients Get Help Ending Their Lives," *Seattle Times*, September 21, 2008, 1. See also Daniel Bergner, "Death in the Family," *New York Times Magazine*, December 2, 2007.

3. Judge McCarter asked the question during oral argument in *Baxter v Montana* in October 2008. Quoted in "Judge: Assisted Suicide is Legal Right, *Billings Gazette*, December 6, 2008.

4. Hillyard and Dombrink, *Dying Right*, 70.

5. Ibid., 71. "Says Mary Jo Tully, a religious educator who serves as chancellor for the archdiocese of Portland, in Oregon: 'This diocese does not have the human resources of the larger and more Catholic archdioceses.'"

6. Oregon Revised Statute, Sections 127.800-897.

7. Ibid., 1241.
8. Hillyard and Dombrink, *Dying Right*, 97. "Humphry reluctantly conceded that *any* level of lawful assisted suicide would be better than the *status quo*, so he agreed not to enter the meetings without invitation."
9. Ibid., 167ff. The ODWDA mandated that the OHD involvement in the creation of "rules to facilitate the collection of information regarding compliance with the Act [and to] annually review a sample of records maintained pursuant to the Act." ODWDA, Section 127.865.
10. The "standing to sue" question is a critical threshold one in a judicial proceeding. "Standing identifies *who* may bring claims that some governmental action violates the Constitution. Stated generally, people have standing to challenge a governmental action only if they are injured by the action." Kermit L. Hall, ed., *The Oxford Companion to the Supreme Court*, New York: Oxford University Press, 1992, 819. See also *Ballentine's Law Dictionary*, Rochester, NY: Lawyer's Cooperative, 1969, 1209.
11. *Lee v State of Oregon*, D.C. No. CV-94-06467-MRH (1994) Nos. 95-35804, -35805, -35854, 95-35949, CA9 (2005), 3.
12. Ibid., 5.
13. Ibid., 5–6.
14. Linda Greenhouse, "Assisted Suicide Clears a Hurdle in Highest Court," *New York Times*, October 14, 1997, A1.
15. Ibid.
16. David J. Garrow, "The Oregon Trail," *New York Times*, November 6, 1997, A 26.
17. Art Levine, "In Oregon, A Political Campaign to Die For," *U.S. News and World Report*, November 10, 1997, 56.
18. Ibid.
19. Ibid.
20. Ibid., 57.
21. Tim Hibbits, quoted in ibid., 57.
22. Ibid., 57, 56.
23. Garrow, "The Oregon Trail," A 26. He observed that the act survived "in the face of the multi-million-dollar media onslaught mounted by supporters of repeal. In addition to the well-heeled opponents—the Oregon Catholic Conference and Oregon Right to Life—the state's dominant newspaper, *The Oregonian*, vociferously championed repeal."
24. The CSA was a comprehensive bill introduced in 1970 by President Richard M. Nixon to try to deal with America's emergent illicit narcotics and dangerous drug problems. The CSA became law in 1970 as Title II of the Comprehensive Drug Abuse Prevention and Control Act of 1970. The new law reflected the regulatory policy of the nation regarding the manufacture, importation, possession, and distribution of five sets of drugs regulators considered dangerous.

25. The Pew Forum on Religion and Public Life, *Legal Backgrounder*, "Supreme Court Considers Challenge to Oregon's Death with Dignity Act, September 2005, 1, at www.pewforum.org.

26. Annas, "Death by Prescription," 1242.

27. After the November 1994 elections, the Republicans controlled both Houses of Congress. The Party retained control of both houses until 2003, when Republican U.S. Senator Jim Jeffords (R-VT) switched allegiance and became an Independent. His action gave the Democrats in the Senate a one-vote margin until the 2004 election. After the mid-term elections of 2006, the Democrats took control of the House of Representatives and narrowly controlled the U.S. Senate.

28. Letter reprinted in U.S. Senate *Report* No. 105-372, 7 (1998).

29. Letter, at www.house.gov/judiciary/constantine/htm>.

30. Quoted in Ibid., 7.

31. Letter, Reno to Hyde and Hatch, June 5, 1998, at www.house.gov/judiciary/attygen.htm.

32. Reprinted in Behuniak and Svenson, *Physician-Assisted Suicide*, 177. See also www.nrlc.org

33. HR 4006/ S 2151.

34. William J. Clinton, "Statement upon Signing the Assisted Suicide Funding Restriction Act of 1997," in *Public Papers of Presidents of the United States: William J. Clinton, Book 1*, 515. Washington, DC, Government Printing Office, 1997.

35. Quoted in Hillyard and Dombrink, *Dying Right*, 180–181.

36. *Pain Relief Promotion Act of 1999* (Introduced in Senate by U.S. Senator Don Nickles), S 1272 IS, 106th Cong., 1st sess., June 23, 1999.

37. *Pain and the Law*, American Society of Law, Medicine, and Ethics, at www.aslme.com.

38. AMA Legal Analysis of the Hyde-Nickles PRPA of 1999, at www.ama.org

39. Quoted in Hillyard and Dombrink, *Dying Right*, 204.

40. This group was a coalition of health organizations and, according to researchers, was "one key" to the eventual failure of the Hyde/Nickles legislation. Hillyard and Dombrink, *Dying Right*, 182.

41. "ANA Opposes Pain Relief Act," *Nursing*, July 1, 2000, 63.

42. Quoted in Behuniak and Svenson, *Physician-Assisted Suicide*, 190–191.

43. His administration's Solicitor General Dellinger had spoken and written briefs against PAD in the two cases, *Glucksberg* and *Vacco*, argued in the U.S. Supreme Court in 1997.

44. See, generally, Howard Gillman, *The Votes That Counted: How the Court Decided the 2000 Presidential Election*, Chicago: University of Chicago Press, 2001.

45. Subject: "Dispensing of Controlled Substances to Assist Suicide," November 6, 2001, in *66 Federal Register* 56, 607.

46. OLC Opinion, "Whether PAD Serves a 'Legitimate Medical Purpose' Under the DEA's Regulations Implementing the CSA," June 27, 2001.

47. Office of the Attorney General, Subject: "Dispensing of Controlled Substances to Assist Suicide," November 6, 2001, in 66 *Federal Register* 56, 607.

48. Edward Lowenstein, MD, and Sidney H. Wanzer, MD, *Sounding Board*, "The U.S. Attorney General's Intrusion into Medical Practice," 346 *NEJM* 447–448, February 7, 2002.

49. Pew Forum, *Legal Backgrounder*, 2.

50. *State of Oregon v John Ashcroft et al.*, No. CIV. 01-1647-JO, U.S. District Court, April 17, 2002.

51. Ibid., Introduction, 1.

52. *Oregon v John Ashcroft et al.*, On Appeal from the U.S. District Court for the District of Oregon, Brief for Appellants, 1.

53. *Oregon v Ashcroft*, 368 *F 3rd* 1118 (2004), 1119. Technically, Judge Tallman wrote, the CA9 (and all the other federal circuit courts of appeal) "have original jurisdiction over 'final determinations, findings, and conclusions of the Attorney General' made under the CSA. . . . Although we conclude that the district court did not have jurisdiction, Judge Jones' opinion on the merits is well reasoned, and we ultimately adopt many of his conclusions." At 1119, and at 1119, n. 1.

54. Ibid., 1123.

55. Ibid., 1125.

56. *Gonzalez v Oregon*, 9, 10.

57. Ibid., 10.

58. Ibid., 11.

59. Ibid., 20.

60. *Auer* was an administrative law decision involving what constituted a "permissible reading" of a section in a federal statute, the 1938 Fair Labor Standards Act (FLSA). The majority deferred to the judgment of the Department of Labor.

61. *Chevron* was another administrative law decision regarding a congressional bill, the 1977 Amendments to the Clean Air Act, which imposed certain require-ments on states that did not reach national air quality standards established by the U.S. Environmental Protection Agency. The Supreme Court deferred to the EPA's interpretation of the amendments.

62. *Gonzales v Oregon*, Scalia dissenting opinion, 546 U.S. (2006), 1–2.

63. *Gonzales v Oregon*, Thomas dissenting opinion, 546 U.S. (2006), 1.

64. Ibid., 1.

65. Ibid., 4.

66. Linda Greenhouse, "Justices Reject U.S. Bid to Block Assisted Suicide," *New York Times*, January 18, 2006, A1.

67. Editorial, "The Assisted-Suicide Decision," *New York Times*, January 19, 2006, A26.

68. A *Not Dead Yet* press release explained the organization's anti-PAD stance: "The disability experience is that people who are labeled 'terminal,' are—or almost inevitably will become—disabled. Furthermore, virtually all 'end-of-life care' issues—access to competent health care, adequate pain relief, [etc.]—have been disability rights issues for decades." www.ndy.org..

69. Dorothy Timbs, "National Right to Life Responds to Ruling on *Gonzales v Oregon, National Right to Life*, January 17, 2006, at www.nrlc.org/press_releases_new.

70. Quoted in Greenhouse, "Justices Reject U.S. Bid to Block Assisted Suicide," A1.

71. Arthur E. Chin et al., *Oregon's Death with Dignity Act: The First Year's Experience,* Oregon DHS, OHD, Center For Disease Prevention and Epidemiology, February 18, 1999, 9.

72. Ibid., 8.

73. Ibid.

74. Ibid., 9.

75. Ibid., 4–6.

76. In the report analyzing the second year of ODWDA implementation, the authors noted that, hypothetically, each physician's report to the OHD "could have been a cock-and-bull story." Sullivan et al, *Legalized PAS in Oregon—the Second Year*, DHR, OHD, Center for Disease Prevention and Epidemiology, March 2008, 5.

77. Chin et al., *Oregon's Death with Dignity Act*, 4.

78. Ibid., 4.

79. John Keown, *Euthanasia, Ethics, and Public Policy: An Argument Against Legislation*, Cambridge: Cambridge University Press, 2002, 171–172.

80. Wesley J. Smith, *Forced Exit: The Slippery Slope from Assisted Suicide to Legalized Murder*, New York: New York Times Books, 1999.

81. Sam Howe Verhovek, "Oregon Reporting 15 Deaths in 1998 Under Suicide Law," *New York Times*, February 18, 1999, A1.

82. Quoted in Michael Vitez, "Oregon Assisted-Suicide Law Little Used But Well Regarded," *Philadelphia Inquirer*, January 19, 1999, 1A.

83. Quoted in John Schwartz and James Estrin, "Oregon's Experience Under the Death with Dignity Act," *New York Times*, June 1, 2004, A1.

84. William Yardley, "Doctor-Assisted Suicide Faces Vote in Washington State," *New York Times*, October 31, 2008, A14.

85. Daniel Bergner, "Death in the Family," *New York Times Magazine,* December 2, 2007. Majorities of women and African Americans [are] opposed to PAD legislation.

86. David Masci, "The Right-to-Die Debate and the Tenth Anniversary of Oregon's Death With Dignity Act," *Pew Forum on Religion and Public Life*, October 9, 2007, at www.pewforum.org/docs.

87. Quoted in Carol M. Ostrum, "Initiative 1000 Would Let Patients Get Help Ending Their Lives," *Seattle Times*, September 21, 2008, 1.

88. www.noassistedsuicide.com.

89. Quoted in Adam Wilson, "What Voters Will Bring to 1-1000," *Olympian*, September 21, 2008, 1.

90. Ibid.

91. Ibid.

92. Ibid. The list of Disability Advocacy groups who opposed the initiative is a long one and included the following organizations: American Association of People with Disabilities; Disability Rights Education and Defense Fund; Justice For All; National Council on Disability, and the National Spinal Cord Injury Association.

93. Barbara Roberts, "1-1000 is Not a Slippery Slope, *Seattle Post-Intelligencer*, September 15, 2008, at www.seattlepi.nwsource.com/opinion/379211_robertsoregon16.html.

94. Carol M. Ostram, "Initiative 1000 Would Let Patients Get Help Ending Their Lives," *Seattle Times*, September 21, 2008, .A1.

95. "Summary of Initiative 1000, Concerns Allowing Certain Terminally Ill Competent Adults to Obtain Lethal Prescriptions," *Washington State Senate Committee Services*, August 14, 2008.

96. Of this amount, $221,414, almost 50 percent of the total, was received from Washington State's Catholic dioceses, parishes, health organizations, and the Knights of Columbus. Joel Connelly, "Supporters of Assisted Suicide Bait Catholics," *Seattle Post-Intelligencer*, September 21, 2008, 1.

97. Quoted in ibid.

98. By election day, more than $6.5 million was spent by both sides in the fight over Initiative 1000. Initiative supporters raised over $4.9 million while the opposition raised nearly $2 million.

99. A great deal of money, nearly one-half (about $1.9 million) of the funds given to the pro-WDWDA movement, came from out-of-state contributors. Examples: Judy Sebba, an educator from England, gave $253,555; Loren Parks, Nevada, gave $250,000; Compassion and Choices, Colorado, contributed $185,000. Out-of-state contributions, collected by that group, totaled $626,500. An Ohio citizen, Andrew Ross, contributed $400,000. See Joe Connelly, "I-1000 Wins Year's 'Sheer Gall Award,'" *Seattle Post-Intelligencer*, November 2, 2008.

100. Quoted in ibid.

101. John Iwasaki, "Physicians' Education on End-of-Life Measure Begins," *Seattle Post-Intelligencer*, February 23, 2009.

102. Quoted in Janet L. Tu, "Death with Dignity Act Passes," *Seattle Times*, November 5, 2008.

103. Chris Carlson, the spokesperson for the Coalition Against Assisted Suicide, quoted in John Iwasaki, "State Second in Nation to Allow Lethal Prescriptions," *Seattle Post-Intelligencer*, November 5, 2008, 1.

104. Quoted in Iwasaki, "Physicians' Education on End-of-Life Measure Begins."

105. Compassion and Choices, March 10, 2011, "Washington: Physician Aid in Dying Two Years Later," www.ccw.org.

106. Washington State Department of Health 2010 Death With Dignity Act Report, Executive Summary, March 2011. www.doh.wa.gov/dwda.

107. See Kathryn Tucker, "Privacy and Dignity at the End of Life: Protecting the Rights of Montanans to Choose Aid in Dying," 68 *Montana Law Review* 317, 2007. The district court judge decided the case on constitutional grounds; however, the state Supreme Court affirmed the lower court judgment on statutory grounds.

108. Kirk Johnson, "Montana Court to Rule on Assisted Suicide Case," *New York Times,* September 1, 2009.

109. Ibid.

110. *Baxter v Montana*, December 5, 2008; 2008 *Mont. Dist.* LEXIS 482.

111. Some *amici* supporting the plaintiffs included human rights groups, women's rights groups, the American Medical Women's Association, American Medical Students Association, clergy, thirty-one Montana legislators, bioethicists, and some legal scholars. Opposing briefs filed came from the Family Research Council, the American Association of Pro-Life Obstetricians and Gynecologists, and the Catholic Medical Association.

112. Only one concurring judge, James C. Nelson, maintained that the Court should have "affirmed the District Court's ruling on the constitutional issues."

113. *Baxter v Montana*, MT DA 09-0051, 2009 *MT* 449.

114. See *Billings Gazette* stories, January 17, 2011, February 9–11, 2011.

NOTES TO CHAPTER 7

1. Quoted in Janet I. Tu, "Assisted Suicide Measure Passes," *Seattle Times*, November 5, 2008, A1. Ms. Coombs in the president of Compassion and Choices, a national right-to-die organization with headquarters in Denver, Colorado.

2. John Schwartz and James Estrin, "New Openness in Deciding When and How to Die," *New York Times*, March 21, 2005, A1.

3. Ibid. One doctor angrily told a pro-PAD organization member who was lobbying for passage of the Oregon death-with-dignity statute: "You've really messed things up. We were doing just fine doing it under the covers." Other doctors disagree. Dr. Howard Grossman, an AIDS specialist and the executive director of the American Academy of H.I.V. Medicine, said: "It's crazy for it to be under the table in this way. It needs to be in the light of day so people can make a

rational decision, not regulated by fear, not based on pain or fear of being a burden."

4. Stopping eating and drinking is another method used by a small number of terminally ill patients but this can be a lengthy dying process lasting two to three weeks.

5. Dan W. Brock, "PAD as a Last-Resort Option at the end of Life," in Battin and Quill, *Physician-Assisted Dying*, 131.

6. Schwartz and Estrin, "New Openness," A1.

7. Rob McStay, "Terminal Sedation: Palliative Care for Intractable pain, post-*Glucksberg* and *Quill*," *American Journal of Law and Medicine*, January 1, 2003.

8. These liberal Justices included William O. Douglas, Hugo L. Black, William J. Brennan, Arthur Goldberg, Abe Fortas, and Thurgood Marshall.

9. See Howard Ball and Philip Cooper, *Of Power and Right: Justices William O. Douglas and Hugo Black and America's Constitutional Revolution*, New York: Oxford University Press, 1988.

10. Charlie Savage, "Appeals Courts Pushed to Right By Bush Choices," *New York Times*, October 29, 2008, A1.

11. Ibid.

12. Nan Aron, quoted in ibid., A14.

13. See Tip O'Neal and Gary Hymel, *All Politics is Local: And Other Rules of the Game,* Holbrook, MA: Adams Media, 1994.

14. Hank Dunn, *Hard Choices for Loving People: CPR, Artificial Feeding, Comfort Care, and the Patient with a Life-Threatening Illness*, Landsdowne, VA: A and A Publishers, 2007, 59.

15. Erich H. Loewy, "Harming, Healing, and Euthanasia," in Linda L. Emanuel, ed., *Regulating How We Die: The Ethical, Medical and Legal Issues Surrounding Physician-Assisted Suicide*, Cambridge, MA: 1998, 53–54.

16. Hal Bernton, "Washington's Initiative 1000 is Modeled on Oregon's Death with Dignity Act," *Seattle Times*, October 13, 2008, A1.

17. Quoted in ibid.

18. *Edwards v California*, 314 U.S. 160 (1941).

19. *Shapiro v Thompson*, 394 U.S. 618, (1969).

20. *Kent v Dulles*, 357 U.S. 116 (1958) and *Aptheker v Secretary of State*, 378 U.S. 500 (1969).

21. *United States v Guest*, 383 U.S. 745, (1966).

22. OHD, "FAQ about the ODWDA," at www.egov.oregon.gov.

Aptheker v Secretary of State, 378 U.S. 500, 1969

Auer v Robbins, 519 U.S. 452, 1997

Bartling v Superior Court, 163 *Cal App*. 3rd 186; 209 *Cal Reporter*, 220 (1984)

Baxter v Montana, December 5, 2008. 2008 *Mont. Dist*. LEXIS 482

Baxter v Montana, MT DA 09-0051, 2009 *MT* 449

Bouvia v Superior Court, 179 *Cal App*. 3rd 1127; 225 *Cal Reporter*, 297 (1986)

Bowers v Hardwick, 478 *U.S*. 186, 1986

Chevron U.S.A., Inc. v Natural Resources Defense Council, 467 *U.S*. 837 (1984)

Compassion in Dying et al. v Washington et al., 49 *F. 3d* 586 (CA9, 1995)

Compassion in Dying et al. v Washington et al., 79 *F. 3d* 790 (CA9, 1996)

Compassion in Dying et al., v Washington, 850 *F. Supp*. 1454 (W.D. Wash., 1994)

Corbett v D'Alessandro, 487 *So. 2d* 368 (Florida, 1986)

Crandell v Nevada, 73 *U.S*. 35 (1868)

Cruzan v Director, Missouri Department of Health, 497 *U.S*. 261 (1990)

Cruzan v Harmon, 760 *S.W. 2nd* 416, at 416–417 (Missouri, *en banc*, 1988)

Edwards v California, 314 *U.S*. 160 (1941)

Eisenstadt v Baird, 20. 405 *U.S*. 438 (1972)

Gonzales v Oregon, 546 *U.S*. 243, 2006

Gonzales v Raich, 545 *U.S*. 1, 2005

Griswold v Connecticut, 381 *U.S*. 479 (1965)

In Re Daniel Joseph Fiori, an Adjudged Incompetent, 543 *Pa* 592; 6783 *A.2d* 905 (1995)

In Re Daniel Joseph Fiori, an Adjudged Incompetent, *So. 2d* 4 (Florida, 1990)

In Re Guardianship and Protective Placement of Edna M.F. v Howard Eisenberg, 95-2719, 1997

In Re Guardianship and Protective Placement of L.W., 167 *Wisc. 2d* 53, 482 *N.W. 2d* 60, 1992

In Re: Guardianship of Theresa Marie Schiavo, Robert Schindler and Mary Schindler v Michael Schiavo, as Guardian of the person of Theresa Marie Schiavo, District Court of Appeal of Florida, Second District, Case No. 2D00-1269 *as Guardian of the person of Theresa Marie*, D. C. Appeal of Florida, 2d District, Case No. 2D00-1269

In Re Quinlan, An Alleged Incompetent, 348 *A. 2nd* 801 (N.J. Superior Court, 1975), 355 *A. 2nd* 647 (N.J., 1976)

In Re Schiavo, 789 *So. 2d* 248 (Florida, 2001), Case No. SC01-559

In Re: Guardians of Schiavo, No 90-2908 GD-003 (Florida 2d District Circuit Court, 2000)

Jeb Bush v Michael Schiavo, Supreme Court of Florida, Case No. SC04-925, September 23, 2004

Kent v Dulles, 357 U.S. 116, 1958

Lee v State of Oregon, D.C. No. CV-94-06467-MRH (1994) Nos. 95-35804, -35805, -35854, 95-35949, CA9 (2005)

Loving v Virginia, 388 *U.S.* 1, 1967

McCleskey v Kemp, 481 *U.S.* 279, 1989

Metropolitan Life Insurance Company v Massachusetts, 471 *U.S.* 724, 1985

Michael Schiavo v Jeb Bush and Charlie Crist, Petitioner's Brief, DCA, Civil Case No. 03-008212-CI-20, 1

Oregon v Ashcroft, 368 *F 3rd* 1118 (2004)

People v Kevorkian, 527 *N.W. 2nd* at 739, 1990

Planned Parenthood of Southeastern Pennsylvania v Casey 505 *U.S.* 833, 1992

Poe v Ullman, 367 *U.S.* 497, 1961

Quill et al. v Vacco et al., 80 *F.3d.* 716 (CA2, 1996)

Quill et al. v Koppel et al., 870 F. Supp (S.D.N.Y., 1994)

Rasmussen by Mitchell v Fleming, 154 Arizona 207; 741 P.2d 674, 1987

Roe v Wade, 410 U.S. 113, 1973

Shapiro v Thompson, 394 U.S. 618, 1969

State of Oregon v Ashcroft, 368 F 3rd 1118 (2004)

State of Oregon v John Ashcroft et al., No. CIV. 01-1647-JO, U.S. District Court, April 17, 2002.

Superintendent of Belchertown State School v Saikowicz, 373 Mass 728, 370 N.E. 2nd 417 (1977)

Theresa Schiavo v Michael Schiavo et al., "Statement of Interest of the U.S., U.S. District Court, Tampa Division, Civ A No. 8:05-CV-530-T-27TBM

Union Pacific v Botsford, 141 U.S. 250, 1891

United States v Guest, 383 U.S. 745, 1966

United States v Salerno, 481 U.S. 739, 745, 1987

Vacco v Quill, 521 U.S. 793, 1997

Washington v Glucksberg, 521 U.S. 702, 1997

Allen, Mike, "Counsel to GOP Senator Wrote Memo on Schiavo," *Washington Post*, April 7, 2005, 1.

Anderson, William S., ed., *Ballentine's Law Dictionary,* 3rd ed., Rochester, NY: Lawyer's Cooperative Publishing Company, 1969.

Angell, Marcia , "After Quinlan: The Dilemma of the Persistent Vegetative State," 330 *New England Journal of Medicine (NEJM)* No. 21, May 26, 1994.

Annas, George J., "Death By Prescription," 331 *NEJM* 1240–1243, No. 18, November 3, 1994.

Anonymous, "It's over, Debbie," 259 *Journal of the American Medical Association (JAMA)* 272, (1988).

Associated Press, "Assisted Suicide Laws State By State," at www.infonet.com.

Balch, Burker J., JD, Director of the National Right to Life Committee Department of Medical Ethics, www. nrlc.org.

Ball, Howard, *The Supreme Court in the Intimate Lives of Americans*, New York: New York University Press, 2002, 2004.

Ball, Howard and Philip Cooper, *Of Power and Right: Justices William O. Douglas and Hugo Black and America's Constitutional Revolution*, New York: Oxford University Press, 1988.

———, *The U.S. Supreme Court: From the Inside Out*, Englewood Cliffs, NJ: Prentice-Hall, 1992.

Battin, Margaret Pabst, *The Least Worst Death: Essays in Bioethics on the End of Life*, New York: Oxford, 1994.

——— and Timothy E. Quill, "The Argument over Physician-Assisted Dying," in Battin and Quill, *Physician-Assisted Dying: The Case for Palliative Care and Patient Choice*, Baltimore, MD: Johns Hopkins University Press, 2004.

Beck, A.L., et al., "PAD and Euthanasia in Washington State: Patient Requests and Physician Responses," 275 *JAMA* 919–925, 1996.

Behuniak, Susan M. and Arthur G. Svenson, *Physician-Assisted Suicide: The Anatomy of a Constitutional Law Issue,* Lanham. MD: Rowman and Littlefield, 2002.

Belkin, Lisa, "Doctor Tells of First Death Using His Suicide Device," *New York Times*, June 6, 1990, A1.

Benoit, L., "State Senate Rejects Physician-Assisted Suicide Bill on Final Day of Session," *Hawaii Catholic Herald*, May 10, 2002, 1.

Bergner, Daniel, "Death in the Family," *New York Times Magazine*, December 2, 2007.

Bernton, Hal, "Washington's Initiative 1000 is Modeled on Oregon's Death with Dignity Act," *Seattle Times*, October 13, 2008, A1.

Beauchamp, Tom L., ed., *Intending Death: The Ethics of Assisted Suicide and Euthanasia*, Englewood Cliffs, NJ: Prentice-Hall, 1996.

Biskupic, Joan, "Unanimous Decision Points to Tradition of Valuing Life," *Washington Post*, June 27, 1997, A1.

Brock, Dan W., "PAD as a Last-Resort Option at the end of Life," in Battin and Quill, *Physician-Assisted Death*.

Bromage, Andy, "With a New Governor in Power, Will Vermonters Finally Win their 'Right to Die'?" Seven Days, January 12, 2011. http://www.7dvt.com.

Brovins, Joan and Thomas Oehmke, *Dr. Death: Dr. Jack Kevorkian's RX: Death*, Hollywood, FL: Lifetime, 1993.

Caplan, Arthur L., et al., ed., *The Case of Terri Schiavo: Ethics at the End of Life*, Amherst, NY: Prometheus Books, 2006.

Caplan, Lincoln, *The Tenth Justice: The Solicitor General and the Rule of Law*, New York: Vintage, 1988.

Cayetano, Benjamin J., "Mom," Honolulu Magazine, December 2006, www.honolulumagazine.com.

Canadian Neurocritical Care Group, "Guidelines for the Diagnosis of Brain Death," 26 *Canadian Journal of Neurological Science*, 1999.

CCC, "No on AB 374: California Compassionate Choices Act," Catholic Lobby Day, 2007, at www.cacatholic.org.

CDC Health, United States, 2006, U.S. Department of Health and Human Services, CDC, National Center for Health Statistics, Washington, DC, 2006.

Cerminara , Kathy and Kenneth Goodman. "Schiavo Case Resources: Key Events in the Case of Theresa Marie Schiavo," University of Miami Ethics Programs, July 25, 2008.

Chin, Arthur E., et al., *Oregon's Death with Dignity Act: The First Year's Experience*, Oregon DHS, OHD, Center For Disease Prevention and Epidemiology, February 18, 1999.

———, "Legalized Physician-Assisted Suicide in Oregon—The First Year's Experience," 340 *NEJM* 577–583, 1999.

Clark, Annette E., "The Right to Die: The Broken Road From Quinlan to Schiavo," 37 *Loyola University Chicago Law Review* 383, 2006.

Clinical Consultation Services, *Medical Ethics*, Bryn Mawr, PA: Clinical Consultation Services, Inc., 1999.

Clinton, William J., "Statement upon Signing the Assisted Suicide Funding Restriction Act of 1997," in *Public Papers of Presidents of the United States: William J. Clinton*, Bk. 1, 515. Washington, DC, Government Printing Office, 1997.

Cohn, Felicia and Joanne Lynn, "Vulnerable People," in Foley and Hendin, *Case Against Assisted Suicide*.

Colby, William H., *Long Goodbye: The Deaths of Nancy Cruzan*, Carlesbad, CA: Hay House, 2002.

————, *Unplugged: Reclaiming our Right to Die in America*, New York: AMACOM, 2006.

Coleson, Richard E., "The *Glucksberg and Quill Amicus Curiae* Briefs," 13 *Issues in Law and Medicine* 3, Summer 1997.

Compassionate Choices, "Who Killed Death With Dignity?" www.compassionat-echoiceshawaii.org.

Connelly, Joe, "Supporters of Assisted Suicide Bait Catholics," *Seattle Post-Intelligencer*, September 21, 2008, 1.

————, "I-1000 Wins Year's 'Sheer Gall Award,'" *Seattle Post-Intelligencer*, November 2, 2008.

Cook, Donald, et. al., "Withdrawal of Mechanical Ventilation in Anticipation of Death in the ICU," 349 *NEJM* 1123, 2003.

Cranford, Ronald, "Diagnosing the Permanent Vegetative State," *American Medical Association (AMA) Virtual Mentor*, 2005, at www.ama-assn.org/ama/pub/category/12720.html.

Crutchfield, Nikki, *To Succeed or Not to Succeed: How Do Political Influences, Culture, and Demographics Affect the Passing of Physician-Assisted Suicide Initiatives?* PhD diss., Auburn University, December 15, 2008, www.etdhelp@auburn.edu.

Curtis, J. Randall and Robert Burt, "Point: The Ethics of Unilateral 'Do Not Resuscitate' Orders," 132 *Chest* 748–751, 2007.

Cutler, Angus Deaton and Adriana Lleras-Muney, "Determinants of Mortality," NIA-sponsored workshop on the Determinants of Mortality, Princeton, NJ, July 16, 2004.

Cutler, David M. and Ellen Meara, "Changes in the Age Distribution of Mortality over the 20th Century," *U.S. National Institutes on Aging*, September 2001.

Death With Dignity, "Living with Dying," Death with Dignity National Center, August 2011. www.ddnc.com.

Didion, Joan, "The Case of Theresa Schiavo," *New York Review of Books*, June 9, 2005.

DiPaolo, Sharon F., "Getting Through the Door: Threshold Procedural Considerations in Right-to-Die Litigation," 6 *Franklin Pierce Law Review* Winter 1997.

Dossetor, J.B., *Beyond the Hippocratic Oath: A Memoir on the Rise of Modern Medical Ethics*, Alberta, CA: University of Alberta Press, 2005.

Dowbiggin, Ian, *A Merciful End: The Euthanasia Movement in America*, New York: Oxford University Press, 2003.

————, *A Concise History of Euthanasia: Life, Death, God, and Medicine*, New York: Rowman and Littlefield, 2005.

Dunavan, Claire Danosian, "Looking Squarely at Death, and Finding Clarity," *New York Times*, August 19, 2008, D5.

Dunn, Hank, *Hard Choices for Loving People: CPR, Artificial Feeding, Comfort Care, and the Patient with a Life-Threatening Illness*, Landsdowne, VA: A and A Publishers, September 2007, 59.

Dworkin, Gerald, R.G. Frey, and Sisela Bok, *Euthanasia and Physician-Assisted Suicide: For and Against*, Cambridge: Cambridge University Press, 1998.

Dworkin, Ronald, *Life's Dominion: An Argument about Abortion, Euthanasia, and Individual Freedom*, New York: Vintage, 1994.

———, "Assisted Suicide: The Philosophers' Brief," *New York Review of Books*, March 27, 1997.

Dyck, Arthur J., *Life's Worth: The Case against Assisted Suicide*, Cambridge: Erdmans, 2002.

Editorial, "ANA Opposes Pain Relief Act," *Nursing*, July 1, 2000, 63.

Editorial, "The Assisted-Suicide Decision," *New York Times*, January 19, 2006, A26.

Editorial, "Palliative Care—A New Paradigm," 363 *NEJM*, August 19, 2010.

Editorial, "Theresa Marie Schiavo," *New York Times*, April 1, 2005.

Flight, Myrtle, *Law, Liability, and Ethics for Medical Office Professionals*, 4th ed., Clifton Park, NY: Thomson, 2003.

Foley, Kathleen and Herbert Hendin, "Introduction," in Foley and Hendin, eds., *The Case Against Assisted Suicide: For the Right to End-of-Life Care*, Baltimore, MD: Johns Hopkins Press, 2004.

Foley, Kathleen, "Compassionate Care, Not Assisted Suicide," in Foley and Hendin, *Case Against Assisted Suicide*.

Garrow, David J., "The Oregon Trail," *New York Times*, November 6, 1997, A 26.

Gillman, Howard, The Votes That Counted: How the Court Decided the 2000 Presidential Election, Chicago, IL.: University of Chicago Press, 2001.

Gorsuch, Neil M., *The Future of Assisted Suicide and Euthanasia*, Princeton, NJ: Princeton University Press, 2006.

Greenhouse, Linda, "Assisted Suicide Clears a Hurdle in Highest Court," *New York Times*, October 14, 1997, A1.

———, "Justices Reject U.S. Bid to Block Assisted Suicide," *New York Times*, January 18, 2006, A1.

Gross, Jane, "How Many of Us Expect To Die?" The New Old Age, Caring and Coping, *New York Times*, July 8, 2008 at www.newyorktimes.com/newoldage.

Hall, Kermit L., ed., *The Oxford Companion to the Supreme Court*, New York: Oxford University Press, 1992.

Harmon, Louise, *Fragments on the Deathwatch*, Boston: Beacon Press, 1998.

Hartocollis, Anemona, "Hard Choice for a Comfortable Death: Drug-Induced Sleep," *New York Times*, December 27, 2009, A1.

Hartwick, John, "Medicalization and Death," 2006 conference of the American Psychological Association, www.apa.udel.edu/apa/publications/newsletters/MedicineNL/vo6n1.htm.

Health, United States, 2006, U.S. Department of Health and Human Services, CDC, National Center for Health Statistics, Washington, DC, 2006.

Hill, T. Patrick and David Shirley, *A Good Death: Taking More Control at the End of Your Life*, New York: Addison-Wesley, 1992.

Hillyard, Daniel and John Dombrink, *Dying Right: The Death With Dignity Movement*, New York: Routledge, 2001.

Hoefler, James M., *Managing Death: The First Guide for Patients, Family Members, and Care Providers on Forgoing Treatment At the End of Life*, Boulder, CO: Westview Press, 1997.

Hull, N.E.H. and Peter Charles Hoffer, *Roe v Wade: The Abortion Rights Controversy in American History*, Lawrence, KS: University Press of Kansas, 2001.

Humphry, Derek, *Jean's Way*, Eugene, OR: Hemlock Society, 1978, 1991.

———, *Dying with Dignity: What You Need to Know about Euthanasia*, New York: Birch Lane Press, 1992.

———, *Final Exit: The Practicalities of Self-Deliverance and Assisted Suicide for the Dying*, New York: Dell, 1996.

Ivan, Leslie, *The Way We Die: Brain Death, Vegetative State, Euthanasia and other End-of-Life Dilemmas*, Groseto, Italy: Pari Publishing, 2007.

Iwasaki, John, "State Second in Nation to Allow Lethal Prescriptions," *Seattle Post-Intelligencer*, November 5, 2008, 1.

——— , "Physicians' Education on End-of-Life Measure Begins." *Seattle Post-Intelligencer*, February 23, 2009.

James, Susan Donaldson, "Tourists Trek to Mexico for 'Death in a Bottle,'" ABC News, July 31, 2008. www.abc.com.

Jennett, Bryan, *The Vegetative State: Medical Facts, Ethical and Legal Dimensions*, New York: Cambridge University Press, 2002.

Johnson, Kirk, "Kevorkian Sentenced to 10 to 25 Years in Prison," *New York Times*, April 14, 1999, A1

———, "Montana Court to Rule on Assisted Suicide Case," *New York Times*, September 1, 2009.

Keown, John, *Euthanasia, Ethics, and Public Policy: An Argument Against Legislation*, Cambridge: Cambridge University Press, 2002.

Kevorkian, Jack, *Prescription: Medicide—The Goodness of Planned Death*, Buffalo, NY: Prometheus Books, 1991.

———, "A Letter From Dr. Kevorkian," *New York Review of Books*, July 5, 2001.

Kinney, H.C., et al., "Neuropathological Findings in the Brain of Karen Ann Quinlan—The Role of the Thalamus in the Persistent Vegetative State," 330 *NEJM* 21, 1469–1475, 1994.

Landler, Mark "Assisted Suicide of Healthy 79-Year-Old Renews German Debate on Right to Die," *New York Times*, July 3, 2008, A8.

Law, Sylvia A., "A Political and Constitutional Context," in Quill and Battin, *Physician-Assisted Dying*.

Lee, M.A., et al., "Legalizing Assisted Suicide: Views of Physicians in Oregon," 334 *NEJM*, 310–315, 1996.

Levesque, William R., "Justices Skeptical of Bush Team's Defense of 'Terri's Law,'" *St. Petersburg Times*, September 1, 2004.

Levine, Art, "In Oregon, A Political Campaign to Die For," *U.S. News and World Report*, November 10, 1997, 56.

Levine, Mark A., "Sedation to Unconsciousness in End-of-Life Care," Report of the Council on Ethical and Judicial Affairs, AMA, CEJA Report 5-A-08.

Liang, Arthur P., MD, MPH, "Foodborne Illness," National Center For Infectious Diseases,CDC, 2002, at http://www.fsis.usda.gov/Orlando 2002/presentations/aliang_text.htm.

Loewy, Erich H., "Harming, Healing, and Euthanasia," in Linda L. Emanuel, ed., Regulating How We Die: Cambridge, MA.: 1998, 53–54.

Lowenstein , Edward, MD, and Sidney H. Wanzer, MD, Sounding Board, "The U.S. Attorney General's Intrusion into   Medical Practice," 346 *NEJM* 447–448, February 7, 2002.

Lynn, Joanne, *Sick To Death and Not Going To take It Anymore: Reforming Health Care for the Last Years of Life*, Berkeley: University of California Press, 2004.

———— and Joan Harrold, *Handbook for Mortals*, New York: Oxford University Press, 1999.

Martin, Marisa, "In Re Schiavo: The Saga Continues," www.law.uh.edu/healthlaw/perspectives/Death/040229Schiavo.html.

Masci, David, "The Right-to-Die Debate and the Tenth Anniversary of Oregon's Death With Dignity Act," Pew Forum on .Religion and Public Life, October 9, 2007.

Mattos, Jenifer, "Court Skeptical About Assisted Suicide," *Time*, January 8, 1997.

McStay, Rob, "Terminal Sedation: Palliative Care for Intractable pain," *American Journal of Law and Medicine*, January 1, 2003.

Memorandum, "Diagnosis of Death in U.K.," Conference of Medical Royal Colleges and Their Faculties in the U.K., 15 Jan 1979, 1 *British Medical Journal*, February 3, 1979.

Moreno, Jonathan D., ed., *Arguing Euthanasia: The Controversy Over Mercy Killing, Assisted Suicide, and the "Right to Die,"* New York: Simon and Schuster, 1995.

Myers, Richard S., "Reflections on Terri Schiavo Controversy," in J. Koterski, ed., *Life and Learning XIV: The Proceedings of the XIV University Faculty for Life Conference*, Washington, DC: UFL, 2005.

National Right to Life Committee, "Come From Behind Victory against Maine Assisting Suicide Referendum Elates Anti-Euthanasia Forces, www.nlrc.org.

Nelson, Roxanne, "Palliative Care Programs Continue to Increase in American Hospitals," *Medscape Medical News*, April 10, 2010, www.news@medscape.net.

Note, "The Mercitron," *Detroit Free Press Magazine*, March 18, 1992.

Nuland, Sherwin B., *How We Die: Reflections on Life's Final Chapter,* New York: Vintage, 1995.

O'Neill, Tip and Gary Hymel, *All Politics is Local: And Other Rules of the Game,* Holbrook, MA: Adams Media, 1994.

O'Reilly, Kevin, "Oregon Still Stands Alone: Ten Years of Physician-Assisted Suicide," *American Medical News,* May 12, 2008, at www.amednews.com.

Orentlicher, David, "The Supreme Court and Physician-Assisted Suicide: Rejecting Assisted Suicide but Embracing Euthanasia," 337 *NEMJ* 23, 1233–1239, 1997.

Ostrom, Carol M., "Initiative 1000 Would Let Patients Get Help Ending Their Lives," *Seattle Times,* September 21, 2008.

———, "Doctors Divided on Assisted Suicide," *Seattle Times,* October 1, 2008, p. 1.

Otlowski, Margaret F.A., *Voluntary Euthanasia and the Common Law,* Oxford: Oxford University Press, 1997.

Pain and the Law, American Society of Law, Medicine, and Ethics, at www.aslme.com.

Pew Forum on Religion and Public Life, Legal Backgrounder, "Supreme Court Considers Challenge to Oregon's Death with Dignity Act, September 2005, 1, at www. pewforum.com.

———, U.S. Religious Landscape Survey, "Religious Composition of the U.S.," September 2008, at www.pewforum.com.

Porter, Roy, *The Greatest Benefit to Mankind: The Medical History of Humanity.* New York: W.W. Norton, 1997.

President's Commission, "Defining Death: Medical, Legal, and Ethical Issues in the Determination of Death," Report of the President's Commission for the Study of Ethical Problems in Medicine and Biomedical Research, Washington, DC: U.S. Government Printing Office, July 1981.

Public Broadcasting System, "The Suicide Tourist," PBS Frontline, March 2, 2010, at www.pbs.org.

Quill , Timothy E., "Death and Dignity: A Case for Individualized Decision Making," 324 *NEJM* 691–694, 1991.

———, *Death and Dignity: Making Choices and Taking Charge,* New York: Norton, 1994.

———, and Margaret P. Battin, ed., *Physician-Assisted Dying: The Case for Palliative Care and Patient Choice,* Baltimore, MD: Johns Hopkins University Press, 2004.

——— "Terri Schiavo: A Tragedy Compounded," 352 *NEJM* 1630–1633, 2005.

Quinlan, Julia Duane, *My Joy, My Sorrow: Karen Ann's Mother Remembers,* Cincinnati, OH: St. Anthony Messenger Press, 2005.

Roberts, Barbara, "1-1000 is Not a Slippery Slope," *Seattle Post-Intelligencer,* September 15, 2008.

Robertson, John A, "Schiavo and Its (In)Significance," University of Texas Public Law Research paper no. 72, March, 2005.

Russo, Frank D., "'California Compassionate Choices Act'" California Progress Report: The Daily Briefing, Sacramento, CA: June 27, 2006.

Savage, Charlie, "Appeals Courts Pushed to Right by Bush Choices," *New York Times*, October 29, 2008, A1.

Schwartz, John, and James Estrin, "Oregon's Experience Under the Death with Dignity Act," *New York Times*, June 1, 2004, A1.

———, "In Oregon, Choosing Death over Suffering," *New York Times*, June 1, 2004, A1.

———, "New Openness in Deciding When and How to Die," *New York Times*, March 21, 2005, A1.

———, "In Vermont, a Bid to Legalize Physician-Assisted Suicide," *New York Times*, March 30, 2005, A1.

Smith, Wesley J., *Forced Exit: The Slippery Slope from Assisted Suicide to Legalized Murder*, New York: New York Times Books, 1999.

———, *Culture of Death: The Assault on Medical Ethics in America*, San Francisco, CA: Encounter Books, 2000.

Steinberg, Donald R., "Limits to Death with Dignity," 1 *Harvard Journal of Law and Technology* 129, 1988.

Stolberg, Sheryl Gay, "Nominee Is Pressed on End-of-Life Care," *New York Times*, August 10, 2005, A1.

Stutsman, Eli D., "Political Strategy and Legal Change," in Battin and Quill, *Physician Assisted Dying*.

Sullivan, et al., *Legalized PAS in Oregon—the Second Year*, DHR, OHD, Center for Disease Prevention and Epidemiology, March 2008.

Swash, M., "Brain Death: Still-Unresolved Issues Worldwide," 58 *Neurology* 9–10, 2002.

Szilva, Jean, MD, "Patients' Rights First; Doctors' Second," *Burlington (VT) Free Press*, October 14, 2008, 5A.

Task Force to Improve Care of Terminally Ill Patients, *The Oregon Death with Dignity Act: A Guidebook*, Portland, OR: Center for Ethics in Health Care, 1988.

Termel, Jennifer S., et al., "Early Palliative Care," 363 *NEJM* 733–742, August 19, 2010.

Thomas, Cal, "St. Theresa Schiavo," *Jewish World Review*, April 1, 2005, at www.jewishworldreview.com.

Timbs, Dorothy, "National Right to Life Responds to Ruling on *Gonzales v Oregon*, National Right to Life, January 17, 2006, at www.nrlc.org.

Tu, Janet, "Assisted Suicide Measure Passes," *Seattle Times*, November 5, 2008, A1.

———, "Death with Dignity Act Passes," *Seattle Times*, November 5, 2008. A1.

Tucker, Kathryn L.,"Privacy and Dignity at the End of Life: Protecting the Rights of Montanans to Choose Aid in Dying," 68 *Montana Law Review* 317, 2007.

———, "In the Laboratory of the States," 106 *Michigan Law Review* 1593, June 2008.

Urofsky, Melvin, *Letting Go: Death, Dying, and the Law,* New York: Scribner's Sons, 1994.

———, *Lethal Judgments: Assisted Suicide and American Law,* Lawrence, KS: University Press of Kansas, 2000.

Verhovek, Sam Howe, "Oregon Reporting 15 Deaths in 1998 Under Suicide Law," The New York Times, February 18, 1999.

Vicini, James, "Kevorkian Murder Conviction Upheld [*sic*] by U.S. Supreme Court," CareCure Forums, October 7, 2002, at www.sci.rutgers.edu.

Vitez, Michael, "Oregon Assisted-Suicide Law Little Used But Well Regarded," *Philadelphia Inquirer,* January 19, 1999, 1A.

Vollmar Valerie, ed., "Recent Developments in Physician-Assisted Death," October 2000, at www.willamette.edu.

———. "Recent Developments in Physician-Assisted Death," February 2004, at www.willamette.edu.

———, "Recent Developments in Physician-Assisted Death," February 2005, at www.willamette.edu.

———, "Recent Developments in Physician-Assisted Death," June 2006, at www.willamette.edu.

———, "Recent Developments in Physician-Assisted Death," June 2007 at www.willamette.edu.

———, "Recent Developments in Physician-Assisted Death," February 2008 at www.willamette.edu.

Wallace, Mike, "A Note on Dr. Kevorkian and Timothy McVeigh," 48 *New York Review of Books*11, July 5, 2001, at www.newyorkreviewofbooks.com.

Walton, Douglas N., *Ethics of Withdrawal of Life-Support Systems: Case Studies in Decision-Making in Intensive Care,* New York: Praeger, 1987.

Wilson, Adam, "What Voters Will Bring to 1-1000," *Olympian (Olympia, OR),* September 21, 2008, 1.

Wolf, Susan M., "Physician Assisted Suicide, Abortion, and Treatment Refusal: Using Gender to Analyze the Difference," in Robert Weir, ed., *Physician-Assisted Suicide,* Bloomington: Indiana University Press, 1997.

Wolfson, Jay, "Foreward," in A.L. Caplan, *Case of Terri Schiavo.*

Yardley, William, "Doctor-Assisted Suicide Faces Vote in Washington State," *New York Times,* October 31, 2008, A14.

Abortion, 2, 6, 11; not a fundamental right, 76

Accelerated rehabilitation, 193n39

Acute trauma, 51

Advanced care directive (living will), 9, 35; Schiavo impact on, 65

Aggressive PAD advocate, anathema to conventional MD's, 68

Alpha One, anti-PAD, disabled group organization, 121

Alzheimer's disease, 18, 49

AMA, 142, 143; Code of Medical Ethics, PAD prohibited in, 106-107; impact on, of Schiavo, 66; opposition of, to Ashcroft directive, 145; secular anti-PAD opponent, 106-107, 109; view of, PAD unregulatable, 107

American Baptist Church, anti-PAD support by, 108

American Bar Association, 143

American Cancer Society, 143

American Civil Liberties Union, role of, in Schiavo case, 58; in PAD Cases, 87

American Medical Association. See AMA

American Nursing Association, 143

American Pain Care Foundation, 143

American Psychological Association, 173-174n11

American transplants, 171-172

Americans, attitudes about dying of, 7-8; life expectancy of, 2-3

Amicus curiae, role of, in PAD cases, 69-70

Amyotrphic Lateral Sclerosis (ALS). See Lou Gehrig's Disease

Anoxia, 13, 22, 32

Antibiotics, 17, 18

Anti-PAD coalition, Hawaii's, 121

Anti-PAD coalition, Maine's, 122

Anti-PAD state policy, 74

As-applied challenges, 97; definition of, 189n42

Ashcroft Directive, 144-147

Ashcroft v Oregon, CA9 decisions in, 145-147

Ashcroft, John, 46, 140, 141, 144-146, 183n91; resignation of, as Attorney General, 147

Assisted Suicide Funding Restriction Act of 1997, 142

Assisted Suicide Prevention Act of 1966, 148

Atkins, Janet, 71

Auer v Robbins, 200n60

Autonomy principle: euthanasia and, 69-70; fear of, 150-151, 152

Baird, Douglas, overturn of Terri's Law by, 58

Bartlett, Paul, 173n4

Battin, Margaret, ix, 3, 18; view of justice of, 1n3

Baxter v Wyoming, 158-161

Baxter, Robert, 159

Berg, Patti, 114, 115, 116, 117-118

"Best interest of PVS patient" standard, 48, 49

Bioethics community, 58

Black, Hugo L., 5, 166

Blackmun, Harry A., 6

Bodily integrity, 30, 31
Bouvia, Elizabeth, 178n11
Bouvia v Superior Court, 30, 178-179n11
Boyle, Frank, 193n41
Brain death, definition of, 175n10
Brain stem, 11
Brennan, William J., 4, 5-6
Breyer, Stephen, 147
Brownback, Sam, 148
Brunetti, Melvin, 137
Bush v Gore, 144
Bush, George H. W., 167, 168; selection of conservative judges, by, 75
Bush, George W., 9, 10, 167, 168; opposition of, to ODWDA, 144-148; role of, in *Schiavo* case, 52, 62; transform makeup of federal judiciary by, 168
Bush, Jeb, 62; Executive order issued in *Schiavo* case, by, 58; religion of, 56; role of, in *Schiavo* case, 52

California, 171
California Bar Association, approval of PAD by, 113
California Catholic Conference, opposition of, to AB 2747, 118; opposition of, to AB 374, 116-117
California Compassionate Choices Act (AB 374), 116
California Compassionate Choices Act (AB 654), 114-115
California Initiative (Proposition 101), defeat of, 112-113
California Medical Association, opposition of, to PAD, 115
California Right to Know End of Life Options Act (AB 2747), 118-119
Californians Against Assisted Suicide, 115
Californians Against Human Suffering, 112
Cancer, 3, 11, 17, 18, 19, 69, 106, 150, 158, 159

Cardiac arrest, 51, 53
Cardiopulmonary-cerebral resuscitation, 14. *See* CPR
Carlson, Chris, 157
Casey. *See Planned Parenthood of Southeastern Pennsylvania v Casey*
Catholic Health Association, 156
Cayetano, Benjamin J., 119-120
Cell necrosis, 13
Center for Ethics in Health Care, 135
Centers for Disease Control and Prevention (CDC), 15-16
Cerebral cortex, 21, 22, 175n11
Certiorari, definition of, 182n67
Chemotherapy, 22
Cheshire, William P., neurology exam of Schiavo by, 61
Chevron, U.S.A. v. Natural Resources Defense Council, 147, 200n61
Christian Americans, denominations of, 191-192n16
Chronic illnesses, emergence of, 18
Chronic Obstructive Pulmonary Disease, 151. *See* COPD
"Clear and convincing evidence" standard, 40; in Schiavo case, 54-55. *See also Cruzan v Missouri*
Clinical death, definitional changes about, 14-17
Clinical medical studies, emergence of, 21
Clinton, Bill, 141-142, 143
Clinton Administration, 140
CNN, 52
Coalition Against Assisted Suicide, 154, 157
Colby, William, appointed Cruzan lawyer, 38; legal strategy of, in *Cruzan*, 38-41
Common law, 9, 30, 42, 52; doctrine of personal autonomy in, 27-28, 30
Communist Party members, right to travel of, 171

Compassion, integral to dying process, 169-170

Compassion, "true," 116, 118

Compassion and Choices, 109, 114, 128. *See also* Hemlock Society

Compassion and Choices of Washington, 158

Compassion and Choices of Oregon, 153

Compassion in Dying v. Washington, 76-77

Compassion in Dying, 77, 109

Competent person, and PVS, 31; right of, to refuse medical treatment, 30-31

Connecticut, 171

Constitutional interpretations, 11

Constitutional question in *Cruzan,* 41

Constitutional right to privacy, 30; status of, in PVS cases, 35

Contagious diseases, 17

Contractures, 37

Controlled Substance Act (CSA): history of, 198n24; use of, by Bush administration, 174n29; use of, to overturn ODWDA, 139-145

Cooper, Jessica, 72

COPD, 3, 18, 106; definition of, 174n13

Covert dialogue, doctor and nurse in, 165

CPR, 22-23, 24

Crandell v Nevada, 2

Critics of PAD, 107. *See also* PAD

Cruzan family, religious beliefs, 52

Cruzan v Director, Missouri Department of Health. See *Cruzan v Missouri*

Cruzan v Missouri, 8, 27, 31, 36, 81; four dissenting justices in, 44-45; impact of, in PAD litigation, 75-76; trial judge decisions in, 39, 45-46; use of, in 1997 PAD briefs, 77-79; various state responses to, 47-50

Cruzan, Joseph, comments of, about *Schiavo,* 64

Cruzan, Nancy, 23, 51; accident of, 37-39; grave marker of, 46

CT scan, 37

"Culture of Death," 169

"Culture of Life," George W. Bush support for, 150

Curry, Tom, 154

Davis, Nancy, 181n49. See *Cruzan, Nancy*

Death, causes of, 14-15; by age group, 19-21; causes of, in 1900, 15-17; causes of, in 2010, 18-21; distinguished between social and biological, 23-24; process of, 13-14

Death penalty, 79

Death tourists, 2

Death with Dignity, 1

Death with Dignity laws, 10, 11

Death with Dignity National Center, 128, 157-158

Death with Dignity Vermont, mission of, 123-124

Deathwatch, 15, 16

Defibrillator, 22

Delayed degenerative disease, 3

Dellinger, Walter, 89-91

Dementia, 17, 18, 19

Detroit Free Press, Kevorkian stories in, 71

"Diane," Dr. Quill patient, 73-74

Dicta, definition of, 179n15

Dideon, Joan, view of *Schiavo,* 63-64

Die, how humans, 13-16; where we, 19-23

Die with dignity, 6, 7

Disability advocacy groups, 202n92

Do not resuscitate order (DNR), 37

Doerflinger, Richard, 143

"Double effect," 2; alternative to PAD laws, 165; definition of, 189n36

Douglas, Jim, opposition of, to Vermont PAD bills, 126-127

Douglas, William O., 4
Dr. Death, 70. *See also* Kevorkian, Jack
Due Process clauses, 28, 41-42, 43, 47,
  51, 172
Dunn, Joe, 116
DWD. *See* ODWDA; WDWDA
Dying, experience of, 175n3
Dying patient, decisional autonomy of,
  92

EEG, definition of, 181n54
Eisenstadt v Baird, 5
Emergency Appeal for Stay of Enforce-
  ment of Judgment Below, 60
Emergency medical technicians (EMT),
  22-23
English common law, 178n2
Equity, definition of, 33, 180n27
Ethics committees, 35, 36
Euthanasia, aggressive PAD advocates
  support of, 68; as social policy, 69-70;
  fear of, 157
Evangelical Lutheran Church, anti-PAD
  support by, 108

Facial challenge, definition of, 189n40
Facial challenges in litigation, 97
Family Research Council, 128
Fannie Allen Health Center of Vermont,
  124
Federal courts, power of, in constitu-
  tional litigation, 164-165
Federal Judicial appointment process,
  167-168
Federal judiciary, conservative judges in,
  74-75
Field Poll, Californians views of PAD
  reported by, 115
Fifty-five Bioethicists and Autonomy,
  Inc., amicus curiae brief filed by, 58
Florida Department of Children and
  Families, 61

Florida House of Representatives, Terri's
  Law passed by, 57-58
Florida Supreme Court, *Schiavo* case in,
  52-63
Focus on the Family, 128
For Relief of the Parents of Theresa Marie
  Schiavo, Bill, 60
FOX News, 52
Freedom of choice, 7
Freedom to travel, 7
Fundamental liberty interest, 6
Fundamental rights, limits on, 28

Gardner, Booth, 131, 154, files WDWDA
  proposal, 154-156
Garrow, David J., 139
Gastrostomy tube, 37
Geller, Eileen, 157
Georgia abortion statute, 6
Ginsberg, Ruth B., 147, 165; comments
  of, about *amici* in PAD cases, 86
Glucksberg, Harold, plaintiff in 1997
  litigation, 77-80
Goldberg, Arthur, 4, 5
Gonzales, Alberto, 147
Gonzales v Oregon, 147-149
Gonzales v Raich, 147-148
Gore, Al, 144
Gregoire, Chris, 155
Griesa, Thomas P., judgment of, PAD not
  a fundamental liberty, 79-80; ruling
  by, in 1996 New York litigation, 78-79
Griswold v Connecticut, 4, 27, 41
"Groundhog day" scenario, 139-144
Guardian *ad litem*, appointment of, in
  Schiavo, 54; role of, in *Quinlan*, 34

Harlan, II, John M., 4-5. *See also* Souter,
  David H.
Harris Poll, *Schiavo* findings in, 62
Hatch, Orrin, 140, 141; view of, on
  Schiavo and abortion, 64

Hawaii, anti-PAD coalition in, success of, 118-121
Hawaii Death with Dignity Act (HB 2487), defeat of, 119-120
Hawaii Death with Dignity Statute (SB 709), defeat of, 119
Hawaii Partnership for Appropriate Compassionate Care, 120
Hawaii Right to Life, 120
Hawaii Woman's Coalition, role of, in PAD legislation, 120
Health care center, Hawaii as, 119
Heart and lung disease, 18
Heart failure, 11, 18, 19, 106
Hemlock Society, 109, 169, 187n2, 192n23; name changes of, 196n72
Hippocratic Oath, 70, 154
Hitler, Adolf, euthanasia and, 69
Hoff, Phil, support of, for Vermont PAD bill, 124
Hogan, Michael R., 136
Homosexual rights, 79
Hospice, 2, 3, 11, 106; hospice facility, 3
Hospitals, as poorhouses, 20
Hughes, Lori, 141
Humphry, Derek, 127-128; role of, in Oregon PAD action, 132, 134; *Schiavo* and, 65
Hutchinson, Asa, 144
Hyde, Henry, 140, 142
Hydration and nutrition tube, 32, 36, 37, 51, 52, 53, 54, 55, 57, 59, 60. *See also* Gastrostomy tube

In re Daniel Joseph Fiori, Pennsylvania PVS decision, 48
In re guardianship of Browning, Florida PVS decision, 48
In re guardianship of L.W., Wisconsin PVS decision, 49
In re Quinlan, 8, 27, 105; facts and legal issues in, 31-35

In re Schiavo, 8
Incapacitated Persons' Legal Protection Act of 2005, 59-60
Industrial revolution, 17, 18
Informed consent, 29
Initiative, 107, 109, 114; definition of, 192n22
Initiative and Referendum process, PAD and, 108-111
Intensive care unit (ICU), 14
"It's Over Debbie," euthanasia supported in, 69-70

Jackson, Ann, 153
Jones, Robert E., 145
Journal of the American Medical Association (JAMA), 69
Judges, balance of interests by all, 29-31

Kennedy, Anthony, 147-148; role of, in *Schiavo* litigation, 55-63; rules on *Schiavo* petition, 60-61
Kevorkian, Jack, 9, 111, 114; assault on medical profession by, 70; background of, 68-73; California Proposition and, 113; end suffering, position of, 72; *Schiavo* and, 65; support for euthanasia by, 69, 71-72; Washington Initiative and, 111
King, Angus, 123
Koch, Thomas, 125
Ku Klux Klansmen, 173
Kunin, Madeleine, support of, for Vermont PAD bill, 124

Law and medicine, clashes between, 24
Lazzara, Richard, role of, in *Schiavo* litigation, 57
Leddy, James, 125
Lee v Oregon, 136-138
Legal guardians, types of, 179n20

Legitimate medical purpose, 139-145; PAD not a, 144-147
Lethal Drug Abuse and Prevention Act of 1998, 141-142
Levine, Lloyd, 114,115, 116, 117-118
Liberty interest, 30, 31, 79; Lawrence Tribe view of, in Vacco, 94-95
Liberty to travel, 2, 171-172
Liberty, as personal privacy and autonomy, 1, 4, 5, 6-7, 8, 10, 11; expansive view of, 163, 166; no extension of, in 1997 PAD cases, 88
Living and Dying with Dignity Committee, 119
Living will, 35. *See also* Advanced care directive
Loewy, Erich H., 170
Lou Gehrig's disease, 72, 151, 158
Lower Federal Courts, view of: liberty in PAD cases, 167; majority of, conservative jurists, 168
Lynn, Joanne, 18-19

Maine Citizens Against the Dangers of PAD, 121, 122; No on One logo of, 122-123
Maine Citizens for End of Life Care, 122-123
Maine Home Care Alliance, 121
Maine Hospice Association, opposition of, to PAD bill, 122
Maine Medical Association, opposition of, to PAD bill, 121-122
Maine Osteopathic Association, 121
Maine public opinion polls, strong support for PAD in, 122
Mainers for Death with Dignity bill (Question 1), defeat of, 121-122
Marriage, prohibitions against, 2
Martinez, Mel, politics of *Schiavo*, and, 63
McCarter, Dorothy, 160

McClellan, Scott, 150
Medicaid, 19
Medical practice, two new schools of, 15-16
Medical technology, 18
Medicalization of death, 8, 20-23, 25, 27, 29; judges wrestle with impact of, 29-30
Medicare, 19-20
Mercitron, 70-71, 187, n 7
Mercy principle, euthanasia and, 69-70
Michigan Supreme Court, 72; right to die view of, 30
Miller, Tony, 171, 172
Miner, Roger, 82-83
Missouri, living will law of, 38, 39
Missouri Citizens for Life, protest of, about Cruzan, 46
Missouri department of health, 38
Missouri Supreme Court, decision of, in Cruzan, 40-41
Montana, 1, 10, 11, 171; lack of PAD regulations in, 161; legislation introduced regarding PAD, 161
Montana Constitution, changes in, 159-160
Montana State Department of Justice, 160
Montana Supreme Court, 10, 131; decision of, on PAD, 158-161
MSNBC, 52
Muir, Robert, *Quinlan* trial judge, 33-36; rejection of *Quinlan* request by, 33-34

National Center for Infectious diseases, CDC, 16-17, 19
National Conference of Catholic Bishops (NCCB), 112, 143
National Hemlock Association, actions of, in Maine, 121-122
National Right to Life, 120, 148

National Spinal Cord Injury Association, 127, 128

New England Journal of Medicine (NEJM), 65; Quill article published in, 73

New Jersey Supreme Court, 8, 31-35; opinion of, *In Re Quinlan*, 34-37

New York State Penal Code, punishment for PAD in, 74

New York Times, 139, 148; Kevorkian stories in, 71-72; *Schiavo* editorial in, 62

Nickles, Don, 142

Noonan, John T., 80

"Not Dead Yet," 120, 127, 168, 201n68; opposition of, to Hawaii PAD proposal, 120

"Oakies," 2, 171

Obama, Barack, 150; view of, about Senate response to Schiavo case, 63

O'Connor, Sandra D., 31, 147; concurs in Cruzan, 43; joins Rehnquist opinions, reasons for, 100-101; states as laboratories, view of, 49; swing vote of, on Supreme Court, 84

ODWDA: battles over, not pretty, 138-140; constitutionality of, in federal courts, 136-138; continuing attacks against, 152-153; data on impact, over ten years, 150-152; euthanasia excluded in, 132; legal challenge to, 135-137; major sections of, 133-134; opposition to, U.S. Congress, 140-145; passage of, by voters in 1994, 134; "prescribing only" bill, 132; type of patient using, 150-152

ODWDA users, personal autonomy primary reason for, 151

OHD, 152-153

Omnibus Spending Bill of 1998, 141

O'Neal, Tip, 169

Operation Rescue, 54

Oral argument, role of, in Supreme Court, 88-89

Oregon, 1, 129; characteristics of population of, 132-133; transplants to, for PAD, 171

Oregon Compassionate Choices, 132

Oregon Death with Dignity Act, 114, 131, 132-135. *See also* ODWDA

Oregon failure, 18

Oregon Health Division, role of, in PAD, 134-135. *See also* OHD

Oregon Health Sciences University, 135

Oregon Hospice Association, 153

Oregon Right to Die, 139

Oregon transplants, 2, 11, 20, 22, 173n5; why necessity of, 172

Oregon v Ashcroft, 145-148

"Originalism," definition of, 182n72

Orr, Robert, 124, 125; proponent of sanctity of life, 124-127

"Our Kind of Man or Woman," 167

Pacemaker, 22

PA, 3; absence of, in American history, 166; after *Baxter*, future of, 161-162; alternatives to, 104, 164, 165-166; anger against, by MD's, 203-204n3; battles over, fought locally, 164; bills for, introduced in states, 194n42; clandestine practice in America, 103-104; compassion reflected in, 169-170; differences between, and withdrawal of feeding tube, 77; end of purely volunteer grassroots efforts to pass, 113; federal courts antipathy toward, 167; givens in battles involving, 164-170; groups supporting, weaknesses of, 105-107; major organizations opposed to, 105-107; outcome of, based on local politics, 169; preventive measures in, to avoid slippery slope, 170-171;

PA (*continued*)
  prohibited in all states, 67; six factors accounting for political outcome of, 128-129; slippery slope argument against, 106, strong public opinion support for, 109-110; use of, term, 173-174n7; Vermont efforts to pass, 123-127; vulnerable groups opposed to, 106, 107
PAD advocate: aggressive type, 68-70: conventional type, 68-71
PAD advocates, litigation initiated against PAD ban by, 74-75; two types, 68-70, 109-112
PAD battles, fundamental question raised in, 163
PAD bill, popular support not enough to pass, 114-125
PAD legislation, state political battles for, 108-127
PAD legislative proposals, slippery slope major argument against, 127
PAD opposition, use of fear by, 127
PAD petitions, arguments made in, 76-77
Pain Relief Promotion Act of 1999 (Hyde/Nickles bill), 142-143
Palliative care, 2, 3, 11, 106, 142; alternative to PAD, 106-107
Palliative Care/Hospice, 165
Palliative sedation, 118. *See also* Terminal sedation
Parens patriae, definition of, 180n33
Park, Sharon, 155
Passive PAD, 2
Patient's right to choose death, 24
Paul, Ron, 143
Pels, Donald, 138
Penumbras, 4, 5; definition of, 174n18
Permanent vegetative state (PVS), 8, 9
Personal autonomy, 27, 29, 30, 53, 58; not a fundamental right, 47

Personal privacy right, 5-6, 8, 74
Petitioners, PAD litigation, 84-85
Pew Research Center, 3
Physician, changes in role of, 20-23
Physician-assisted death, 1. *See* PAD
Pitts, Joe, 60
Planned Parenthood of Southeastern Pennsylvania v Casey, 75; dissenters in, 76-77; use of, in 1997 PAD briefs, 77-79
Plum, Fred, 21
Pneumonia, 17
Pope Benedict XVI, 155
Pope John II, opposition of, to PAD, 116; *Schiavo* case and, 54
Port, Richard, role of, defeat of Hawaii bill, 195n60
Potassium chloride, 72
Powell, Lewis, 5
Private bill, 185n30
Pro bono publico, 181n56
Public Health Organizations, 17-18
Pugh, Ann, 126
PVS, 14, 21, 24, 27, 51, 52, 53; definition of, 21-22, 174n26

Quesada, Frank, order of, in *Schiavo* case, 55-56
Quill, Timothy, 65; background of, 73-74
Quinlan, Joseph, 34, 35
Quinlan, Julia, 33
Quinlan, Karen Ann, 23, 32; autopsy report of, 180-181n45; PVS status of, 32

Reagan, Ronald, 167; selection of conservative judges, by, 75
Referendum, 107, 109, 114; definition of, 192n22
Rehnquist, William H., 5-6; *Cruzan* author, 31; distinction between

PAD and PVS by, 90, 100; majority opinions of, in 1997 PAD litigation, 97-104; understanding of terminal sedation by, 190n48

Reinhardt, Stephen, 80-81

Reno, Janet, 144; decision of, in ODWDA battle, 140-141

Repeal Measure 51, overturn ODWDA with, 137-138

Respect for Life Sunday, 112-113

Respect Life Office of Roman Catholic Diocese of Hawaii, 120

Right of privacy, 4, 29, 33, 34, 35-36, 38, 40, 41-42, 43, 47;

balance of, against state interests, 43; meaning of, 5-6

Right to be left alone, 29

Right to die, 51, 65, 80, 99

Right to marital privacy, 4, 5

Right to privacy, 51, 53

Right to travel, liberty to, protected by Due Process clause, 173

Rights of personality, 34-35

Riser, Fred, 193, n 41

Roberts, Barbara, 155

Roberts, John, comments of, about *Schiavo*, 62-63; dissent of, in *Gonzales*, 147

Roe v Wade, 6, 8, 11, 27-28, 75

Roman Catholic Archdiocese of Maine, opposition of, to PAD, 121-122

Roman Catholic Bishops, role of, in *Schiavo* case, 54

Roman Catholic Blog, opposition of, to PAD, 117-118

Roman Catholic Church, 168-169; financial strength of, 107-108; major political opponent of PAD, 107, 114; number of American members in, 107; opposition of, to WDWDA, 154-155; relation with Protestant churches, 108; role of, in defeat of Hawaii PAD bill, 120; role of, in Oregon battles, 132-145

Roman Catholic Diocese of Seattle, 155, 156

Roman Catholic Diocese of Vermont, opposition of, to PAD bill, 124

Rothstein, Barbara J., ruling by, in 1996 Washington litigation, 77-79

Sanctity of life, 36, 52, 75, 87, 113, 120, 124; *Cruzan* judgment and, 40; major support for, by groups, 51, 57, 164, 168-169; power of concept of, in PAD battles, 164; presidential support for, 167; Republican politicians and, 140, 141, 144

Scalia, Antonin: concurs in *Cruzan*, 43-44; dissent of, in *Gonzales*, 147-148; "Scaliaisms" in PAD cases, 91-92, 93, 94; ideological fervor of, 63-64

Schiavo case: impact of, on PVS patients, 52; litigation in, 53-63; number of appeals in, 54; skewed media coverage about, 64-65

Schiavo, Michael, husband of Terri, 51-63

Schiavo parents, accusations of, against Michael Schiavo, 53-63

Schiavo, Terri, autopsy of, 53; death of, 62; husband of, 23; PVS of, 51-52; suffers cardiac arrest, 51; tragedy of, 51-63; withdrawal of feeding tube, 54-63

Schwarzenegger, Arnold, view of, about PAD bill, 115-116, 119

Seattle Post-Examiner, 155

Seattle Times, 154-155

Self-determination right, 27, 29, 47, 183n99

Shumlin, Peter, support of, for Vermont PAD bill, 127

Sixty Minutes, Kevorkian on, 72

Skrzynski, John, prosecutes Kevorkian, 72

Slippery slope argument, 68, 110, 112-113, 127, 152, 155, 156, 170; argument against PAD by critics, 68-70; basic principle of anti-PAD groups, 170-171; euthanasia and, 68-69; use of, against WDWDA, 155

Snelling, Barbara, support of, for Vermont PAD bill, 124

Social security, 19

Soros, George, 138

Sorrell, William, 125-126

Souter, David H., 147; concern about slippery slope, 90, 92-93, 103; impact of, in PAD political battles, 127; use of "ordered liberty" concept, 190, n49

Sox, Harold C., 142

Standing to sue, 137; definition of, 198n10

Starr, Kenneth, 41-44

State legislative process, PAD introduced in, 113-125

State police powers, 28-29

State powers, ban PAD, using, 109

Stevens, John P., 44-45, 147; opinion of, in PAD cases, 102-104

Stewart, Potter, 5,

"Strict scrutiny" standard, 49; 183n103; 190n47. *See also* Suspect class

Stroke, 23

"Substituted judgment" standard, 29, 29, 47, 48

Suicide tourists, 2

Suspect class, 189n46

"Switzerland syndrome," 1-2

Tallman, Richard C., 146

Task force to Improve the Care of Terminally Ill Oregonians, 135

Temporary injunctive relief, 61

Temporary restraining order (TRO), 145

Terminal sedation, 103; definition of, 190n50. *See also* Palliative sedation

Terminally ill patient, 1, 3, 6-7; liberty of, 10; options for, 163-164

Terri's Law, 9

Terry, Randall, 54

Texas abortion statute, 6

Thibaudeau, Pat, 154

Thomas, Cal, 63-64

Thomas, Clarence, dissent of, in *Gonzales*, 148-149. *See also* "Originalism"; Scalia, Antonin

Total brain death, 14-15

Tribe, Lawrence, 93-95

Tuberculosis, 17

Tucker, Kathryn L., 91, 93-95

Tuohey, John F., 153

"Undue burden" standard, 78. See also *Planned Parenthood of Southeastern Pennsylvania v Casey*

Uniform Determination of Death Act, 175-176n12

United Methodist Church, anti-PAD support by, 108

Unregulated PAD ("back alley"), emergence of, 110

U.S. Congress, 9; Republicans in, and *Schiavo* case, 52-54

U.S. Constitution, 1, 9, 25, 172; 1st amendment, 4, 33-34; 3rd Amendment, 4; 4th amendment, 4; 5th amendment, 4; 8th Amendment, 33-34; 9th amendment, 4, 72-73; 10th Amendment, 28, 109; 14th amendment, 2, 74; Article I, 28; Bill of Rights, 4; Due Process clauses, 1, 28, 77; Equal Protection argument by PAD advocates, 77-78; Equal Protection Clause, 77, 136; federalism in, 28; Liberty clause in, 10; Liberty in, 4; Preamble, 28

U.S. Courts of Appeals, decisions in 1996 PAD cases, 79-82

U.S. Drug Enforcement Agency (DEA), use of, to overturn ODWDA, 140-144

U.S. House Committee on Government Reform, and *Schiavo* case, 60

U.S. Justice Department, 10, 141

U.S. Public Health Services, U.S. Department of Health and Human Services, 176n23

U.S. Senate, *Schiavo* private bill passed by, 60

U.S. Solicitor General, brief of, in *Cruzan*, 41-43; power and influence of, in litigation, 95. *See also* Dellinger, Walter; Starr, Kenneth

U.S. State Department, travel restrictions by, 171-172

U.S. Supreme Court, 2, 6, 7, 8, 10, 27, 29, 30, 35, 131; balancing of interests by, 28-30; certiorari denied by, in *Kevorkian* case, 72-73; changes in makeup of, 170-171; conference sessions of, 95-96; conservative justices on, 75; decision of, in *Cruzan*, 36, 40, 43-45, 47; decision-making process of, 96-97; individual privacy decisions of, 27-28; justices divided in PAD decisions, 96-98, 97-98; makeup of, in 1997, 84; power of, interpret the Constitution, 166-167; review by, of Ashcroft directive, 147-149; right to refuse medical treatment, view of, 30-31; *Schiavo* case in, 52-63

Vaccines, development of, 17

Vacco, Dennis, 83-94, 165

Vacco v Quill, 76, 108, 109, 113, 114, 166, 167; amicus curiae briefs filed in, 86-88; basic constitutional question in, 89; briefs filed in Supreme Court, 84-88; CA2 opinion in, 82-84; *Cruzan* and *Casey* opinions cited in, 86-87; Equal Protection basis of decision in, 93-95, 99-100, 102-103; oral argument before Supreme Court in, 93-95; Supreme Court grants certiorari in, 83-84; Supreme Court decision in, 95-103

Vermont Alliance for Ethical Healthcare (VAEH), mission of, 124-125; opposition to PAD, 124

Vermont Bill of Rights for Hospital Patients, 126

Vermont Death with Dignity (H 274), inaction on, by legislators, 127

Vermont Death with Dignity bill (H 044), defeat of, 126-127

Vermont Medical Association, 125

Vermont, political culture of, 126; town meeting ethic of, and PAD debates, 125

Vlazny, John, 153

Voluntary stopping eating and drinking (VSED), 118, 194n54, 204n4

Vulnerable anti-PAD groups, fear of legalized euthanasia and, 107

Wallace, Mike, Kevorkian interviewed by, 72

Walters, Dick, 196n70

Warren, Earl, 4, 5

Warren Court, right of privacy concept and, 41

Washington Death with Dignity Act (WDWDA), 131, 154-156

Washington Hospice and Palliative Care Association, 154

Washington Hospice Association, 157

Washington Initiative (Ballot Initiative 119), defeat of, 110-112; Roman Catholic Church opposed to, 111-112; slippery slope argument defeats, 110-111

Washington State Department of Health, 158

Washington State Medical Association (WMA), 154

Washington State Natural Death Act, 1979, 110-111

Washington State PAD Initiative, 1990, 65-66

Washington State Penal Code, punishment for PAD, in, 74

Washington State public opinion polls, reports of, voter support, 157

Washington State transplants, why necessity of, 172

Washington State, 1, 129; transplants to, for PAD, 171

Washington v Glucksberg, 108, 109, 113, 114, 127, 166, 167; *amicus curiae* briefs filed in, 86-88; balancing of rights by judges in, 81-82; basic constitutional question in, 89; briefs filed in Supreme Court in, 84-88; CA9 opinion in, 81-82; *Cruzan* and *Casey* opinions cited in, 85-86; due process basis of decision, 98-99; liberty interest discussed in, 99-100; meaning of Due Process discussed in, 88-93; oral argument before Supreme Court, 88-93; Supreme Court grants *certiorari* in, 83-84; Supreme Court decision in, 95, 98-99

Watershed year 1990, 65-66

WDWDA (Initiative 1000), 154-156; campaign for/against intense, 156-157; data on use of, 158; fear of euthanasia and, 157; major sections copy ODWDA, 155-156; passage of, 157

Webster v Reproductive Health Services, 86

Weldon, David, 59, 60

White, Byron, 4-5, 6

Whittemore, James D., role of, in *Schiavo* litigation, 61

Williams, William A., 89-90

"Winks and nods," reality of, in terminal cases, 165-166. *See also* Ginsberg, Ruth Bader; *Washington v Glucksberg*

Wyden, Ron, 63, 141, 149

Youk, Thomas, 72. *See also* Lou Gehrig's disease

◈ ABOUT THE AUTHOR

HOWARD BALL, a graduate of Hunter College-CUNY and Rutgers University, is Professor Emeritus/Political Science and University Scholar at University of Vermont. He has authored nearly three dozen books about the Supreme Court, judicial policy/politics, and international justice, including *The Supreme Court in the Intimate Lives of Americans* (NYU Press); *Genocide: A Reference Handbook; Hugo L. Black: Cold Steel Warrior;* and *Justice in Mississippi: The Murder Trial of Edgar Ray Killen*. He and his wife Carol reside in Vermont and Arizona.